HEALEYS AND
AUSTIN-HEALEYS

Symbolizing the popularity of the marque amongst motor sport enthusiasts, an Austin-Healey Sprite and a '3000' in a typical club setting.

HEALEYS

AND

AUSTIN-HEALEYS

*An illustrated history of the marque
with specifications and tuning data*

PETER BROWNING

AND

LES NEEDHAM

G T FOULIS & CO LTD
HENLEY-ON-THAMES · OXFORDSHIRE

Distributed in the USA by
CLASSIC MOTORBOOKS
1415 West 35th street, Minneapolis, Minnesota 55408

First published June 1970

© Peter Browning and Les Needham 1970

ISBN 0 85429 101 6

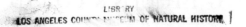
MADE AND PRINTED IN GREAT BRITAIN BY
MORRISON AND GIBB LIMITED, LONDON AND EDINBURGH

CONTENTS

ILLUSTRATIONS

vii

PREFACE

The motoring historian who undertakes to be the first person to write the history of a marque has a difficult but rewarding task. It is difficult because you have no one else's findings to refer to; it is rewarding when you track down information and have the opportunity to hear first-hand accounts from the people involved. This has certainly been the case with this story of Healey and Austin-Healey cars.

The past bibliography of the marque has consisted of just one rather sketchy volume named *Austin Healey* 'ghosted' for Donald Healey and Tommy Wisdom. When I therefore joined the staff of the B.M.C. Sports car magazine *Safety Fast* in 1965 and was acting as General Secretary of the Austin-Healey Club, I set about the task of writing for that magazine the first complete history of the marque. This appeared in serial form under the title 'Perranporth to Abingdon' and it is on this series that I have based this book. The story has been corrected in a number of minor details and brought up to date but it has also been augmented with many first-hand reports and interviews by people involved in the development and competition programme of the cars and who are far better qualified than I to tell the tale.

I am firstly indebted to Donald Healey for his unfailing interest and enthusiasm in this book. I have also received invaluable help from his sons—Geoffrey, who has provided a great deal of the technical background story and Brian, who has supplied a lot of information on the Healey Company and unearthed many of the early photographs.

Of the Healey drivers who have given up a great deal of their time to talk to me about their experiences I must particularly thank John Gott, Tony Ambrose, Rauno Aaltonen and Tommy Wisdom. I am also very grateful to Pat Moss and William Kimber & Co Ltd, the publishers of her book *The Story So Far*, for permission to reprint many extracts from Pat's very personal account of her rallying activities.

Other people who have provided valuable contributions include John Thornley, the late James Watt, Charles Mortimer, Lance Macklin, Peter Riley, John Sprinzel and Christabel Carlisle.

Many of the illustrations have come from the archives of the Donald Healey Motor Company and I am very grateful for their permission to reproduce them. Most of the remaining pictures have come from the B.M.C. Photographic Department who, as always, have been very co-operative in searching deep into their past files.

Finally I am indebted to Les Needham who has taken over all my past Healey files and compiled them into an invaluable Appendix to the main story.

PETER BROWNING

Abingdon,
January 1970

CHAPTER 1

DONALD HEALEY

The tiny mining village of Perranporth on the north Cornish coast can claim to be the home of just one world-famous name – Donald Mitchell Healey, who was born there in July 1898. He spent his childhood in the then unspoilt village and amongst his earliest motoring memories are those of his father starting his Panhard Levassor and, on one occasion, breaking his arm in the attempt.

His father, a Perranporth grocer and builder, bought the Panhard in London and drove it back to Cornwall, a journey that took three days. At the age of 11, Donald remembers his first serious motoring adventure when he went with a friend of the family to London to collect a new 30 h p Beeston Humber. The return trip of some 300 miles was completed in two days after repairing numerous punctures. It was on this trip that Donald recalls seeing England's first filling station, situated between Yarcombe and Honiton, and run by the A.A. There were no pumps, petrol being dispensed from large cans at the roadside.

For a young lad brought up in a fishing village, Donald showed an unusual interest in things mechanical although, like most Cornishmen, he and his family have always had a love of the sea. After schooling at Newquay College it was no surprise when young Donald announced that he was off to become an apprentice at the Sopwith Aviation Company in Kingston-upon-Thames where he earned the princely sum of six shillings a week for a ten-hour working day. Part of his training included the opportunity of learning to fly and his many trips to Brooklands thus enabled him to maintain his interest in cars at the same time.

By increasing his age by a couple of years Donald was able to volunteer for the Royal Flying Corps in 1915 and he saw active service as a pilot in France. However, an unfortunate episode involving an encounter with our own anti-aircraft guns, caused him to be invalided out of active service in 1917 when he found himself involved in less exciting work with the Aeronautical Inspection Department.

After the war it was back to Perranporth where motor cars became
the main interest and by 1919 Donald had opened a little garage and
was soon to be seen tinkering with a variety of sporting machinery.
Inevitably, he was soon involved with local car club activities and in
1922 he became a founder member of the Truro and District Car
Club, who held their first hill climb on the public road just outside
the town. Donald had a new six-cylinder Buick at the time and made
fastest time of the day – his first motor sporting success.

The Buick was followed by a little A B C with a 10 h p air-cooled,
horizontally-opposed twin cylinder engine, which, being very light,
had quite a good performance. Donald entered this car in a variety
of local events and soon his name was well known in motor sporting
circles.

In 1923 Donald tried his luck with the A B C in the classic London
to Lands End Trial, but he over revved the engine on Porlock Hill,
a push rod jumped out and the engine seized solid. Later that year,
while out on a test run with a 10 h p Ariel, Donald found a disused
track with a steep gradient and a very acute hairpin. He approached
the Committee of the M.C.C. (organizers of the Lands End Trial)
and in 1924 the now famous Blue Hills Mine was introduced into the
route for the first time.

For the 1924 event, Donald entered a 10 h p Riley 'Red Winger'
but on its way to London a leaking petrol tank caused the car to
catch fire and it was completely destroyed. Donald rushed back to
Perranporth, grabbed his old A B C , made the start in time, and had
a faultless run to win his first M.C.C. Gold Medal. Later in the same
year he won the premier award in the M.C.C. Lands End Trial,
driving a new Ariel Ten with his father as co-driver.

Further Gold Medals were collected in the Lands End Trial with a
variety of cars – an Ariel in 1925, a Fiat Seven in 1926, a Rover Ten
in 1927, a supercharged Triumph Seven in 1929 and a Fiat Ten in
1930. During this period Donald also started to widen his motoring
activities, mainly with the Triumph Seven, and he has the distinction
of winning the first ever R.A.C. Rally in 1928.

In the following year the Monte Carlo Rally was his first attempt
at this winter classic but bad snow conditions resulted in his Triumph
Seven arriving just two minutes outside the time allowance in Monaco.
However, a small consolation was winning his class on the Mont des
Mules Hill Climb which followed immediately after the rally. Donald's
first Monte success came in 1930 when, still driving the Triumph

Seven, he finished seventh overall, the best performance by a British entrant.

Allegiance was transferred to a $4\frac{1}{2}$ litre Invicta in 1930 and this paid big dividends for not only did Donald win the premier award on the Alpine Rally but in January of the following year he became the first British driver to win the Monte Carlo Rally outright. Driving with Louis Pearce and the famous motor cyclist Victor Horseman, Donald used the low chassis Invicta modified with 23 in. wheels fitted with $7\frac{1}{2}$ in. section Dunlop tyres which gave the low slung car an incredible ground clearance.

In those days, the Monte starting controls were allocated points according to their estimated difficulty, thus Athens was considered the most difficult route and had the maximum marks, and Stavanger was next on the list. No one had ever succeeded in getting through within the time allowed from Athens, so Stavanger was considered the best start for those competing seriously for the major award.

Donald, along with the 12 British crews, started from there and ran into trouble even before the rally began. Their boat sailed from Newcastle into a raging North Sea gale and eventually arrived at Bergen 11 hours late, thus missing the connection to Stavanger. Another boat was found, but it was such a crush to get all the cars on board that the doors could not be opened and the drivers had to get out through the windows or sliding roofs. The starting point was eventually reached with just one clear day available for pre-rally formalities. Two of the foreign entrants failed to reach the start, however, including Louis Chiron, who eventually joined the rally at Oslo!

Leaving Stavanger for the dreaded Tronaagen Pass, many competitors were soon in trouble, including Donald, who slid off the road and demolished a 9 in. diameter telegraph pole. This pushed the rear axle of his Invicta $1\frac{1}{2}$ in. out of true on one side and meant disconnecting the brake at that side. For the rest of the rally the Invicta proceeded in a somewhat crab-sided fashion, with only three brakes working!

The journey through Norway and Sweden was as tough as expected, and by the time Copenhagen was reached over 10 cars had dropped out and one or two others were running late. Whilst the Northern starters were floundering through snow and ice, eight gallant heroes were endeavouring to force their way through from Athens. Here the problems were non-existent roads, and miles and miles of really glutinous mud. Only two cars succeeded in getting out of Yugoslavia, one retired at Munich, and the last one arrived at one of the time controls just five minutes after it closed.

The remaining Stavanger starters eventually made their way to Monaco, six of them arriving without penalty, so the fate of the major award rested with the crucial acceleration and braking test.

In previous years, ties had been decided by a regularity run, but for 1931 a new test was devised. Cars had to accelerate as fast as possible over 250 metres and then, by braking hard, cover the next 10 metres as slowly as possible. Times were taken from the start to the end of the 250 metres, and from there to the end of the 10 metres. In addition, to stop people braking early, the last 10 of the 250 metres were timed separately and had to be covered in the shortest possible time.

Donald was handicapped in the test by his still faulty brakes and had to start braking part way through the fast 10 metres, but nevertheless he put up the second best performance for the day, being beaten only by a Lagonda which had lost points elsewhere. Thus Donald achieved one of his life's ambitions by winning the Monte Carlo Rally outright. The following day, he went on to put up fastest time of the day at the traditional Mont des Mules hill climb.

On the Monte of the following year, again with an Invicta, Donald started from Umea, and came second overall and the first British car to finish for the third year running. The third Monte attempt with the Invicta was not so successful. Conditions were very bad indeed and the car left the road in Poland when trying to avoid a runaway horse sledge.

Later that year, in the Alpine Rally, whilst driving a Brooklands Riley, Donald was baulked on the Galibier Pass and dropped his first mark ever on the Alpine, bringing to an end his run of four consecutive Glacier Cups, which must be a unique pre-war Alpine record.

Then followed a period of experimental work with the Riley Company when Donald began a long lasting friendship with Victor Leverett who was later to play such an important role in the production of the later Riley-powered Healeys.

In 1934 Donald joined the Triumph Motor Company and was put in charge of design and experimental work, being responsible for the birth of the Gloria and Dolomite cars. A 10 h p Gloria was used for the 1934 Monte with co-driver Tommy Wisdom, and was fitted with some extra large 9 in. Dunlop low-pressure tyres. The starting point was Athens, which had the reputation of being the most difficult start in the whole Rally because, if it was cold, parts of Yugoslavia could be virtually impassable because of snow drifts, whilst if it was warmer, the route became a sea of mud. Healey's gamble with the low-pressure tyres paid off, for although they restricted his maximum speed, they enabled him to get through the mud and floods, the 11 in. ground clearance also helping with the latter problem. A larger car, also starting from Athens, won the Rally outright, but the tiny Triumph came third overall, won the light car class and was the best British car. In an amusing sequal, one of the French competitors protested that the engine of the Triumph must be oversized because it performed so well, but subsequent measurements proved that all was well.

The Healey story nearly came to an abrupt end in the 1935 Monte when Donald was driving an eight-cylinder Dolomite in thick fog through Denmark; the car was hit by a train at an unguarded level crossing, which completely removed the nose of the car. Luckily both Donald and his passenger were unhurt, but that was the end of that year's trip to Monte Carlo.

The following year saw the Dolomite through clean from Tallinn, but the final wiggle-woggle test at Monaco dropped the car down to eighth place, although Donald's was the first British car home for the fifth occasion. On the route down he had a near repeat of the previous year's disaster when the car he was following through Lithuania collided with a train at a level crossing, this time with fatal results.

Donald's last Monte was in 1937 when he started from Palermo with Tommy Wisdom and Norman Black as his co-drivers. The car was the new Triumph 12 which retired with engine trouble near Munich. Later on that year he was appointed Technical Director of the Triumph Company and this brought his active competition work to a temporary close.

When the war started, Donald, now General Manager of Triumph, got involved in various forms of development work, including the design of the Hobson aircraft carburetter. Later he moved to the Humber Company where he was to be principally involved in the development of armoured cars. It was here, however, that Donald met up with three people who were instrumental in influencing him to consider the manufacture of his own car. One was A. C. Sampietro, an Italian, who had formerly served his time with Alfa Romeo, then gone to Maserati and on to Thomson & Taylor in England. The second man, equally skilled, was Ben Bowden, a stylist, early Farina, then working as a body man with Humbers. The last man was James Watt, a cheery salesman whom Donald had met at Triumphs and who was at this time involved in the R.A.F.V.R. with Donald, who was then Squadron Leader of the Warwickshire A.T.C.

Just before his sudden death in 1965, James Watt wrote the following, which gives us a pretty accurate account of the formation of the Company and the building of the first Healey car:

'It was Ben Bowden who began with the body design. Ben in fact worked in the dining-room of his home in Coventry, drawing directly on to the wallpaper and then taking tracings from the originals! That's why there have never been any original body drawings for the first cars. Ben worked throughout the Blitz on the basic designs for two versions of the body; a fixed-head four-seater two-door coupé (eventually to be known as the "Elliot") and a similarly styled drop-head version (which became known as the "Westland").

'While Ben was busy with his sketches, Sammy (Sampietro) was experimenting with various suspension ideas. Hitler's Volkswagen, designed by Porsche, had made quite an impression on the motor industry, particularly the trailing link front suspension. We thought about various ideas of making i f s, remembering the troubles that Alvis had had as the first British touring car to have this form of suspension. Standards also had not been all that successful when they applied it to an inexpensive production car. We all felt that if we were going to have i f s, then trailing links would be the best.

'And so this was how our little team set about the creation of the new car, Ben sketching away at his body drawings in his spare time on his dining-room wall while Sammy (in Humber's time of course!) worked on the suspension ideas. Another Humber employee enters into the story here, a fellow by the name of Ireland who worked in the drawing office and who was responsible for designing the chassis, again in Humber working hours!

'Donald and I began to feel that our little team was really getting somewhere and we now felt that we very nearly had a good enough design to think about production and that the time had come for us to try and sell our ideas to Triumphs. I had already made two fairly successful approaches to Triumphs and in February 1944 the opportunity arose for another meeting. Very conveniently my Commanding Officer had a new aeroplane to collect at Doncaster that week so I reckoned that this would be a handy way to get to Sheffield. So I flew up to the all-important meeting.

'At first things seemed most encouraging and they genuinely thought that our scheme and ideas had merit. However, Triumphs had had a board meeting recently and I was tremendously downcast to learn that they had decided not to back Healey, mainly for the very simple reason that we were not motor-car manufacturers.

'I was very disconsolate, went back to the aerodrome, took off, the elastic broke on the port side and I came down in the back garden of a local hotel. So I did well that day – lost the deal with Triumphs and pranged the C.O.'s aeroplane!

'And so we had to put aside all thoughts of building our car at Triumphs. But we were not beaten, indeed with Donald as the ever-cheerful leader of our little group, Ben, Sammy and I were even more enthusiastic, led on by the conviction that we *were* going to build that motor-car somewhere, somehow.

'One of our troubles in those days was that you had to be an established Company with a manufacturing licence to get any material supplies. We did not have a Company, let alone a licence, and until our plans were a little more advanced would not be able to get such a licence. Again it was another Humber employee, Peter Skelton, who saved the day. Peter was Director of Westlands, the Humber distributors in Hereford and, like a lot of people in those days, he had started up a small aero parts business in his garage doing small contract work for Humbers. And so we got Peter interested in our car (we still had no name for it by the way. We had begun to call it "the Triumph" but when we lost the Triumph deal we just called it "the car" again.)

'Peter showed the greatest enthusiasm for our plans and we even asked him at one stage to put some money into the project. Very wisely he declined! However, he did agree that we could use his garage to work in; furthermore he offered to make one or two parts for us. It was in Peter's garage one day that Sammy spied an 8 ft folding machine, a piece of machinery which enabled metal up to 8 ft long to be folded at right angles. For no other reason than the availability of this machine, Sammy designed his top hat section frame 8 ft long, which led to the Healey's 8 ft 6 in. wheelbase.

'By early 1945 our enthusiasm was really running wild. All activities were now based at the Westland Garage at Hereford where the ever-enthusiastic Peter Skelton, always ready to meet any challenge, had by now agreed to make our frames and bodies. Now we were really making progress and all we needed at this stage was a supply of engines and transmissions and somewhere to assemble the car.

'It was an old friend of Donald's, Victor Leverett, who did much to influence our decision to use the 2·4 litre Riley engine, a well-proven power unit which had an extremely good reputation. It could be tuned easily and was, of course, the basis of the famous E.R.A. engine. This we thought would be the ideal power unit for our project.

'Vic was now working at Riley's and we asked him whether he could let us have some engines. This led to a meeting with Victor Riley who not only agreed to let us have an engine, gearbox and any other Riley components we required but, later, when we were in production, offered to let us have a month's supply of engines in advance. We were to get them one month and would not have to pay for them until the next. This was going to be tremendously important because, of course, we had not got any money to pay for anything until we had found a customer for the car!

'So we had an engine. All that remained now was to find a place to build and assemble our first car. And yet again it was an ex-Triumph man who helped us out. One of the former Triumph directors, Wally Allen, was at this time running a firm called Benfords at The Cape in Warwick, which was manufacturing concrete mixers! Wally kindly agreed to lend us a little office in Warwick, plus a corner of his factory at The Cape.

'At last it seemed everything was set. I had been away for a short spell of service in the Middle East and was delighted to hear from Donald that he really believed the time was ripe for us to get a licence for some material. Donald applied to the Ministry with no money behind him and no Company, but, heaven knows why, we got our licence.

'This was indeed a great milestone and in the summer of 1945 we all moved camp from Westlands in Hereford to a pitch among the concrete mixers at Warwick and began to assemble the first car. It was a great day when Riley's delivered their first engine – incidentally a pre-war reconditioned one, as Riley's had not really got going yet.

'First recruit to the new company was one Roger Menadue, an old buddy of Donald's. Roger had been with Armstrong-Whitworth and, as you know, in the aircraft industry nuts and bolts are never used twice and over the years Roger had collected a splendid array of once-used nuts and bolts! So Roger with his collection joined the Company.

'It became pretty obvious at this point that the supply of bodies was going to cause us trouble. Peter Skelton, although struggling splendidly with the supply of chassis and the open two-seater bodies, was obviously going to run into trouble when it came to making the saloon.

'With this in mind we went down to meet some people in Reading called Elliots. I believe they had made a car body of some sort at one time or another but their main business was building shop fronts! Certainly they knew how to fashion timber and we set them to work on a wood frame and aluminium saloon body. We gave them an order for 50 units.

'Soon the prototype "Westland" was nearing completion and we decided to announce it to the Press on 6 January 1946. And how well I remember the thrilling moment as Donald and I went down to Westlands to collect the car, somehow all our troubles seemed worth-while as we set off up the road. We had not gone far, however, when the darn thing boiled which was a bit of an anti-climax!

'For the press announcement we invited old friends from the *Autocar* along and also Kay Petre, then motoring correspondent of the *Daily Sketch*.

'As our catalogue listed two models – and we only had one Westland – we had some photos taken of a model of the saloon and touched it up to look like the real thing. I think everyone really thought we did have two cars to sell!

'The reception the Press gave to the car was somewhat embarrassing. New cars were, of course, extremely difficult to get hold of in those days and the embarrassing thing was that we had not got any to sell!

'The very first car, with the open Westland body, was given the chassis number 1501. Why we chose this figure I cannot imagine, but I remember we agreed not to start at 1 as that would look too amateurish. Talking of numbers, the Westland carried the registration number VVV 214 for no other reason than that we found a stack of old letter "V"s and some odd numbers lying around in a corner of the workshop and we made up an imaginary number plate at the last minute. I don't think we ever registered the car at all!'

Looking at the design of the car in more detail the chassis for the original Westland and Elliot was a very successful design, remaining unchanged for all future Healey models until 1954, except the longer-

wheelbase Nash-Healey. Built up from 18 gauge sheet steel forming
a sturdy but light box section, two straight 6 in. side-members ran
from the front to the rear wheel-arch, stoutly braced at the front
and in the centre. The completed chassis weighed only 160 lb.

The independent front suspension was unique in permitting a
large wheel movement without variation to castor or camber angles.
A trailing arm design was adopted, the light alloy suspension arms
moving upon large ball and roller bearings carried in boxes bolted to
the chassis. Single coil springs were used in conjunction with built-in
Girling piston-type hydraulic dampers.

Whenever possible in his design, Healey incorporated well-proven
components already available, and at the rear a conventional Riley
spiral bevel axle was located by a torque tube and a track bar, coil
springs being fitted over the axle with lever arm Girling dampers.

The steering layout was unusual, the steering-box movements
being transmitted to the wheels via a swivelling plate and link rods,
a design which gave precise movement yet transmitted the minimum
of road-wheel movement up the steering column. Bolt-on disc
wheels were used with hydraulic Lockheed brakes, 11 in. drums at
the front, 10 in. drums at the rear.

For the power unit, the well-tried and sturdy 2,443 cc four-cylinder
Riley engine was used. This twin-camshaft pushrod o h v engine
was fitted with twin horizontal SU carburetters and an improved-
flow exhaust system, raising the output to 104 b h p at 4,500 rev/min.
The compression ratio was 6·8 to 1. Coupled to the engine was the
four-speed Riley gearbox. The standard 3·5 to 1 rear axle ratio gave
22 mile/h per 1,000 rev/min in top gear.

The aerodynamic body designs were subjected to extensive wind-
tunnel tests, and throughout development the greatest consideration
was given to weight saving. The bodies were panelled in magnesium
alloy on a timber frame.

It is worth noting that the first Elliot saloon in 1946 recorded a
time of 17·8 secs. for the standing quarter-mile and was timed at
104 mile/h. Comparing this time with road-test figures for four-
seater saloons of today, it is clear that the standard Elliot was no
sluggard!

CHAPTER 2

THE HEALEY ELLIOT AND WESTLAND

While the Company referred to their two first models simply as
2·4 litre Roadsters, they are more clearly defined as the 'Elliot' Saloon
and 'Westland' Roadster. These two models were produced simul-
taneously from October 1946 to October 1950 and some classification
of the type specifications and detailed improvements to each model
might be useful at this stage.

The original chassis was named the A-type, and Elliot and Westland
bodies were fitted in almost equal numbers for the first six months.
The B-type chassis was then introduced; this had an adjustable steering
column, the petrol pumps were removed from the bulkhead and
placed in the boot, and twin 6-volt batteries were replaced by a single
12-volt unit, this being repositioned in the boot with the petrol pumps.
With the introduction of the B-type chassis, the production of Elliots
was double that of Westlands (many chassis were, of course, also sold
to other specialist coachbuilders). In the autumn of 1950 the C-type
chassis was introduced with modifications to the front suspension units;
the boxes were now made in Elektron with side-plates, and the units
were bolted on to the chassis. On the later Elliots and Westlands the
frontal appearance was altered, with improved headlamps repositioned
in the front wings instead of on the body panels close by the radiator.

With the factory at Warwick busy producing the first batch of cars,
a standard Elliot was taken to Italy in December 1946 for road-testing
by *The Motor*. The results proved – on the very doorstep of some of
the world's fastest sports and touring car manufacturers – that the new
Healey was not to be ignored. On the Milan-Como autostrada, the
flying quarter-mile was covered at 104·65 mile/h and the standing
quarter-mile was timed at 17·8 secs. The Healey was therefore claimed
to be the fastest British production car.

Alpine début

The new Healey made its competition début in the International
Alpine Rally held in the summer of 1947, when a Westland was

entered for Tommy Wisdom to drive. The event was divided into three stages, the 61 starters leaving Marseilles to travel over the many passes to Aix-les-Bains, where the first of the special speed tests took place. Here the Healey beat all the opposition in its class, and after a night's rest the crews set off on the second stage via Chamonix to Annecy where the cars were put through a timed speed trial over a standing kilometre. Again the Healey won its class by a handsome margin. The final stage provided the toughest road section, from Annecy to the finish at Cannes, but the Healey and Tommy Wisdom put up a fine show to be amongst the three cars to climb these difficult sections unpenalized, and the sole British entry to do so. Amongst the 27 finishers, Wisdom brought the Healey across the line a comfortable winner in the 3 litre class and gained class awards for all the speed tests. Yet another trophy was collected when the Healey was placed first in the concours for open cars. In its first competition, the marque had certainly not disgraced itself. Wisdom returned the car to Warwick with four major trophies!

Following the 1946 timed run with the Elliot in Italy, running on Swiss petrol, there was some speculation as to whether similar speeds could be achieved using the rather poor fuel then available to the British public. Donald Healey was pleased to accept the challenge and in August 1947 made further timed runs under R.A.C. observation, this time in Belgium on the Jabbeke-Aeltre highway. The Healey proved the point, improving on its previous performance to achieve 110·8 mile/h over the measured mile.

Sicilian success

In 1948 the Healeys enjoyed their first year of participation in international rallying and racing, and the season began with the classic Sicilian road race, the Targa Florio. Practically all the entries were from Italy, including works-entered Cisitalia, Maserati and Ferrari. The sole Healey, facing strong class opposition from Lancia and Fiat, was a privately-entered Elliot driven by Count Johnny Lurani. With co-driver Serafini, Lurani had collected the car from London only a few days before the event and driven direct through France, Switzerland and the length of Italy to the start at Palermo. There had been little time to prepare the car for this punishing event.

The 98 starters began their 600-mile journey from Palermo at midnight, the course following the coastline around the island, turning inland at about half-distance to include the more difficult sections in the mountains of the interior. Co-driver Serafini took the wheel from the start, taking things easy to begin with, as the pair were determined to finish. Lurani took over for the more difficult sections and the Healey was running well up on schedule by the time the first fuel stop was made. Already many of the Lancia opposition had been passed, but maintaining such high average speeds over the rough roads had tested the Healey suspension to its limit and, approaching the most tricky stages of the event, the panhard rod came away from the chassis. Lurani pulled the car to a stop and, while helpers lifted the car, Serafini crawled beneath to dismantle the broken parts. Ten valuable minutes had been lost before they were back on the road, and with the damaged suspension it was not easy to maintain the required speed, let alone catch up on lost time. But, determined to finish, Lurani and Serafini struggled on, finally bringing the Healey back to Palermo to complete the course in almost exactly 14 hours to average 48·2 mile/h. Their efforts had been worthwhile, for they finished 13th overall amongst the 30 crews who completed the course, and they won the unlimited touring car class and were placed second in the general classification for touring cars. This was a convincing demonstration against strong Italian opposition.

A record-breaking Mille Miglia

Straight from his Targa Florio success, Lurani entered the same car for the 1948 Mille Miglia. A second Elliot was entered for Nick Haines and R. Haller, while a third Healey entry was a Westland to be driven by Donald Healey and his son Geoffrey. The record entry of 187 starters confirmed growing enthusiasm for this classic 1,100-mile road race, the course climbing twice across the stormy Apennines besides covering many hundreds of miles of the fastest roads in Europe. The three Healeys were the sole foreign entries, and again they faced the cream of Italian sports and touring cars.

For days before the event there had been heavy rain, leaving the roads in poor condition, but at least the skies cleared at midnight as the first cars left Brescia. Lurani had suffered a last-minute setback when his co-driver, Serafini, was taken ill; his new partner was Carlo Sandri. The three Healeys set a cracking pace from the start, so fast in fact that by the time Padua was reached the Lurani/Sandri car had broken all previous touring car records, averaging 78 mile/h. Compared with the booming exhausts of the sports-racers, the Healeys caught the admiration of the crowds as the cars whistled quietly through the crowded towns and villages along the route.

After 206 miles the first control was reached. All three cars were through and making good time, but as the roads from Pesaro turned inland, climbing over the first crossing of the mountains, the two saloons were in trouble. Both Lurani and Haines experienced the same rear suspension troubles that bothered Lurani on the Targa Florio, and, with 850 miles to go to the finish, the prospects were not very bright for the Healey team. The Haines saloon spent 50 minutes off the road while repairs were made. Lurani, however, was more fortunate and was not delayed so long. Meanwhile, Donald and Geoffrey Healey with the Westland had made good time to Rome, running second in their class, and despite the mishap to Lurani's saloon, he also reached Rome to break previous touring car records by 26 minutes.

From Rome, northwards along the coast to Florence, the course led up over the mountains for the second crossing. Now the twisty roads were going to tell on the two Healeys with damaged suspension. To make matters worse, the weather began to turn bad. The Haines/Haller car was the first to strike trouble, although it was a gearbox leak which caused their retirement, not the suspension troubles. Then Donald and Geoffrey Healey had the wretched luck to have a 100 mile/h collision with a large dog, which smashed the front wings of the Westland and put the lights out of action. They were delayed nearly 30 minutes, leaving them behind time and facing the most difficult section of the route to cover in darkness without lights. Donald Healey met the challenge with typical determination, for he crossed the mountains safely after a hair-raising drive, and in company with the Lurani/Sandri saloon (which was still running despite the damaged suspension) he sped on to the finish at Brescia along the Turin-Milan-Brescia autostrada. Along this final 150-mile stage, the Healeys had a chance to demonstrate their top speed, the Lurani saloon covering this section at an average of 87·4 mile/h; amongst the six best averages of any competitor. Finally Brescia was reached and the two Healeys came in after 17½ hours of motoring. Donald and Geoffrey Healey in the Westland were placed ninth overall and second in the unlimited sports car class. The Lurani/Sandri saloon was 13th overall, winning the touring car class outright, and established a new touring class record by 90 minutes.

Spa racing début

After its road-racing successes in the Targa Florio and Mille Miglia, the Healey made its circuit racing début in the Belgian 24-Hour Race run upon the famous Ardennes road course at Spa in July 1948. In this, the splendid outright victory of the St John Horsfall Aston Martin somewhat overshadowed the fine performance of the sole Healey entry, an Elliot driven by Tommy Wisdom and Nick Haines.

The race was run under appalling weather conditions; throughout the 24 hours the track was never dry. The Healey saloon, placed in the sports car category because of insufficient entries in the touring class, faced opposition from a number of 3 litre Delages, and these faster French cars led the Healey for most of the race. The sleek, silent Healey contrasted oddly with the sports-racing Delages; the French drivers were completely exposed to the dreadful weather in their open cars, while Wisdom and Haines sat comfortably in the saloon (Wisdom in familiar tweed suit and trilby hat!).

'That got me into a little bit of trouble with my old friend Sammy Davis,' recalls Tommy Wisdom.

'He did not think it was quite the thing to do to go motor racing in a tweed suit and trilby hat and smoking at the same time. Well, the tweed suit was comfortable and I intended to be comfortable in the Healey for the 24 hours. Anyway, it was the sort of car you should wear a tweed suit in – racing or not. The idea of the trilby hat was so that I could protect my eyes from the low sun in the evening. I certainly was not going to wear a crash helmet for 24 hours. And as for smoking – well, I always smoke!

'I remember a funny incident at the start of this race. It was a Le Mans start and we, of course, had a right-hand-drive car and lined up along side us was an open BMW which had left-hand drive. The very pleasant German driver of the BMW came up to me as we stood on the grid and said: "Please, you will go first because we cannot both get into the car at the same time because the doors will touch".

'I replied: "No, please you will go first."

' "No," he answered, "you will go first because I have the faster car and I will soon catch you up. That is only fair."

'And so I did go first and he never saw me again. I bet he was hopping mad!'

By sheer reliability, the Healey reduced the opposition to one single car as the finish approached. With four laps to go, the sole remaining

Delage held only a slender lead over the Healey. It was not until two laps to the finish, when the Healey swept past the French car, that the Delage pit realized their position. Only by establishing a new class record on the last lap was the Delage able to repass the Healey to win the class by less than a mile. It had been an exciting finish to a 24-hour race, and in the atrocious weather conditions the Healey had averaged 66 mile/h, covering 1,585 miles.

Another Alpine class win

Encouraged by the success of the marque's competition début in the 1947 Alpine Rally, Donald Healey and Nick Haines entered a Westland for the 1948 event, held in July. From the familiar starting control at Marseilles the 61 starters left on the first stage to Aix-les-Bains, over a 286-mile route which included the 15-mile timed climb of Mount Ventoux. Here the Healey recorded fastest time in the class, and at this stage Healey and Haines were amongst the 23 crews unpenalized. The 300-mile second stage from Aix-les-Bains to Lugano, through Geneva and Lausanne, caused little trouble. It was the final stage from Chamonix to Nice that brought the greatest penalties.

Col followed col in quick succession. Despite a puncture, Donald Healey was still in the running with the 11 unpenalized drivers for an Alpine Cup. On the timed climb of the Col d'Izoard, the Healey once again made the fastest time in its class.

But it was Donald Healey's sportsmanship that cost him the chance of a coveted Alpine Cup – a success that would have meant valuable publicity for the Company. On the descent of the Col d'Allos, the Healey was being followed by the Hiskins/Marsden Sunbeam-Talbot. On a dangerous bend the Sunbeam's brakes locked and the car left the road, turning over several times as it rolled down the mountainside. Healey and Haines, hearing the crash, turned back to the scene of the accident to help the injured crew from the car. The 45 minutes' delay sacrificed their chances of an Alpine Cup, but, even so, the Healey made the final control at Nice in time to finish amongst the first 14 crews. By putting up the fastest time of his category in the acceleration and braking test at the finish, Healey made sure of winning the 3 litre class for the second year running.

Two trips to Montlhéry

In early September of 1948, the Paris 12 Hour Race took place on

the Montlhéry circuit. Run in conjunction with the awards for outright and class victories, there was a British-versus-French challenge
match between two teams of eight cars. Representing the British team
were the Healey Elliot of Johnson and Haines, the Westland of Wisdom
and Black, two Aston Martins and four HRGs. These were matched
against a French team of Simcas, Gordinis and Delages. The Healeys
made a good start, Leslie Johnson in the saloon leading the field away
from the Le Mans start. But on the first lap the saloon had dropped to
11th place, being passed by the faster Ferraris, Talbots, Simcas, Delahayes and Delages. A rough section of the track provided punishing
treatment in this long-distance event, and within the first three hours
the Wisdom/Black Westland had to make an unscheduled tyre change.
The Johnson/Haines saloon also had to stop for brake adjustment.

In the match race the French team established an early lead, whilst
Talbot, Delahaye and Ferrari led the race. By half-distance the Elliot
had climbed to ninth position and the British team had built up a
commanding lead over the French, but the continuous high speed on
the banked track was causing trouble to the Healeys, and the rough
track was taking its toll. With three hours to go the saloon was retired
with suspected big-end failure; shortly afterwards, transmission troubles
caused the retirement of the Westland. It was a disappointing performance by the Warwick cars, but at least their retirement before
the finish had not prevented the British team from winning the team
match.

The Healeys had not had a very successful outing to Montlhéry,
but when Tommy Wisdom returned to the circuit a month later with
a saloon to undertake long-distance record runs, the results were far
from disappointing. The Healey completed 103·76 miles in the hour
from a flying start, 101·7 miles in the hour from a standing start. The
Healey could now claim to be the first production saloon car to cover
100 miles in the hour.

Private owners

By now many Healeys were being raced successfully in club meetings
by private owners, and the Junior Car Club, now adopting the mantle
of the Brooklands Automobile Racing Club, attracted these enthusiasts
to their first race meeting at Goodwood in September 1948. Healey
saloons had the honour of sharing the front row of the grid for the
first race at the Sussex circuit, and although they were robbed of

outright victory, Ken Downing and Peter Hall were placed second and third in the first race and Nick Haines had the honour of establishing the first lap record, with a speed of 68·3 mile/h.

Undoubtedly one of the fastest Riley-engined Healeys was the Elliot owned and driven by Edgar Wadsworth. This car was extensively modified and developed over several years of competitive use. This particular car's outstanding success was in the B.R.D.C. Production Touring Car Race at Silverstone in 1952, when in the hands of the late Ken Wharton, the Elliot finished second overall to Stirling Moss' Mark VII Jaguar at an average speed of 74·8 mile/h.

Another Mille Miglia class win

The final outing for the works-prepared Elliots and Westlands was in April 1949, when two cars were entered for the Mille Miglia. A saloon car was to be driven by Donald Healey and Geoffrey Price (now Service Manager of the Donald Healey Motor Company), a Westland by Tommy Wisdom and Geoffrey Healey.

It was during practice for this event that Tommy Wisdom recalls an amusing experience:

'I was out practising with the late Peter Collins who was then driving for Aston Martin. We were bowling along at a steady rate of knots somewhere between Verona and Bologna when we carved up a couple of trucks.

'When we got outside the town I turned round and said to Peter, "I think you've had it my old mate because there are a couple of police motor cycles on your tail."

' "Oh, to hell with them," replied Peter and put his foot very firmly on the loud pedal.

'We certainly lost them in a very short space of time but after about ten miles I said to Peter, "I think you've still had it my old mate because there's a level crossing around the next corner and I think it's shut."

'The crossing was indeed closed and after we had been stationary for a couple of minutes our two friends on the motor cycles arrived on the scene. While one of them parked his machine across the front of the car, the other parked his across the back. Then they both came round to Peter's side of the car, gave a smart salute and in broken English said, "A very impressive performance. Permission, please, to examine the engine of this Mille Miglia racer."

'And they never said a word about our little carve up down the road!'

For the 1949 Mille Miglia the course had been modified slightly so that it was faster, although the final section of autostrada had been eliminated. As the cars left Brescia on the 993-mile course, it was clear that there was to be a fierce battle in the touring class between Healey, Bristol, Alfa Romeo and Lancia. The Alfa and the Bristol led away with the Healeys in third and fourth positions, chased by the Lancias not far behind. For the first 420 miles to Rome the order remained unchanged, although the four leading cars were seldom far apart. Along the high-speed run from Pescara to Ancona, Wisdom and Geoffrey Healey were able to forge ahead in the Westland, using their superior top speed, and at Ravenna the British car was able to hold a slender lead.

But on the mountain course the local knowledge of the Italian drivers gave them a temporary advantage. For miles the Healey and Alfa Romeo fought for the class lead, and after 993 miles it was a close finish with the Wisdom car crossing the line less than two minutes ahead of the Alfa. The Bristol came home third followed by Healey and Price in the saloon. Only four minutes separated the first three cars in the touring class. Wisdom's winning speed had been 68·6 mile/h, and for the second year running the Healeys had put up a magnificent performance by winning their class.

Enter the 'Silverstone'

As a production touring car, not specifically designed for competition work, the Elliot and Westland models had achieved a fine record of competitive achievements, success which had helped to swell the order books of the Warwick factory. Only once in international competition had the Healey failed to finish, and from eight major events the marque could claim six class wins and one class 'second'.

The name Healey was now firmly established amongst those of the world's fastest and most successful touring car manufacturers, but with the revival of club racing at home and in the States there was a demand for a Healey more suited to the track. It was clear that the existing Healey chassis and Riley engine, fitted with a lightweight two-seater sports-racing body, would provide the answer, so towards the summer of 1949 the design department at Warwick began work on a new sports car.

CHAPTER 3

THE HEALEY 'SILVERSTONE'

In the spring of 1949 the prototype of a new Healey sports car was completed at the small but industrious factory of the Donald Healey Motor Company at Warwick, and in July the Healey 'Silverstone' was added to the list of British sports cars.

Of all the Warwick-built Healeys, the 'Silverstone' is perhaps the best known, yet only 105 cars were built in the production period to September 1950. In common with all Donald Healey's designs, the 'Silverstone' broke away from tradition, but with the revival of club racing and speed events after the petrol shortage, there was a ready market for this two-seater sports car, the first production Healey costing (less purchase tax) under £1,000.

The 'Silverstone' offered, in the simplest form, an open two-seater sports car bereft of all items of equipment which were not specifically doing a job of work as part of the Healey design for optimum performance and good road-holding. The 'Silverstone' offered its passengers few creature comforts; it was a car you drove simply for the joys of safe, fast motoring.

By using the basically standard Healey chassis, together with the 2,443 cc Riley engine, gearbox and rear axle, the 'Silverstone' was founded upon a rugged design, developed and proved through four years of competition use with the Healey Elliot Saloon and the Westland Roadster. Apart from moving the engine 8 in. farther back and modifying the rear frame and petrol tank layout, the original chassis remained unchanged. Modifications to the suspension included the addition of an anti-roll bar between the trailing links of the front suspension and the fitting of firmer coil springs at the rear. The 5·75 × 15 tyres fitted to the early models were replaced by 5·50 × 15 tyres on the 'Silverstone'.

The purposeful body was of the simplest and most functional design, yet it was not unattractive. To reduce the internal framework, the body was constructed from a single, stressed-skin, light alloy shell. Cycle-type wings were fitted front and rear, and these were made

James Watt, who was closely associated with the Healey Company in its earliest days with the first 'Westland' Roadster. This prototype had retractable flaps over the headlamps; later models had conventional fixed lamps

Chassis construction at the Cape, Warwick

The Healey chassis fitted with the 2½ litre Riley engine that was the basis of all the Warwick-built models up to the Austin-Healey '100'

Donald Healey with the 'Westland' Roadster on a visit to a Hollywood filmset

The production 'Elliot' saloon

Donald Healey's stand at the Paris Motor Show of 1947 showing an early production 'Elliot' on the left and the pillarless 'Duncan' saloon on the right

Tommy Wisdom takes the 'Elliot' around Montlhéry in 1948 to record 103·76 miles in the hour. Note the revised headlight position on this later model compared with the earlier car in the above picture

Donald and Geoffrey Healey set out with the 'Westland' from Brescia at the start of the 1948 Mille Miglia in which they finished ninth overall and second in the unlimited sports car class

The two Healeys entered for the 1949 Mille Miglia. The 'Westland' on the left scored a win in the touring car class, the 'Elliot' finished fourth in the same class

The 'Elliot's' international racing achievements included a class second in the Spa 24 Hour Race of 1948 (Tommy Wisdom and Nick Haines above) and 13th overall at Le Mans in 1949. (Les Onslow-Bartlett and Nigel Mann below)

First competition outing for the 'Silverstone' was on the Alpine Rally of 1949 when Donald Healey and Ian Appleyard won their class and finished second overall

Racing debut for the 'Silverstone' was in the BRDC Silverstone international in 1949 when a team of three cars won the Manufacturers Team Prize. This is the car driven by Louis Chiron

The 'Silverstone' was an ideal car for the clubman and amongst those who started their motor racing career in this model were Charles Mortimer (seen above with his wife) and Tony Brooks, both at BARC Goodwood Meetings

'Silverstones' continue to be raced by a small but enthusiastic band of owners. This is Brian Dermott who contributed most of the Riley engine tuning data in the Appendix to this book

Based on the 'Silverstone' chassis the 3·8 litre Nash-Healey was introduced in 1950 and had the biggest production run of all the Warwick-built Healey models

Driven by Tony Rolt and Duncan Hamilton this 'Silverstone'-based Nash–Healey prototype finished fourth overall at Le Mans in 1950 averaging 87·6 mile/h

For the 1951 Le Mans race the 1950 Nash–Healey prototype was rebuilt as a closed coupé and, driven by Tony Rolt and Duncan Hamilton, finished sixth overall. Here Rolt leads the 'C' type Jaguar of Stirling Moss

For Le Mans the following year the coupé was converted back to an open car and driven by Leslie Johnson and Tommy Wisdom finished third overall behind the works Mercedes

Nash–Healey entries in the Mille Miglia included the production model (*above*) driven by Donald and Geoffrey in 1951 (finished 30th overall) and the 4·1 litre special (*below*) driven by John Pitch and John Willday in 1953 (retired)

The 'Duncan' bodies on the Healey chassis offered less expensive coachwork designs. Both the two-seater sports (*above*) and the open roadster (*below*) are rare examples

The 'Tickford' (*above*) was the most popular of the Healey saloons. The similar styled drop-head coupé model (*below*) was made by 'Abbott'

Contrast in cockpit appointments of the luxurious 'Abbott' above and the more sporting 'Silverstone' below

If the 'Sportsmobile' introduced in 1949 lacked style and attractive body lines, it did offer remarkable comfort and lavish appointments. Some 23 examples were built

The last of the Warwick-built models, the Alvis-engined 'Sports convertible', bore a close resemblance to the prototype shape of the Healey '100'

easily detachable for competition use. Another design feature to attract the enthusiast was the full-width retracting windscreen, which could be lowered into the scuttle for speed events. To improve the aerodynamics, the lines of the body shell were kept as smooth as possible, the headlamps being tucked away behind the radiator grille and the spare wheel housed in a 'letter-box' opening in the tail. Just enough of the tyre projected to form a convenient rear bumper.

The early 'Silverstone' chassis was designated the 'D'-type. In April 1950 the 'E'-type was introduced. This had a slightly wider body and had more leg room in the cockpit; a bench-type seat, individually moulded, replaced the twin bucket seats. A detachable front portion gave easier access to the front suspension. An adjustable telescopic steering column was employed, the windscreen was enlarged, and Perspex wind deflectors were fitted. There was an improved hood design and a full tonneau cover. Front bumpers were also supplied. The 'E'-type was most readily distinguished from the earlier model by the air intake on the bonnet top.

Saving 4 cwt over the earlier Healey models, the 'Silverstone' weighed $18\frac{1}{2}$ cwt and, with the $2\frac{1}{2}$ litre Riley engine producing 104 b h p, it was not surprising that the new Healey proved to be a 100 mile/h-plus performer with a useful third gear maximum around the 80 mile/h mark.

Alpine début

The announcement of the 'Silverstone' in July coincided with the Alpine Rally, and it did not take Donald Healey long to decide that this would be an ideal test run for his new car.

Retaining its reputation amongst the world's toughest trials, the 1949 event was to cover 1,830 miles, encompassing 35 major Alpine passes. With co-driver Ian Appleyard, Donald Healey and the new 'Silverstone' set out from Marseilles among the 92 starters. The first of the special tests was a timed regularity climb of Mount Ventoux in the dark, and here Healey and Appleyard put up a fine performance. After 12 hours on the road, at the end of the first section at Monte Carlo, the 'Silverstone' was an easy class-winner and well in the running for a Coupe des Alpes. On the special 5 km timed section on the autostrada, included in the 445 mile second stage to Cortina, the Healey recorded an average speed of 83 mile/h, but soon after this the crew were unfortunately delayed at a level crossing. Despite

H.A.H.—4

Donald Healey's efforts in forcing the low-slung 'Silverstone' beneath the closed gates (much to the annoyance of the gatekeeper), the crew lost two minutes on this section. As this was the only penalty they gained throughout the whole event, undoubtedly this piece of hard luck cost them the chance of the coveted Coupe des Alpes and perhaps outright victory. But the Healey certainly had not disgraced itself, for after class-winning climbs of the Stelvio and Col de Vars (the 'Silverstone' actually recording the fastest time on the Col de Vars and second fastest on the Stelvio) Healey and Appleyard reached the finish at Nice to be placed the first British car, second overall in general classification and first in the class. The 'Silverstone' had enjoyed a glorious competition debut and its performance against 53 other British crews, with Allard, Bristol, Sunbeam and MG, was a praiseworthy effort for a new model.

Silverstone success

Not long after the Alpine Rally, came the B.R.D.C. International Trophy Meeting at Silverstone and the popular Production Car Race. Donald Healey secured the services of three well-known drivers, Louis Chiron, Tony Rolt and Tommy Wisdom, and entered a team of three 'Silverstones'. The race was dominated by the new XK Jaguars, and became the occasion of closely-fought class battles which entertained the record crowd. The three 'Silverstones' were well placed in the $2\frac{1}{2}$ litre category, doing battle with the Frazer-Nashes. Towards the finish, the retirement of one of the Jaguars gave the 'Silverstones' the Team Prize. Rolt finished fourth overall in the race and was placed second in the class with a race speed of 78·4 mile/h, while Chiron was fourth in the class and Wisdom fifth. Soon after the order books at Warwick reflected the 'Silverstone' model's success at its 'own' racing circuit.

But the 'Silverstone' was also making a name for itself in the States, mainly thanks to the enthusiasm and ability of Briggs Cunningham, who had shipped the first 'Silverstone' across the Atlantic. Not satisfied with the performance of the Riley-engined car, Cunningham fitted a $5\frac{1}{2}$ litre Cadillac power unit, and scored many successes. Competing in the 105-mile Palm Beach Road Races held in Florida in January 1950, Cunningham gained second place overall with the 'Silverstone', and later in the year with the same car he took second place again in the 100-mile Watkins Glen Sports Car Grand Prix.

Wisdom on the Targa

In the gruelling Targa Florio Road Race held in April 1950, an event plagued with atrocious weather conditions and dominated by Italian entries, Tommy Wisdom and Tony Hume brought a 'Silverstone' home as the first British car, 16th overall out of 185 starters, and fourth in the unlimited sports class.

Tommy Wisdom remembers an amusing little incident concerning his co-driver on this event:

'Whenever we stopped for refuelling (usually in the middle of a market place in a village) I would always take the opportunity to spend a penny if the urge was there. Tony, however, obviously had not given much thought to this problem and after we had done about 400 miles he lent over and shouted to me asking whether I would mind stopping for a moment. When I asked him what the devil he wanted to stop for, and he told me, I said that it was just hard luck and he would have to wait until the next fuel stop. Damned if I would stop for such a performance in an important international road race!

'After about another half hour Tony began to fidget about in his seat and obviously the poor fellow was in some distress. I then suggested to him that if he was that bad then he had better solve his problems while we were going along because I was then even more determined not to stop for him. But Tony, poor fellow, replied that he did not think this was a very practical solution as there were rather a lot of spectators lining the route. Furthermore, he did not think he could accomplish what he wanted to do sitting down and he made it very clear to me that he was not going to stand up in the car and perform!

'We reached the next control; there was a lot of work to be done on the car and we hurried with refuelling and tyre changing, checked the oil and were soon away. I had promised Tony that he could take over the wheel on this the last leg and with the excitement of doing the driving Tony, of course, forgot about his past troubles.

'No sooner had we gone about 20 miles than Tony screeched to a stop and leapt out of the car.

' "What the hell do you think you are doing?" I yelled at him.

' "I'm sorry, Tom. I forgot all about it at that last stop."

' "If you're not back in this car in 10 seconds," I screamed at him, "I'm going on without you."

'Poor Tony leapt back in behind the wheel with his trousers half
undone and shot off up the road in such a state that when we came
to a level crossing about half a mile on he was going so fast that we
missed the road altogether and the "Silverstone" went roaring off up
the railway lines! Never mind, he soon had us back on the road
without any damage and we pressed on to the finish.

'I must say we had a good laugh about that afterwards!'

A bad Mille Miglia

After the Targa Florio, attention was turned to the Mille Miglia,
but again the weather was bad for this 1,000-mile road race. This was
an unhappy event starting a succession of eliminations by accidents
for the Healeys. 'Silverstones' were entered by Peter Monkhouse/
Philip Wood, Robin Richards/Rodney Lord and the Italians Mosters/
Castelbarco, and of these three entries only the Italian crew reached
the finish, being placed 38th out of 383 starters. Accidents eliminated
the other two 'Silverstones' soon after the start. It had been a disappointing outing for the Warwick cars after the marque's outstanding
record of Mille Miglia successes in 1948 and 1949 with the Elliot and
Westland.

Fortune did not change for the Alpine Rally run in July, when
'Silverstones' were entered by Gordon Wilkins, Edgar Wadsworth,
Leslie Onslow-Bartlett and G. Walker. All but Gordon Wilkins
retired after accidents early in the event, Wilkins making a promising
start to lead the class by a handsome margin, performing well on the
regularity tests and putting up third fastest time (at 95·7 mile/h) over
the timed kilo, beaten only by the leading Talbot and Jaguar. Then
on the final stage of the event a stone jammed the throttle open, the
remaining 'Silverstone' crashed and was too badly damaged to
continue.

Silverstone racing

The Healey's luck remained poor until August 1950, when the
two-seater made a return to Silverstone for the B.R.D.C. Production
Car Race. No fewer than eight 'Silverstones' were entered: one works
car for Duncan Hamilton and seven privately-entered cars. With his
characteristic style, Hamilton entertained the crowd to a fine class
win at 79·9 mile/h, holding off a strong Aston Martin challenge. The

best of the private entrants, Charles Mortimer and Guy Gale, were placed fifth and sixth in the class behind Hamilton.

Charles Mortimer, in his book *Racing a Sports Car*, has left us a full account of the race:

'We took up our places on the other side of the course, and the minutes ticked away relentlessly. Four minutes, three, two, and I began to wonder whether the old car would start as perfectly as she always had. I looked at Duncan who was next door and who was still sitting on a straw bale nonchalantly watching the starter. I wondered; would the car start, would it start? Why I should have thought so I can't imagine, because of all the cars I have ever owned, the Healey was the best starter ever. But on every other occasion it hadn't mattered particularly whether it started first push of the button or not. This time everything depended on it. Suddenly I heard the announcer on the loud speaker. "Twenty seconds to go." My feet felt as though they were filled with lead and as I looked down the line I thought, "How ridiculous we look." Fat men, thin men, men wearing visors, men wearing goggles, boxing boots, plimsolls, queer shirts, as incongruous a collection as one would meet anywhere. And now we were going to run! It seemed fantastic!

'Then suddenly: "Ten seconds to go." I put my goggles down. "Five, four, three, two, one" and down goes the flag and we scuttle across the concrete as though our very lives depend on it. At last – the car – open the door – hurl myself in – left-hand switch on – right hand slam door – left hand engage first gear – right hand press starter.

'Dead silence all along the line – but no! No! – the engine's running. A fraction of a second to build up some revs and we're away before Duncan or Guy Gale on either side have moved. As we gather way, the entire line, it seems, get going and we roar down to Woodcote Corner right on the tail of the three Aston Martins driven by Sommer, Reg Parnell and Eric Thompson. Suddenly I realize that there is a car alongside trying desperately to get through and out of the corner of my eye I recognize Duncan – very determined, grimly determined, in fact, and obviously in no mood to argue. Well, he can have it, as far as I am concerned. It's early yet, and I'd rather see whether the circuit had dried out at all, although I haven't any objection to hanging on to his tail. Copse Corner and the pace is much hotter than I expected under these conditions – Maggots Corner, still very slippery, and as we round Becketts – it happens.

'Quite what happened I've never been able to recall accurately. It was very wet and I think the thing started as a tail slide. It finished, however, as a glorious dyed-in-the-wool four-wheel slide, quite out of control with no steering way and no object in braking because the car was going sideways anyhow. I had a glimpse of the grass verge roaring up at terrific speed and had quite decided that the car was going to roll when, to my amazement, I found that I was still motoring albeit with only two wheels still on the track. Obviously, though, the crisis was over and now was the time to accelerate and rejoin the contest. The rest of the lap is completed, I am afraid, at greatly reduced speed and if ever I had any doubts regarding my ability to become a racing driver, I have them now.

'As I approach Stowe, I am aware of another car alongside and as we pull away from the corner altogether, I take a look – and am duly shocked for I find that it is G. H. Grace's $2\frac{1}{2}$ litre Riley full four-seater saloon. Worse is to follow, for it takes me over a lap to get ahead of him and another lap before I really feel that he is shaken off. After five laps, we become fairly well strung out; there is a blue Allard ahead which seems to be gaining slightly although steadily, and in the mirror I see my team mate Guy Gale in his dark green Healey. Duncan, of course, has vanished into the blue, and by now the circuit has really dried out with the exception of one or two bad patches which are easily remembered and which present no real difficulty.

'The race has now become comparatively dull, for we are cracking along without seeing anyone. Guy is gradually falling astern, the Allard has now disappeared from view and for several laps I am motoring entirely alone with no one else in sight at all. I begin to wonder about the progress of the race. We had agreed that unless some very great crisis arose I would not expect to receive any pit signals, for we felt that the race was not long enough to warrant any and that we could more or less foresee the result anyway. I knew that the Jaguars and big Allard would be way out in front and that the three Aston Martins and Duncan would be filling the first four places in the up to 3 litre class, although I was not sure that there were no other 3 litre cars ahead of me.

'Normally, I would have felt fairly sure of the position, for it is not too difficult at the start of a race to see who had gone on ahead, but when I had trouble at Becketts on the first lap, I was dimly aware that a number of people had gone by without my knowing who they were. I had subsequently passed both David Lewis and W. Freed's Healeys who had obviously slipped by but could not recall having seen anything of either Sir Francis Samuelson or my other team mate Robin Richards.

'I wondered what my pit staff were thinking, for the start really had been a good one although my position in the race at the end of lap one must have been a complete mystery to them. The car was now going perfectly and I felt much more comfortable and had really settled down and was beginning to enjoy myself. I was now expecting to be lapped by the outright leader of the race, and sure enough at the end of lap 13 discerned in the mirror the form of a green Jaguar which, as it passed, turned out to be driven by Peter Walker, closely followed by Tony Rolt on another Jaguar.

'Although I didn't know it at the time, my lap times were steadily improving throughout the race and I now began to lap some of the steadier runners in the race. There were several incidents, one of them, at Maggots Corner, involving Peter Whitehead's Jaguar to no small degree. I found that it was not easy to see exactly what had happened because as I came around for the first time I must have been closely on the tail of the incident, for the marshals on the spot had not yet had time to sort out the correct flags. What I did see, however, caused me not to allow my attention to wander for, out of the corner of my eye, I spotted one marshal hastily grabbing the flag denoting oil on the track.

'I wondered whether he'd grabbed it by mistake, but almost at the same moment I felt sure he was right for, on the opposite side of the track, there was apparently a large hole in the fence through which the tail of a car protruded. No sooner had I had time to take all this in than the Healey gave a lurch and, if I had ever had any doubts, I now knew that there was indeed oil on the track. To make it more difficult, the oil patch was right on the apex of the bend, but the marshals on the spot must have dealt with it most capably for it was no worse to cross on the next lap and appeared to get steadily better as the race progressed.

'A few laps later, having negotiated it once more without incident, I emerged from Becketts to find David Lewis' light blue Healey facing back to front, its driver obviously waiting until there should be a lull in the activity before turning the car round and continuing.

'Shortly after this, I saw in my mirror another car coming up astern rather more slowly than the two Jaguars and for several laps I was a bit mystified as to what it was.

'It turned out to be Sommer's Aston Martin which went by me

quite slowly, on the straight between Chapel Curve and Stowe
Corner. Rather to my surprise, it was not followed by the other two
Astons and as it had gone by more slowly than I had expected I made
an effort to hang on for as long as possible.

We approached Stowe, according to my rev. counter, at between
105 and 107 miles an hour, the Aston's stop lights blinked for a
moment and before I had really grasped the situation, we were into
the corner, the Aston in the most perfectly controlled four-wheel
drift imaginable. I was also conscious of being in a slide although in
my wildest dreams I could not claim that it was perfectly controlled,
but I did get around and, to my great delight, I came out of the corner
still on Sommer's tail. We more or less repeated the performance at
Stowe, even appeared to gain slightly at Abbey Curve, went past the
pits in line ahead and into Woodcote Corner at a pace I just couldn't
quite manage.

'As we came out, I estimated that I had lost between 15 and 20
yards and I don't think I lost any more at Copse although Sommer
appeared not to have a worry in the world as he crossed the oil patch
at Maggots and here again I appeared to have lost about the same
distance on this one bend alone. I was now convinced that there was
virtually no difference whatever in acceleration between the two cars
although the Aston Martin seemed to have about five miles an hour
more maximum. But the point was that there were so very few places
on the course where we were reaching maximum and it boiled down
therefore to the fact that, as I saw it, ninety per cent of Sommer's gain
over my own car had been obtained by his terrific technique on the
bends. I continued the losing battle for a few more laps but was
forced to admit that despite all I just couldn't come near to coping.

'By now, the race was nearing its end and as Sommer disappeared
from view a well-known silhouette appeared in my mirror—Duncan
with the works Healey! So Duncan was ahead of the other two Astons
and at that rate was not so very far behind Sommer. He passed me at
the approach to Stowe, the car sounding very good and taking the
corner very fast indeed although, I thought, not as steadily as the
Aston Martin. Duncan was obviously on top of his form, shaking
with laughter and sticking his tongue out at me as he passed and I
decided again to tail him for a bit if I could. But it seemed to me
that he was, if anything, faster everywhere than the Aston and I had
the greatest difficulty to stay with him for even half a lap. The
acceleration of the car was much better than mine and coupled with

Duncan's carefree style of driving was obviously likely to, and did in fact produce the results required, for just before the end of the race he caught and passed Sommer, thereby finishing winner of the 3 litre class.

'Almost immediately, it seemed, we were given the chequered flag and, on coming in, I was besieged by my staff as to why, after my good start, I had been so slow in the opening laps. Having furnished the explanations, we all went off to the timekeeper's box to obtain copies of the official results and finishing times which were, after all, rather more encouraging than I had expected. They showed that we had finished fifth in the 3 litre class.'

Tourist Trophy

In September came the Tourist Trophy, run over 34 laps of the 7·4-mile Dundrod road circuit. Again the marque was represented by many private entrants with 'Silverstones'. All but one of the Healeys finished the race, Ernie Wilkinson bringing the highest-placed car into ninth position overall, averaging 70·6 mile/h for the 211 miles. The 'Silverstones' occupied fourth to eighth places in the class behind three formidable Aston Martins driven by Parnell, Abecassis and Macklin.

Again, Charles Mortimer's book gives us a graphic description of this race:

'At one minute to go, the conditions were as bad as ever and, as the final seconds ticked away, I watched the various preparations of those in the pits to combat the elements for the next three hours. If the drivers looked strange at Silverstone, they looked even stranger now and when I looked down the line and saw Lance Macklin waiting to drive his Aston Martin in a pixie hood I felt that I had witnessed everything that motor racing had to offer.

'At last – five seconds to go, four, three, two, one – and down goes the flag. Again the mad scramble across the track – again the breathless silence having hurled oneself into the car and again the sudden realization that my engine was running before I, at least, had heard anyone else's. Into first gear – and away – and as I pull out, the entire line seems to pull out as well.

'But again the start is a good one – there is no doubt about that, for there are no Healeys, or Frazer-Nashs ahead, only Allards, Jaguars and directly ahead, the three Aston Martin DB2s. I just manage to scramble past the Austin A90 before the narrow section which is good from my

point of view for, as the most "touring" car in the race, he is likely
to hold up very fast cars behind him quite appreciably. Now we are
really cracking along the straight at Rushyhill, but as we approach
the fast bends at the end of the straight there is considerable caution
among those at the head of the procession and the stop lights of the
three Aston Martins directly ahead of me blink, it seems, hundreds of
yards earlier than they have done even in the worst weather in practice.

'Leathemstown bridge is also treated with respect by all, but the
superior acceleration of the Aston Martins tells slightly in the steep
pull away afterwards. Nevertheless after the breathtaking dive down
to Cochranstown, I am again right on the tail of the third one, driven
I can now see by George Abecassis, as we pull away from the corner.
I know very well that this state of affairs cannot and will not last – that
the field is gradually sorting itself out and that we are all having a
chance to assess carefully, the fearful state of the roads. Because the
process is taking slightly longer than usual and the pace is, in consequence, considerably slower, it would be a fatal mistake to try to pass
even if it looks possible to do so at this stage.

'At Wheelers Corner the form is now taking shape, for the Astons
have drawn seventy or eighty yards ahead and I am now trying really
hard to keep up instead of, as at the start of the lap, feeling I could
get by. We round the hairpin which always gives one an impression
of standing still after the fast bends preceding and following it and,
having successfully negotiated the Quarry bends, we are passing the
pits for the first time.

'Reading later from the official bulletins issued by the R.A.C. I
found that at the end of this lap I lay fourth in the class, our respective
averages for the first lap being: Reg 65·59 mile/h, Lance 63·14, George
62·82, all with Astons, of course, while I followed at 62·09 mile/h with
Ernie Wilkinson on the next Healey, fifth at 61·23 mile/h. Leslie
Johnson led the big boys on his Jaguar at 69·34, followed by Stirling
Moss, similarly mounted, at 69·16 mile/h. Allard with one of his own
products being third in this class at 65·92 mile/h. No one obviously
was prepared to risk getting into trouble on the first lap as these speeds
showed.

'Although I didn't know it at the time, there was a smash on the
second lap of the race which might well have had serious consequences,
for my team mate, Walter Freed, who was just behind me at the time,
came badly unstuck at Irelands Corner, the car apparently hitting the
offside bank first, careering across the road and collecting a tree head

on. The marshals at this spot must have been right on their toes for, granted the fact that the accident happened immediately behind me, there could only have been an interval of six and a half minutes at the outside before we were round again. At no time did I see any sign of the wrecked car and in that time they must somehow have dislodged the wreck from the tree and parked it somewhere well clear of the course – really smart work by all concerned. Freed was fortunately quite unhurt, apart from having broken his glasses which, having seen the car, seemed to me a miracle. Fairly early on lap two, I spied a dark green car in my mirror which obviously had the speed to pass, and pulling aside I found that it was Ernie Wilkinson. He passed, going great guns, and when we reached the pits at the end of that lap he was eight seconds ahead of me according to our timing.

'To my great dismay, however, the brakes of the Healey were already showing signs of tiring. The symptoms were not the same as those I had had in practice, for there was now plenty of brake power, but the pedal was going farther and farther down to the boards which meant that, if we went on at this rate, there would be literally nothing left even by half distance. The state of affairs was exactly what I had been warned would happen if the brakes were not bedded down and progressively adjusted over a substantial mileage so I could place the blame on no one but myself although I felt that we had not really had the best of luck on this particular trip right from the outset. Nevertheless, there it was, the brakes were bedding down, and mighty quickly under these conditions, so I decided to give up trying to stay with Ernie and to brake earlier everywhere and use the gearbox wherever possible in an endeavour to keep going to the end somehow. One by one, the Frazer-Nashes of Culpan, Gerrard and Crook came by, as I had expected, for we knew too well that due to their very light weight we couldn't hope to stick with them on the Healeys although at the start they had been slightly farther down the line due to their smaller capacity, but before long I found another Healey, this time Robin Richards, on my tail and again I had to let him pass.

'Both Ernie Wilkinson and Robin were taking the bends at terrific speed and it was quite hopeless for me to try to tag along and still have any brakes later in the race; but before long I found yet another Healey, this time the green car driven by Masters, on my tail. He passed me just before Jordans Cross, the car sounding very good indeed and on the run up to Wheelers Corner I noticed that it appeared to have rather more acceleration than either of the two Healeys that had passed me previously. Masters, however, was exercising much more caution on the bends than either Robin or Ernie, and as soon as he had gone by I tucked in behind him to watch points.

'I found that, despite his superior acceleration I could gain a lot on him on the fast bends on the uphill stretch from Ireland Corner to the hairpin. He would pull away at the hairpin, I could gain on him again through the twisty bends before the pits whereupon he would pull right away on the long straight from the pits to Leathemstown Corner. Over Leathemstown bridge I found that I was catching him again and by using the brakes fairly hard at Cochranstown I found that I was right on his tail once more half-way between Jordans Cross and Wheelers Corner. This went on for several laps until I noticed that already things were noticeably worse in the braking department and, bearing in mind the fact that we had not yet completed one hour's running out of three, I decided to save the brakes even more in my endeavours to finish the race. Weather conditions had, for the past fifty minutes, been even worse but now it appeared as though it might be going to improve. Unfortunately the improvement was only temporary for by three-thirty they were as bad as ever.

'Even the pool in which I sat, and it really was a pool of some standing – for the water was pouring in a steady stream off the scuttle of the car – even this pool was mildly warm for, without using the brakes I was having to drive the old car to the maximum and the hard worked engine and gearbox were warming the cockpit nicely in consequence.

'Strangely enough, visibility did not seem to me to be too bad when one was alone, but in the company of other cars it was at times down almost to nil when the rain was at its height.

'I was keeping a careful eye on both the time and the petrol gauge for we had checked on consumption and if it were wet we should just be able to run through the three hours without stopping for fuel by virtue of the reduced mileage we should cover under these conditions. If fine, we thought we should have to stop but, of course, although we couldn't possibly have had it wetter our calculations were now completely upset by the brakeless state in which we now found ourselves.

'Not only was I having to drive the car much harder than I had intended to in order to put up even a reasonable performance, but in addition, I was having to use third and even second gears probably a hundred per cent more than I had in practice in order to assist in pulling the car up. Towards the end of the race the situation from our point of view was so desperate that on two occasions I had to use first gear instead of second in order to get the car round the hairpin.

'At the end of one and a half hours' running, the needle of the fuel gauge showed the tank between half and three-quarters full, but I knew that in common with most other gauges it was prone to fall much more quickly from the half full to zero positions than from the full to half full points. Until later in the race, I should not be able to learn much from it but I knew that when the car went on to reserve, I could then do only four more laps at the outside without running out of fuel.

'Meanwhile, despite the awful conditions, or perhaps even because of them, the race was not by any means lacking in excitement. However the only incident I had noticed was when I discovered one of the HRG team stationary in the road right on the approach to the hairpin. As I passed, I could see that it was Peter Clark's car and to my great surprise it was still there when I came round again six and a half minutes or so later and I couldn't at the time imagine what malady had befallen it to make it immobile for so long. Looking back, although I am not absolutely sure, I think it was still there when I came round for the second time. At any rate I was vastly puzzled by it all and subsequently heard that its brakes had seized on which must have been a considerable source of worry to the marshals on the hairpin and, of course, even more so to Peter himself.

'By 4 p m the conditions were absolutely indescribable, for, in addition to the wind and driving rain, the section of the course between Wheelers Corner and the hairpin was becoming shrouded in mist. On one lap it would be quite bad then on the next it would have improved, while on the lap following it would move a few hundred yards down the road just to make it harder still. I found this complication, coupled with my brake troubles, almost the last straw that broke the camel's back and for a time I felt like packing the whole thing in. However, we had come a long way for the race and were now two-thirds through it and it seemed a pity to drop out at this stage, if we could possibly keep going, although we were, of course, nowhere in the running even for a class place. But the thing that decided me above all else to keep going was the marvellous enthusiasm and doggedness of the spectators and even more so the spirit among the marshals and observers all round the course. In all the races both on two wheels and on four that I have run I can never recall a race or a course where flag signals were of greater importance, and I can certainly say without fear of contradiction that I have never at any time seen those duties carried out more efficiently or under more unpleasant circumstances.

'From the driver's point of view it was often impossible to know that there was a car behind one wishing to pass unless one received a flag signal, for at times the mirrors became coated in mud and water so that they were temporarily almost useless. Towards the latter part of the race in fact the Aston Martins were using their sidelights and these showed up so well in my mirror when they came up behind that I at once followed suit and found passing quite a bit easier in consequence.

'Just after four-thirty the car ran right out of fuel on the main supply just between Quarry Corner and the pits and this, too, presented another headache for I now knew that in the 26 minutes left before 5 p m when the race was due to finish, I should cover almost exactly four laps. Whether to make sure of completing the race by stopping on my last lap or whether to chance it and to keep going I couldn't decide. The car hadn't gone quite so far on main supply as it should have, according to calculations we had made during practice, but this was obviously because I had had to use the gears so much more to assist in braking and this state of affairs would certainly be no better over the final four laps.

'I thought and thought about it, and just couldn't decide. As we were not in the running we could lose little by coming in except that it would put us further still down the list of finishers. On the other hand, if the car ran out of fuel between the hairpin and Quarry Corner, as it probably would on the last lap, it should, I felt, be able to coast the remainder of the way to the pits, most of this being downhill. Another awful possibility occurred to me. I had estimated that I should arrive at the finish almost spot on 5 o'clock. Supposing I arrived seconds before to find no flag flying, I should then be faced with having to do yet another lap which was, I knew, quite impossible without a fuel stop.

'Anyhow, I didn't decide until I was nearly beginning what I hoped and thought would be my last lap. To tell the truth, I felt so disgusted with the prevailing conditions, that, although I realized it was a chance, I decided to take it and to keep going. If the thing ran out, nothing was lost; if it didn't, so much the better. I did, however, take one precaution in driving the car not quite so hard for the final lap. In this way I may perhaps have saved the few drops of fuel necessary to take the car over the line, but I also ensured that it was fractionally after 5 o'clock rather than fractionally before it when I rounded Quarry Corner for the last time. Anyhow, we made it and it was a great relief to see the chequered flag flying, although rather limply, as we arrived at the pits, followed closely by Robin who had just failed to lap us and by Mike Oliver who, having passed us once, had then had to stop for fuel and had just failed to catch up and pass for the second time.

'The scene at the pits was quite chaotic for the gale which was now certainly worse than ever, had blown down most of the refreshment tents, the rain was falling as never before and as, one by one, the storm-battered cars and drivers arrived the confusion and shouting increased. Needless to say, my wonderful wife was waiting, soaked to the skin, to welcome me, for all our efforts to combat the elements whether in the car or in the pits had been as naught.'

A 'Silverstone' on the Liège

By September 1950, production of the 'Silverstone' had ceased, for the Warwick factory were now concerned with the full-time production of the dollar-earning Nash-Healeys. But in private hands the 'Silverstones' continued to gain successes in international competition for many years.

The story of Peter Riley and Bill Lamb's class win and eighth place overall in the 1951 Liège-Rome-Liège Rally was told in *Safety Fast* magazine by Peter Riley:

'It was in the summer of 1951 when Bill Lamb telephoned me and asked if I'd like to enter my Healey "Silverstone" in the Liège-Rome-Liège. I'd never *heard* of the Liège-Rome-Liège, and no Englishman had done it since Bill Everett with a Singer in the early 'thirties. Bill and I thought it would be a nice, quiet trundle down to Rome and back, run by some unknown Belgian club – and there was nobody to disillusion us.

'I was racing my "Silverstone" fairly regularly around the club circuits in England, and it was in the usual knock-about, mid-season trim. It wasn't modified, just an ordinary standard machine with a low-compression (6·9 to 1) motor, no side-curtains, and oil-drum dents all over it. The idea of a bit of Continental travel appealed to me, since I'd never seen the Alps or in fact anywhere south of Le Mans, and I agreed to Bill's suggestion for a pleasant 10-day holiday.

'We duly entered and arranged to cross to Ostend on Sunday, 12 August. The Sunday before I was racing at Ibsley in Hampshire, and during practice ran a big-end on the Healey. However, Archie Scott-Brown and I set to and, working through most of the night, changed the big-end and got the Healey to the starting line.

'On the Monday I went up to Norwich and, leaving the car with a local garage, overseen by Bill Lamb (who was stationed nearby), went back to Cambridge for a final week's lecture-cutting before the "off". The garage fitted new plugs, new brake-linings, new tyres, and plastered as many lights on the front as would fit. We were rather concerned about tyres, but since works service was non-existent and finance short we arranged for four retreads to be delivered to a garage in Viterbo; this, we hoped, would see us through. By mid-day the following Monday we were in Liège.

'We were received with great kindness by Monsieur Garot, the organizer, and personally escorted to our hotel. The next day we fitted the rally plates and checked over the car. I was a bit worried about the engine, since it had been put together by two amateurs and I'd never hand-scraped a bearing before, but it seemed its usual lusty self. We'd hit a big bump on the way over the Belgian *pavé* and both tail-lamp glasses had shot out of their rubber mountings; replacements were unobtainable, so we had to make do with red-painted bulbs.

'On Wednesday evening, we left Liège in the official procession for the midnight start at Spa. The opposition certainly impressed us: Johnny Claes (Jaguar); Gendebien (Alfa-Romeo); von Hanstein and Guilleaume in the brand-new prototype Porsche coupés; Trintignant in a Le Mans Simca-Gordini, and many other fierce-looking operators in fierce-looking motor-cars.

'The start was magnificent. A huge grid – 40 rows of three cars each – was assembled up the main street of Spa, and every three minutes the front row was released by a gesticulating Monsieur Garot. Our turn soon came, and off we shot into the misty night. We rapidly outdistanced our group and, arriving at the Spa circuit, just as rapidly got lost. After milling round for some time in the forest we came upon a forester's house with a light in the upper window. A head appeared and we shouted "St Vith?" in an enquiring tone. The head disappeared and, in a flash, a pyjamaed figure shot out of the front door and with a cry of "Suivez-moi" leapt into a 203 Peugeot. We followed the Peugeot, travelling absolutely flat out, until after a few kilometres we rejoined the rally convoy behind a sports-racing $4\frac{1}{2}$ litre Lago-

Talbot two-seater. This was a great challenge to Monsieur Pyjamas in the Peugeot, and he diced happily with us both for about 10 miles before he "retired when leading" with a cheery wave. We arrived at Luxembourg 34 minutes early after a splendid motor race.

'By morning we had crossed France to Belfort, near the Swiss border, but already there were ominous thumps coming from the rear suspension. The shock-absorbers were beginning to wilt but there was little we could do, so we pressed hopefully on. The first pass was the Col de la Faucille, and since I had never seen one before, Bill drove. I was perfectly sure that no motor-car could stand this sort of thing for long, but the Healey came gallantly over without missing a beat and we made it by $2\frac{1}{2}$ minutes, so I supposed that we would have to continue at the same breakneck pace. By the time we got to Annecy with 450 miles behind us, the rear tyres were showing signs of wear, so we decided on a front-to-rear change. I bent down to undo the front wheel-nuts and promptly passed out on the ground. Bill hauled me up and, propping me up against a shady wall, did the job himself. On the way again the cool air of the Haute Savoie revived me. After eating a hard-boiled egg and having a swig of water, I felt fine.

'We were now in the traditional rally country for the first time, and I began to enjoy the whole thing enormously. During the course of the afternoon we did the Col de Porte, the Cucheron, the Granier, the Lautaret, and in the early evening that dreaded 7,000 ft, single-track gravel pass known as the Col d'Izoard. Halfway over we came across the crew of a Belgian Aston Martin, fighting one another beside their very bent motor-car; we assumed the owner had not been driving.

'However, we made the control at Arvieux with 1 min. 59 secs in hand and we were well content. Then came the Col de Vars and the Cayolle – and now it was our turn to hit trouble. The weak rear shock-absorbers had allowed the axle to hammer on the bottom of the petrol tank, which soon began to leak, and our fuel consumption rose alarmingly. At Barcelonnette we had 24 secs in hand, at Guillaumes 1 minute. With the engine working hard, a core plug in the cylinder block started leaking water and the valve-cover seal gave way, so that both us and the car were covered in a thick layer of filth. We bought chewing-gum for the petrol tank and made a wooden plug for the block. After a triumphant 80 mile/h arrival down the Promenade des Anglais, we had nine minutes to gulp a coke and a hot dog in the Nice control; 750 miles done, and we still had not lost a mark. . . .

H.A.H.—5

'Now we turned the Healey's stubby nose towards Italy and tackled the Col de Nice, the Col du Braus and the Col de Saint-Jean, and descended the Col di Tenda on to the plain of Italy. The tank was beginning to leak again, and I remembered lying under the car in Cuneo, wedging more chewing-gum into the cracks while a voluble Italian pushed little cups of hot black coffee to me. By now fatigue was taking its toll and, inexperienced as we were, we soldiered on in a fair daze. Bill was driving along the Italian Riviera into Genoa while I sat swaying in the passenger's seat, hoping and praying that he would shunt it so that we could at least stop. It was difficult to remember any other life than driving this Healey and difficult to conceive of actually being allowed to sink into a warm, clean bed. We still had three days and two nights to go. . . .

'By midday we were in Siena and the petrol tank situation was grim. We suddenly saw a garage with a Ferrari sign outside. Thinking they would understand the urgency of our problem, we drove straight into the workshop. They were magnificent. A small boy was sent pedalling off on a bicycle and the Healey put up on the lift. They stripped off the chewing-gum, made up a paste of soap and petrol, and plastered the bottom of the tank. The boy returned with a pot of thick red-lead paint, which was smeared over the soap. Inside 12 minutes we were on our way with a tank which at last fulfilled its proper purpose.

'The running average in Italy was 72 km/h (45 mile/h) generally, but rose to 105 km/h (65 mile/h) on any section containing autostrade. By now we were nearing Viterbo and our four new tyres, so we put on speed and arrived with nearly an hour in hand to do the job.

'To our horror we found that the tyres were not there; they were still at Milan airport, and we were in bad trouble. Bill has red hair, so it was obviously his job to lose his temper with the tyre man, which he did magnificently, while the tyre man lost his temper back in Italian. But after the shouting died down, the local schoolmaster, a little, bald, stooping Italian, shuffled forward and offered his services in English. After much impassioned argument we were given four very cheap and nasty Italian tyres on the credit of the Tyresoles company. Two were fitted on the front wheels, two were tied to the tail, and we left for Rome very late but mobile. We had 52 minutes to get to the Rome control and the signpost said "Roma, 99 Kms". That, to us, meant an average of 115 km/h (71 mile/h).

'We stormed along absolutely flat with cheering crowds waving encouragement. I remember passing Johnny Claes' Jaguar XK120 with 113 mile/h on the clock of the Healey.

'After a few miles we were travelling at about 100 mile/h when there was a sudden flapping from behind. Bill's blazer, tucked behind the seats, had flown off into the countryside – and it contained our passports and all our money. So I braked to a sliding stop and we pelted back down the road, picking up all the money we could find on the way to the vital documents. We left the rest behind.

'The situation now looked black indeed, and we seemed sure to lose time. In fact, as we reached the suburbs of Rome, Bill said "Eighteen kilometres to go, and two minutes left". Suddenly we saw a knot of cars and people. Across the road in front of us was stretched a banner saying "CONTROLE". They had moved the position out to the by-pass to avoid the congested traffic – we passed under the banner with 13 secs to spare!

'Our next problem was to get those new tyres on the rear wheels, so we borrowed a jack and removed them. Suddenly the car rocked and fell off the jack on to the brakedrums, but with much shouting and heaving the job was finally accomplished, and we headed back over the Apennines into the gathering dusk. On through the night we drove across Italy, the banging from the rear suspension getting worse and worse. Finally we struggled into Ferrara very, very tired, with one of the rear springs collapsed. We knew that springs were a weakness of this car and, since we carried a spare, started to change it. It is a fairly simple job to do, and with the encouragement of a holidaying Yorkshire couple we managed it.

'Soon dawn was breaking and we were faced with the Dolomites. On we went with hairpin following hairpin, the Pordoi, the Falzarego. One of the Italian tyres burst on the Pordoi, and since we had just had much difficulty in passing a touring coach, we changed wheels in the middle of the road, to a horn fanfare from the irate coach-driver. By nine in the morning we reached the bottom of the Stelvio, where Bill was to drive, and off we shot on the toughest section to date. For the first time we began to lose on the average, and at the Bormio control we were 2 minutes late. A quick change of drivers, then off on the grandaddy of them all, the Passo di Gavia – a tiny, narrow mule-track stretching 8,500 ft into the sky. Fifty-four minutes later we were in Ponte di Legno with another three minutes of penalty.

'The afternoon brought us to Aosta, where, walking round the car, we were horrified to see that the rear rally plate had fallen off. This meant 25 marks lost, the equivalent of 2½ minutes. We were bemoaning our loss to Huschke von Hanstein, the Porsche competition manager, when he said, "Read the regulations. It doesn't say *your* rally plate, it says 'The official rally plate must be fixed to the car'. How about that timekeepers' car over there?" So we crept round behind the crowd, and soon had a nice new plate on the Healey.

'Now we had the Alps before us again. As we entered the first valley, we were approaching a railway bridge when Bill said, "I think the brakes are going". Somehow we scrambled round, and, coasting to a halt, discovered that one of the brake bleeders had slackened off, so that we had lost most of the fluid. We jacked up and bled the system, tightened the bleeder, and wondered just how much longer both us and the poor old car would last.

'Back in France, in Val d'Isère, the crowds were huge and the P.A. announcer hysterical. "Arrivée, arrivée, équipe Britannique, Riley-Lamb sur Healey" – it all felt very Mille Miglia. Over the Col de l'Iseran, the Galibier, the Lautaret, and so to Grenoble. In the middle of that night Bill passed out cold, and, convinced that he was lying drunk at a party, kept murmuring, "No more whisky, no more whisky". By morning he was back on the rally.

'At last the toughest part of the event was over, and we had 750 kms. – from Dijon to Liège – to cover during the last day. It wasn't half so tiring now that the end was in sight. We rushed happily along with the Healey in fine fettle. When we got to Spa circuit, we wound her up to 110 mile/h just to prove she'd do it, then, after four nights and four days of fantastic motoring, rolled down the hill into the Spa, with the finish banner, the flowers and the champagne waiting. Monsieur Garot was there to welcome us with the astounding news that we were placed eighth overall in the rally and had won the 3 litre G.T. Class from three works Lancia Aurelias, which were second, third and fourth. We wandered back to the hotel in a happy daze. Our first Liège was over – and the rally bug had bitten deep.'

Private owners

In June 1951, P. J. Simpson's 'Silverstone' gained fifth place overall in the Manx Cup Races on the Isle of Man, and in the 1951 Alpine Rally, Edgar Wadsworth and Cyril Corbishley won a very creditable Coupe des Alpes and tied for the 3 litre class win. In the 1951 Tourist Trophy, again run at Dundrod, John Buncombe's 'Silverstone' finished 14th overall and fifth in the class matched against Aston Martins and Ferraris. In the 1952 Goodwood Nine Hours Race, the 'Silverstone' of D. Boston and R. Shattock finished eighth overall and fourth in class behind two Ferraris and an Aston Martin.

The private entrants have therefore played a leading role in the story of the 'Silverstone' and rightly too, for, of all the Healey models, the 'Silverstone' was produced exclusively for the enthusiastic clubman who wanted a reliable, safe and easy-to-maintain sports car. It is a fair testimonial to the model's rugged reliability, sound design and construction that today there are still quite a few 'Silverstones' around giving a fair account of themselves in club races, sprints and hill climbs.

CHAPTER 4

THE NASH-HEALEY

In December 1949 Donald Healey embarked on a sales tour of the United States and it was a chance meeting aboard the *Queen Elizabeth* with George Mason, President of the Nash Kelvinator Corporation of America, which began the story of that unusual Anglo-American car, the Nash-Healey.

Although many 'Silverstones' had been exported to the States, the Riley-engined Healeys had not really satisfied the demand for a Healey sports car. It was natural that these overseas buyers should expect more than 2·4 litres under the bonnet to compete on level terms with the more powerful American models. Furthermore, they preferred a car with which they were mechanically familiar, a car which they knew how to service and for which spare parts were readily available. Donald Healey was quick to realize the demand for a new Healey sports car with British-built body and chassis, but incorporating mechanical components of well-known American manufacture.

The meeting between the patrons of the Nash and Healey concerns happily resulted in complete agreement on a combined Anglo-American design, and soon after Healey's return from the States the Nash and Healey engineers began work on the new model.

Early 1950 saw the first of the 3·8 litre Nash engines delivered to the Warwick factory for trials with a modified 'Silverstone' chassis. The Healey chassis frame had to be slightly modified to accommodate the larger engine, gearbox and overdrive, but apart from these alterations the Nash mechanical components fitted snugly into the 'Silverstone' frame. The traditional Healey trailing-link suspension was retained at the front, but coil springs were fitted at the rear with the axle located by a track bar. The 'Dual Jetfire' six-cylinder o h v Nash engine was fitted with twin SU carburetters, an aluminium cylinder head, seven-bearing crankshaft and a special sports camshaft. An unusual feature of this engine was the arrangement of the manifold passages, which were formed directly into the main engine casting. They were thus water-cooled on two sides, providing even fuel distribution and improved temperature control. On an 8·1 to 1 compression ratio the power output was rated as 125 b h p at 4,000 rev/min, and in unit with the three-speed Nash gearbox and Borg Warner overdrive this engine gave a useful increase in top speed and general performance over the Riley-powered 'Silverstone'.

The Nash-engined prototype was completed in April 1950, just in time for a test run in that year's Mille Miglia. With his son Geoffrey as co-driver, Donald Healey entered the new prototype for this classic 1,050-mile road race around the northern half of Italy. As recounted in the last chapter, the 1950 event was run in atrocious weather and the Healey was amongst the many entries delayed by off-the-road excursions. But the new model completed the course, finishing ninth in the over 2 litre sports car class and 177th overall from 383 starters. The trip to Italy had been an effective test run for the new car, encouraging the Warwick engineers to start preparations for an entry in the 1950 Le Mans 24 Hour Race.

Le Mans début

For long-distance racing on the very fast Sarthe circuit, the Nash-powered 'Silverstone' prototype was fitted with a prominent head-fairing for the driver, and the rear bodywork was modified to accommodate long-range fuel tanks. To drive the car, Donald Healey engaged the services of two experienced sports car men, Duncan Hamilton and Tony Rolt.

There was a strong entry for the 1950 event, with nine British marques matched against French Talbots and Delahayes, Italian Ferraris and the American Cadillacs. As expected, the Talbots and Ferraris set the pace, but Rolt and Hamilton found themselves amongst the first dozen and the Healey pit were content to let the faster cars wear themselves out in the initial stages. This proved a wise policy; by half-distance there had been so many retirements amongst the leaders that the Healey had climbed to fourth place behind the two leading Talbots and the only surviving Jaguar.

As dawn came, the efforts of the Warwick team nearly met with a sad end when a French car rammed the Healey in the stern. The Healey shot off the course, but Duncan Hamilton performed some spectacular agricultural manoeuvres, and, finding himself back on the track and facing in the same direction as the rest of the traffic, pressed on to the pits. A hasty inspection revealed damaged suspension and rear axle, but it was decided that they should rejoin the race and hope for the best. The Healey struggled on. With four hours of racing to the finish, the Jaguar retired from third place, so Rolt and Hamilton moved up behind the two Talbots, which were touring round with an unassailable lead. Now interest focused on an exciting battle for third place as a 5 litre Cadillac-Allard moved up to challenge the Healey. They were two sick cars racing for the flag; the Allard jammed in top gear, Rolt and Hamilton nursing their damaged suspension and now having to drive with failing brakes. After a desperate battle in the 23rd hour the Allard managed to take the lead, but not before Rolt had recorded a splendidly fast lap at 94·3 mile/h. So the Nash-Healey took the flag in fourth place overall, the second British car to finish, covering 2,103 miles at 87·6 mile/h and breaking the previous class distance record.

Nash-Healeys in production

The combination of the Nash power unit and Healey chassis had now been successfully tested in the Mille Miglia and at Le Mans, the world's most gruelling road and track events for sports cars. The time had come for series production, so, towards the end of summer 1950, production of the Riley-engined Healeys ceased and the entire re-sources of the Warwick factory were set to building the new Nash-Healeys. This 100 per cent export and dollar-earning production was a move which made the Company unique in the history of the British motor industry, and the Nash-Healey was the first British car to be sponsored by an American manufacturer since the mid 1920s.

The new model made its début at the London and Paris Motor Shows in October 1950, appearing for the first time in the States at the Chicago Show in February 1951. The British-built body was a striking new design with unusual three-abreast seating on a single bench-type seat. Incorporated in the styling were the Nash radiator grille, headlamps, bumpers and other embellishments which were shipped over from the States with the Nash mechanical components. The complete car weighed 21½ cwt (around 3 cwt more than the 'Silverstone'), but with 3·8 litres under the bonnet the new Healey was a brisk performer with a top speed around 110 mile/h and a 0–60 mile/h acceleration time of 9½ secs. British sports car enthusiasts saw the car for the first time at the 1950 Motor Show and expressed dislike of only one feature; that was the 'Export Only' ticket on the wind-screen!

Mille Miglia and Le Mans

With full order books and a steady flow of new cars being despatched to the States at the rate of 10 cars per week, Donald Healey concentrated his competition programme on works-supported entries for the two events in which the Nash-Healey prototypes had exhibited such promise, the Mille Miglia and 24 Hour Race at Le Mans.

First appearance of a production-bodied Nash-Healey was in the 1951 Mille Miglia run over a shortened course of 970 miles from Brescia to the Adriatic coast, down to Rome, north across the Apennines and back to Brescia. Donald and Geoffrey Healey were paired for their fourth Mille Miglia with the marque, one of eight British crews in an entry of over 300 cars. Torrential rainstorms, traditional Mille Miglia weather, washed the Italian highways and mountain tracks into a deplorable state, making it even tougher for the British crews to compete on level terms with the local drivers. The Healey was unable to match the performance of the class-winning Aston Martin and the fastest of the Italian-entered Ferraris but after a consistent 15-hour drive, Donald and Geoffrey Healey returned to Brescia fourth in their class, and a commendable 30th in general classification.

Two months later came Le Mans, for which Healeys prepared a single car, carrying their streamlining ideas even further by building a new coupé body around the lines of the original prototype. Panelled in aluminium on a lightweight steel frame, the new bodywork featured a deep windscreen and side windows offering exceptional visibility for a closed car. Special attention was paid to the cooling of the brake-drums, with fresh-air scoops set in the front body panels. The driving compartment was also ventilated by an ingenious system of fresh-air ducting. Duncan Hamilton and Tony Rolt piloted the Healey for the second year running and again they chose to take things easy for the first few hours, letting the Jaguar, Talbot and Cunningham opposition set the pace.

Again this proved a wise policy and by midnight the Healey lay well placed, Rolt and Hamilton enjoying a comfortable and uneventful drive in the coupé. The retirement of the leading Talbot and Jaguar in the early hours of the morning brought the Healey up to sixth place, improving to fifth when another Talbot retired shortly afterwards. Lapping consistently at a little over 90 mile/h, the Healey even snatched fourth place for a short time, but Rolt and Hamilton soon had to concede this position to a very fast Cunningham. For the second

year running the Healey had to fight every minute of the 24 hours for
its place amongst the leaders. This time Rolt and Hamilton put up
a brave fight against an Aston Martin challenge, but failed by less than
half a mile to hold position. The Nash-Healey finished sixth overall
and fourth in the class, averaging 89·3 mile/h.

Farina styling

In February 1952 it was announced that future Nash-Healeys would
be available with new coachwork by the Italian stylist, Pinin Farina.
The Healey was thus named the 'three-nation sports car'. Engines and
transmissions were shipped over from Nash Motors of America to
Warwick for installation in the British-built Healey chassis, these
assemblies were then sent over to the Farina coachworks in Turin, and
completed cars were finally despatched back to the States.

The new Farina body gave the Healey a sleeker line. The V-
windscreen was replaced by a one-piece curved screen and the headlamps were now incorporated in the Nash radiator grille, permitting
a lower bonnet-line. At the rear the flowing wing-line was embellished
with restrained tail-fins to appeal to American buyers. Farina later
introduced a 'Le Mans' fixed head coupé form of this body, but the
convertible coachwork remained unchanged.

From February 1952 the Farina-bodied cars were fitted with an
improved version of the Nash engine. The bore size was increased to
raise the swept cylinder volume to 4,138 cc, the compression ratio was
raised to 8·25 to 1, and twin Carter horizontal carburetters replaced
the SUs. These modifications brought the peak power output up to
135 b h p at 4,000 rev/min.

Mixed fortunes on Mille Miglia

In 1952, Italian mastery of the Mille Miglia was threatened by the
highly organized entry of new Mercedes to be driven by Caracciola,
Lang and Kling. The British flag was carried by Aston Martin and
two Nash-Healeys; the coupé prototype for Donald and Geoffrey
Healey and a second car for Leslie Johnson and W. McKenzie. From
the traditional starting control at Brescia, local interest was centred
on the exciting duel between the new Mercedes and the local Ferraris,
but British enthusiasts were more excited to find the two Healeys
pacing both German and Italian teams and running high in general

classification. After 200 miles Donald Healey's run was brought to an unhappy finish when a tyre burst on a tricky bend. The coupé was badly damaged in a spectacular crash, but fortunately both the crew stepped unscathed from the incident. Meanwhile Johnson and Mc-Kenzie were enjoying better fortune with the other Healey entry, and they were well placed despite shockabsorber troubles which had caused them some delay on the mountain stages. At the finish their Healey had climbed to seventh place overall and they were fourth in their class behind the winning Ferrari and the two team Mercedes. This performance of the Nash-Healey had surpassed even the past Mille Miglia achievements of the Healey Elliots and Westlands.

A magnificent Le Mans

At Le Mans, it was the turn of Mercedes in 1952 too, but it was also a great year for Warwick. Healeys entered two cars, one of them the 1951 coupé now remodelled as an open car to be driven by Leslie Johnson and Tommy Wisdom. The second entry was the original 1950 prototype entered for two French drivers, Giraud-Cabantous and Pierre Veyron. This car was fitted with a British-designed experimental cylinder head with hemispherical combustion chambers and inclined valves with vertical and horizontal pushrods, these modifications raising the power output to around 200 b h p.

From the start it was the customary 'Grand Prix' between Ferrari, Cunningham and Jaguar with Mercedes playing the waiting game. The Healey team suffered an early disappointment when the Cabantous/Veyron entry was retired with engine troubles. The battle continued amongst the leaders, and it was not until after 16 hours of racing that the Johnson/Wisdom car appeared on the leader-board in sixth place. The order now was Talbot, the two Mercedes, Aston Martin, a second Talbot and then the Healey. The order remained unchanged through the morning, but just before mid-day the Healey, lapping consistently at around 94 mile/h, moved up to fifth place behind the Aston Martin.

With four hours of racing to the finish, the results seemed established, the leading Talbot touring round with a 4-lap advantage over the two Mercedes, and the Aston Martin comfortably in fourth place ahead of the Healey. No one, least of all the Healey team, anticipated the sudden change of fortunes which was to alter the whole pattern of the race. First the Aston Martin came into the pits with rear axle trouble, allowing Johnson and Wisdom to take the Healey through into fourth place behind the Mercedes. Then, in the last hour, the leading Talbot retired with bearing failure, leaving Mercedes with a safe first and second places and the Healey secure in third place. The German cars held an unassailable lead, and all that was asked of the Healey was to last the distance as the final minutes ticked by.

Besides finishing third overall, the Healey also collected a class win, second place in the Index of Performance and, of course, the *Motor* award for the first British car to finish. Johnson and Wisdom had covered a distance of 2,196 miles averaging 91·5 mile/h. This certainly brought great credit to the small Warwick factory, for with a car which had already completed one Le Mans race, Donald Healey and his team had defeated the might of works entries from Ferrari, Cunningham, Talbot, Aston Martin and Jaguar – all, in fact, except the invincible Mercedes. It was truly the marque's finest racing achievement.

Final sorties

The final sortie to the Mille Miglia with the Nash-Healey was made in 1953, with a special-bodied car fitted with the larger 4·1 litre engine. A Laycock overdrive was used in place of the Borg Warner unit. The two-seater streamlined bodywork reduced drag to a minimum; with its overall length of 15 ft and its 4·1 litre engine, this car must surely rank as the largest Healey ever built. American John Fitch drove this mighty Healey special, but unhappily did not have a fair chance to demonstrate its potential. A brake pipe fractured towards the end of the first stage from Brescia to Ravenna, and although every effort was made to effect a satisfactory repair, the car had to be retired.

At Le Mans in 1953, the Healey team's main responsibility was, of course, the running of two new Austin-Healey '100's, making their racing début at Le Mans. The story of their remarkable display of high-speed reliability is reserved for a future chapter of Healey history. Also entered in the 1953 24 Hour Race were a pair of Nash-Healeys for Leslie Johnson and Bert Hadley and the French drivers Cabantous and Veyron. The Healey team could hardly have expected to repeat the previous year's success, running cars which had already completed many hours of racing, and against even stronger works entries from rival teams. For the second year the French crew retired their car in the early stages, but Johnson and Hadley soldiered on to finish 11th overall, completing a greater distance than in 1952 at an average speed of 92·5 mile/h.

Apart from the achievements in the Mille Miglia and at Le Mans, the Nash-Healeys gained few successes in other events either at home or overseas. In June 1951 Tony Rolt took sixth place in the B.R.D.C. Production Sports Car Race at Silverstone, the Healey and the late Reg Parnell's Aston Martin battling hard to break up the complete domination of the race by the new XK Jaguars. The Nash-Healey's race speed on this occasion was 81·8 mile/h. Shortly after this Reg Parnell drove a Nash-Healey in the British Empire Trophy Race in the Isle of Man, but he was forced to retire with a broken gear-lever when well placed. The sole international rally entry for the Nash-Healey has been traced to the 1952 Alpine Rally, when Edgar Wadsworth lost a potential Coupe des Alpes through a crash on the Stelvio.

These achievements were somewhat eclipsed by the efforts of the works entries which, in the years 1951 to 1953, furthered the marque's reputation in the Mille Miglia. Indeed, in six consecutive years the Healey entries in this Italian classic established a record of successes unequalled by any other British marque.

CHAPTER 5

THE HEALEY DUNCAN, SPORTSMOBILE, TICKFORD, ABBOTT AND SPORTS CONVERTIBLE

Our story of Healey cars has so far been confined to those models which were associated with the marque's record of competition achievements: the 2·4 litre Elliot Saloon and Westland Roadster, the 'Silverstone' and the Nash-Healey. These models accounted for just over half of the 1,185 Healey chassis built at Warwick. The remaining chassis were fitted with specialist coachbuilt sports and touring bodies, and it is with a description of these models that we now complete the story of the Warwick-built Healeys.

Healey 'Duncan'

Duncan Industries of Norfolk were the first coachbuilders to offer an alternative body design for the Healey, 39 examples of their two-door saloons appearing on the 'A'- and 'B'-type chassis during the production period of the standard Elliot Saloon and Westland Roadster.

The all-aluminium four-seater 'Duncan' body offered greater interior room and comfort than the Elliot, and there was also improved luggage accommodation. The styling was similar to the Elliot, differing only in the detail of the rather bulbous front wings and the pillarless side windows. This Duncan body was actually a 'master' design also made available to Alvis and Daimler, who incorporated their own traditional radiator grilles with slightly different front wing styles. This was the first time in the British motor trade that unrelated manufacturers had offered the same body design.

Duncan also built an open two-seater sports body on the Healey, and this was offered as a less expensive version of the 'Silverstone'. The frontal design was unique, with the radiator grille running back beneath the bonnet to the scuttle on either side. The cockpit layout was similar to that of the 'Silverstone', but at the rear the spare wheel was carried on top of the tail section instead of being housed in the conventional 'Silverstone' letterbox compartment. Very few of these Duncan sports bodies were built and only one or two examples have been traced in this country.

Healey 'Sportsmobile'

Present-day sports car enthusiasts would probably consider the 'Sportsmobile' one of the less attractive bodies to be built upon the Healey chassis. Yet when this model was seen for the first time in October 1948, it was hailed by the motoring press as one of the most striking post-war sports car designs.

The Sportsmobile was introduced after two years' production of the Elliot Saloon and Westland Roadster (with which it shared the same technical specification), preceding the 'Silverstone' by some six months. The Sportsmobile bodies were built upon the standard 'B' type chassis, although the rear frame members had to be extended to carry the long tail section of the new body. The model was available for a little over a year, until early 1950, and 23 examples were built.

The body offered exceptional comfort for four passengers and there was a large boot; unusual features for a 100 mile/h sports car. The convertible-type hood was designed for single-handed operation from the driving seat, and the rear window panel of the hood was removable for warm-weather ventilation, as on the later Austin-Healey '3000' Convertible. On the road, the Sportsmobile compared favourably with the 100 mile/h-plus performance of the Elliot and Westland models, and this alternative sports body attracted enthusiasts who wanted spacious and well-appointed four-seater convertible coachwork on the well-proven Healey chassis.

Healey 'Tickford' and 'Abbott'

In October 1950, the four-year production run of the Elliot and Westland was brought to a close with the introduction of more modern coachwork designs. The new aluminium bodies, hand-built upon timber frames, gave the Healey a lower flowing line with a more spacious and luxurious interior. Two versions of the new body were available: the two-door, four-seater sports saloon with 'Tickford' coachwork, and the drophead coupé version by 'Abbott'.

These models shared the same technical specification as the 2·4 litre Riley-powered models which preceded them, and the first of the Tickford and Abbott bodies were built upon the 'C'-type chassis. In the summer of 1951 the 'BT'-type was introduced. This had better headlight units and the twin pass lamps, previously set into the front body panels, were replaced by triangular ventilation grilles on either side of the radiator. A larger diameter steering wheel was also fitted at this time, with the horn and trafficator controls in the wheel hub. The 'F'-type Tickfords and Abbotts (from November 1951) had an open propeller shaft and hypoid rear axle in place of the torque tube transmission. Telescopic rear dampers were also fitted instead of the piston-type dampers.

A total of 241 Tickfords and 77 Abbotts were built up to the beginning of 1954, the Tickfords having the most successful production run of all the Healey models except the Nash-Healeys. The Tickford and Abbott satisfied the Healey enthusiast who was prepared to pay a fairly high price for a fast, yet economical four-seater sports tourer offering the highest standards of hand-built coachwork.

Healey 'Sports Convertible'

To meet the demand for an open sports car of similar size and performance to the 'export only' Nash-Healey, the 3 litre Alvis-engined 'Sports Convertible' was added to the Healey range at the London Motor Show in October 1951.

The body, by Panelcraft of Birmingham, was a replica of the Nash-Healey fitted with a different radiator grille, less prominent bumpers, British headlight units and Healey wheel discs. The Nash power unit was replaced by the six-cylinder 2,993 cc Alvis engine which developed 106 b h p at 4,200 rev/min, the same maximum power output as the 2·4 litre Riley engine but achieved at a lower engine speed. This gave the Sports Convertible improved low-speed torque and better acceleration than its Riley-powered stablemates although the maximum speed was almost identical, the car just achieving 100 mile/h.

The Sports Convertible was one of the best-appointed sports cars of its time with an exceptionally well-furnished interior, wind-up windows, lockable doors, a large luggage boot and a quickly erected hood. The Healey 'Convertible' was produced until late 1953, and 25 examples were made.

Enter the Healey '100'

These fast and luxurious Healeys, outstanding in their day, were all built in quantities too small to bring them within the reach of the average keen driver. Inevitably, prices were comparatively high, and only the fortunate few could afford to enjoy the many good features of the Warwick-built cars.

So it might have remained had Donald Healey not decided on a new approach which was a complete break with previous Warwick practice. He designed a new sports car: light, compact, ingeniously simple in layout, and powered by an untuned version of a rugged, straight-forward engine that was manufactured in large quantities. This car's appeal lay in its clean, balanced lines, high performance and good roadholding, rather than the luxurious appointments of its coachwork. This was, of course, the Healey '100', later to become the first in the line of Austin-Healey models.

CHAPTER 6

THE AUSTIN-HEALEY '100'

The Healey '100', creator of the new Austin-Healey marque and forerunner of the famous line of '100S', '100-Six' and '3000' models, appropriately enjoyed world-wide acclaim upon its announcement. The new Healey became the sensation of the London Motor Show in October 1952. At the World's Fair in Miami, Donald Healey's design won the Grand Premier Award, and at the New York Motor Show the new model was voted the International Show Car of the Year. Turning the pages of the Healey scrapbook, one finds that the press cuttings on the Austin-Healey '100' fill as many pages as the complete history of all the earlier Healeys. Reporters in all the leading motoring journals praised the new Healey in monotonous repetition, using their most complimentary phrases, whilst announcements and pictures of the new Warwick-designed sports car appeared in even the smallest provincial newspapers.

The story of how the '100' came into being is told by Geoff Healey:

'We were faced with the problem of the old Riley engine going out of production, we had already been forced to drop the Riley axle in favour of the Salisbury unit for the same reason. It was my father's idea to make use of the Austin A90 Atlantic engine, which was available in large quantities and at the right terms. Certainly they were very much cheaper and lighter than the Riley units.

'We started with a clean sheet of paper, my father dictating the rough outline of the sort of car he had in mind. I designed the chassis at home along with the help of Barrie Bilbie while Gerry Coker handled the body styling. It is rather amusing now to think that we worked secretly at home so that the people we were dealing with on the Morris side with the Riley power units would not know that we were considering using Austin components in our new car!

'The very first prototype was not quite the same as the final production model. The grille was slightly different and it had rather ugly tail fins on the back wings. These my father had removed immediately and we repositioned the grille by a couple of inches.

'Ian Duncan, the man who made the old Duncan bodies, was responsible for getting the overdrives for us. He was then working at Austins and had been working with Laycock on this particular overdrive type. He reckoned it would be ideal for the Healey; we tried it and he was proved right.

'If I remember right we had only one car completed just in time for the Motor Show and we only had a couple of chassis standing by.

'We did, however, assemble the first 25 cars at Warwick after the agreement with Austins while Longbridge were laying down the production line.

'There was very little change in production from the original prototype. The headlamps and the front wing line were raised just a fraction to comply with the American regulations and I did some small redesign work on the steering.

'Apart from this, Austins built the cars to our drawings and even to the last days of the '3000', parts were being made to Healey drawings over-stamped Austin Motor Company.'

The story of how, overnight, the Healey changed its name to Austin-Healey is well known. Donald Healey's new model was a last-minute entry for Earls Court; indeed, it arrived too late to enjoy most of the pre-Show publicity. But on the opening day it did not take long for the enthusiasts to find the shapely new sports car tucked away behind a pillar on the Healey stand. As one journal reported, it was fortunate that the car was safely protected behind a hefty barrier to hold back the thousands who pressed forward for a closer look.

As a refreshingly new approach in design – incorporating well-proven mechanical components in a good-looking body giving 100 mile/h-plus performance at the right price – this was the sports car that so many enthusiasts had been waiting for. The Healey '100' needed no sales talk, in fact the Warwick salesmen were hard pressed to keep pace with the ever-increasing batch of orders. It was not long before over 3,000 cars had been sold, mostly destined for the States. These orders alone represented some $7,000,000 worth of business. On the one hand this was just reward for the folk at Warwick, but on the other it presented the problem of how the limited resources of their small factory could lay down a production line to satisfy the demand.

The problem was solved by a far-seeing business move on the part of Sir Leonard Lord, then Chairman of the Austin Motor Company at Longbridge, and Lord Nuffield, head of the Morris group. Sir Leonard had been associated with the new Healey sports car since early 1951 when, in conjunction with Donald Healey, development work had been carried out using Austin components in a new Healey chassis. Thus Sir Leonard's offer at the time of the London Motor Show – to take over the entire production of the Healey, putting the vast resources of the Longbridge works behind the assembly of the cars and backing the venture with the worldwide Austin sales and service facilities – was not quite as spontaneous as many contemporary reports suggested. The new model was to be called the Austin-Healey '100', and it was promised that a £100 reduction in the price would be made.

Although Sir Leonard's offer heralded the ultimate end of vehicle production at the Warwick factory, the proposals suited the Donald Healey Motor Company, for they would continue the closest association with development work on all future Austin-Healeys. Initially at least, they would handle sales and the preparation of works-entered competition cars. And so the important announcement was made at Motor Show time. Overnight the Healey '100' changed its name, and when the public gathered around the stand on the next day the pale blue prototype was proudly wearing the Austin-Healey wings for the first time.

Plans for an entirely new Healey sports car had begun early the previous year when Donald Healey returned from a tour of the U.S.A., confident that he had the right formula for a new design which would have common appeal to both home and overseas markets. In his own words, 'I wanted to produce a very fast everyday road car with genuine sporting characteristics, capable of 100 mile/h, which would also be exceptionally cheap to buy and easy and economic to maintain.'

Working with his son Geoffrey, Donald Healey and his design team discarded the old Healey chassis which had formed the backbone of all the past Healey models since 1946. The new two-seater sports chassis was to be constructed on different lines, consisting of two straight 3 in. square box-section side-members running parallel the length of the car, some 17 in. apart. These were braced by parallel and cruciform cross-members, also of box section, and to them was attached the steel floor pressings. The scuttle structure was built up as part of the basic frame, welded to it and triangulated by means of struts running forward to the front of the chassis frame. The new Healey design represented an interesting compromise between the traditional rigid box-section sports car chassis and the lighter integral chassis/body construction of the more modern saloon car.

The traditional Healey trailing-link front suspension was superseded by coil and wishbone suspension, with lever arm hydraulic shock-absorbers. These units were also fitted at the rear with half-elliptic leaf springs. In line with most of the mechanical components used on the new Healey, these suspension units were built up from stock Austin components.

Next came the choice of a suitable power unit, and here Donald Healey selected the 2·6 litre four-cylinder o h v Austin A90 engine. Developing 90 b h p at 4,000 rev/min, the A90 engine did not offer a particularly exciting specification on paper. But Donald Healey was not mistaken in believing that it would prove a reliable unit possessed of a useful reserve of power and reliability when the time came for extensive tuning.

On the original prototypes the four-speed A90 gearbox was used in its standard form except, of course, for the adaptation of the column-change mechanism used on the saloon to a central remote control lever for the Healey. During road tests of the prototype it was found that the power-to-weight ratio was not suited to the very low first gear, and that second gear could be used quite satisfactorily for standing starts. Thus first gear was locked out of action, and on production models the Healey was offered with a three-speed gearbox, synchro-mesh on all ratios. Subsequent road tests indicated that the 2·6 litre engine, coupled to the three-speed box and 4·1 to 1 rear axle, produced an ample reserve of power to take an overdrive, and so a Laycock de Normanville unit was fitted, operating on second and top gears.

Finally came the body design – undoubtedly the sensational feature of the new car. The sleek two-seater body, with sporting but comfort-able cockpit and a fair-sized boot, presented an entirely new look in sports car design, avoiding imitation of Continental stylists. In the true Healey tradition the design was 'way ahead of its time. After 10 years, the Austin-Healey '3000' wore an almost identical body yet it was still considered as one of Britain's most handsome and functional sports cars.

After 25 cars had been built at Warwick to satisfy the immediate demand from Austin distributors, series production began at Long-bridge in May 1953. The new model received the factory designation BN 1, this code becoming more widely used in later years to differen-tiate it from the BN 2 introduced in August 1955. The BN 2 was fitted with the new four-speed B.M.C. C-type gearbox and a hypoid rear axle in place of the original spiral bevel unit. Other modifications included improved front suspension with longer coil springs, and improved brakes with wider brake shoes.

113 mile/h at Jabbeke

On the road the Healey's performance matched its sporting looks. Just a few days before the announcement of the new model at the London Motor Show, Donald Healey took one of the prototypes for speed tests upon the famous Jabbeke highway in Belgium, the same road that he had used to test his first Healey saloon in 1946. The trip to Belgium was certainly worthwhile, for the new Healey recorded a top speed of 113 mile/h and collected Belgian Class records for the flying kilometre at 111·7 mile/h and the flying mile at 110·9 mile/h. Contemporary road test performance figures for the BN 1 are a little misleading, for the car submitted for test was usually one of the original Warwick-built prototypes. These were somewhat lighter than the production cars from Longbridge, and present owners should bear this in mind when comparing performance figures. Performance testing was usually undertaken with the hood down and the windscreen folded flat. The BN 2 was fractionally faster than the BN 1, both in overall top speed and acceleration, in view of the more suitable gear and axle ratios.

Competition début

The first competition outing for the marque was to France in March 1953, when one of the original prototypes was made available to the late Gregor Grant who, with Peter Reece, entered for the Lyons-Charbonnières Rally. A 1,250-mile run over the snow-packed passes of the Massif Central and Haute Savoie seemed an inappropriate competition début for a new 100 mile/h sports car, but the Austin-Healey enjoyed a good run, Grant and Reece really getting into their stride on the timed hill-climbs. But their rally came to a disappointing end when, after a high-speed encounter with a deep pot-hole, the rear suspension damper snapped its mounting. The crew carried on, determined to bring the Austin-Healey to the finish in its first event, and the final stages became a nightmare drive with the rear axle almost adrift and the unattached springs cutting their way through the body. Heavily penalized, the Austin-Healey completed the course in an exciting, if not particularly successful, competition début for the marque.

A disappointing Mille Miglia

Soon after the Lyons-Charbonnières Rally came the Mille Miglia, by now an annual outing for the folk at Warwick after their run of successes with the earlier Healeys. The 1,000-mile non-stop road race around Italy, upon contrasting autostrada and rough mountain passes, was going to be a fair test for the new Austin-Healeys, and two cars were prepared at Warwick to be driven by Hadley/Mercer and Lockett/Reid. In turn with over 480 starters, the sleek new Austin-Healeys took their place upon the traditional flood-lit starting ramp at Brescia, and there were high hopes that the cars would maintain the marque's past record in this classic event. But unhappily the new cars did not fare well. Both cars suffered from clutch troubles when, with the continual high speeds, the gearbox oil built up pressure and forced its way into the clutch. Hadley/Mercer had to retire within the first 180-mile stage to Ravenna. Lockett/Reid were a little more fortunate and managed to keep going almost to the finish, but they, too, were eliminated about twenty miles from Brescia. In addition to the clutch troubles the rough going had shown up a weakness in the throttle linkage, so, although the works cars had a disappointing outing, at least some useful lessons had been learnt for improvements on production models.

Reliability at Le Mans

When a pair of works cars were taken over to Le Mans in June 1953 to make their racing début in the 24 Hour Race, it seemed that ill-luck was to remain with the new Austin-Healeys. On this occasion, however, the misfortunes could hardly be blamed on the cars. A bout of food poisoning struck the team during the days of practice, then one of the cars was involved in an accident on its way from the circuit on the eve of the race. The car was badly damaged and Donald Healey sought the organizer's permission to substitute his reserve entry. But the officials would not allow this, so the mechanics had to get the car roadworthy. After an all-night session the car was repaired and the two Austin-Healeys took their place in front of the pit for the traditional Le Mans start.

From their outward appearance the cars looked entirely standard, for they ran with bumpers in position, small aero screens and the standard tonneau cover. But some significant mechanical modifications had been made to give the Austin-Healeys a little more pace against the stern competition from specialized sports-racing entries. Basic engine modifications included a high-lift camshaft with improved inlet manifolding, which raised the power output to 100 b h p at 4,500 rev/min. A higher rear axle ratio was used with modified over-drive ratios, giving the Austin-Healeys a timed top speed of 119 mile/h. The braking department was improved with a twin-shoe system all round, with lightweight drums. A substantially larger fuel tank filled the boot.

A truly international quartet were to pilot the Austin-Healeys; Frenchman Marcel Becquart was paired with British journalist Gordon Wilkins, and Dutchman Maurice Gatsonides paired with British motor-cycle ace Johnny Lockett. Reserve driver was Ken Rudd, a Healey enthusiast later to become well known for his tuning conversions for the '100-Six' and '3000'.

The Austin-Healey entry at Le Mans was to be no more than a high-speed demonstration of reliability, though perhaps the cars would be well placed in their class if things went well. Certainly they did all that was asked of them, both Austin-Healeys putting up an almost monotonous performance of high-speed lappery for the 24 hours. After an uneventful and trouble-free run, Gatsonides/Lockett took the chequered flag in twelfth position, Becquart/Wilkins finishing in fourteenth position. The team also collected second and third places in their class. The leading car covered 2,153 miles at an average speed of fractionally less than 90 mile/h – pretty fair achievement for a car that had been titled 'the world's cheapest 100 mile/h sports car'.

142 mile/h at Bonneville

The entry of a lone works car for Lockett/Rudd in the B.A.R.C. 9 Hour Sports Car Race at Goodwood in August 1953 endorsed the Le Mans demonstration of reliability, the Austin-Healey finishing tenth overall behind the flight of Jaguars and Aston Martins.

But to close the 1953 season and publicize the Austin-Healeys in America, Donald Healey planned a record-breaking trip to Bonneville Salt Flats, Utah. It was decided to attack two groups of records, the International Class 'D' and American Stock Car Records. For the International Records a tuned car was used, with modifications similar to those of the season's works cars. For the Stock Car Records a perfectly standard production model was used, as selected by officials of the American Automobile Association from a local Austin dis–

tributor. No modifications were permitted on this standard car apart from careful running-in, final tuning and adjustments. With Donald Healey leading the team of drivers, Capt. George Eyston, John Gordon Benett, Roy Jackson-Moore and Jackie Cooper, the two Austin-Healeys captured a total of over 100 records. The stock car gained all American records from five to 3,000 miles and from one to 24 hours, putting up an overall average speed of 104 mile/h for the 24 hours. The attempt with the tuned car progressed well up to 12 hours, but then adverse weather conditions cut the 24-hour run short. Nevertheless, all the 12-hour records were taken. Undoubtedly the most publicized feature of the Austin-Healey outing to Utah was the performance of the tuned car to achieve a timed speed over the mile of 142·6 mile/h. The publicity boys at Longbridge were not slow to announce the Austin-Healey as the fastest production under 3 litre car in the world.

CHAPTER 7

THE AUSTIN-HEALEY '100S' AND '100M'

By 1954 the Austin-Healey '100' had achieved outstanding popularity in both home and overseas markets, yet success in international competition, so important to a sports car manufacturer, had been restricted to nothing more noteworthy than one or two demonstrations of high-speed reliability in long-distance events.

International sports car racing at this time seldom offered categories for series-production cars, so the Austin-Healeys were forced to compete against the specialized, limited-production sports/racing machinery from constructors such as Ferrari, Maserati, Lancia, Aston Martin and Jaguar. Clearly, if the marque was to present a serious challenge in international events, a true competition version of the Austin-Healey would have to be built.

Thus in early 1954, whilst the Austin-Healey '100's were coming off the production lines at Longbridge, it was decided that the Donald Healey Motor Company at Warwick should develop and produce a more powerful and lightweight model of the production BN 2, not only to serve as a more useful weapon for use in international events, but to be marketed in limited production for sale to private owners who wished to purchase a competition version of the Austin-Healey. At the same time it was decided to market an engine tuning kit which the owners of the standard BN 1 and BN 2 models could fit themselves; alternatively, completely modified cars could be ordered from Warwick. These new competition models were to be known as the Austin-Healey '100S' and '100M'.

Sebring success

Naturally these competition versions of the Austin-Healey were to be developed through racing, and when the 1954 season opened with the 12-hour race at Sebring a prototype '100S' was entered for

Lance Macklin and George Huntoon. Although the Austin-Healey wore the normal '100' bodywork, there were non-standard disc-type centre-lock wheels with Dunlop disc brakes fitted front and rear. Beneath a louvred bonnet there were extensive engine modifications, later to form the basis of the '100S' specification.

The 12-hour race began with the anticipated battle between the works Lancias, Ferraris, Cunninghams and Aston Martins, and in those early stages nobody took very much interest in the lone Austin-Healey or believed that it would feature prominently in the results. After some three hours' racing and the first of the pit stops, it was clear that the leading Lancia trio of Fangio, Ascari and Taruffi had set too fast a pace. Soon the Lancias began to drop out with engine troubles and a Ferrari momentarily took the lead, only to fall out with axle failure. As the race wore on the Cunninghams also retired, whilst the Aston Martin challenge failed when their leading car retired, brakeless. By half-distance Macklin and Huntoon found themselves in fourth place overall, the Austin-Healey prototype – running with complete reliability – having climbed up the leader board along with the incredibly fast 1·5 litre Osca of Moss and Lloyd, which now lay in second place sandwiched between the two surviving Lancias.

Now the main interest centred on the leading foursome, and with a little over one hour's racing to the finish, the leading Lancia retired with a broken oil-pipe. Moss in the Osca now took the lead, with the sole surviving Lancia close behind and Macklin's '100S' in third place. Within this last hour, outright victory seemed within Macklin's grasp, for Moss was driving with practically no brakes, while the Lancia was a very tired machine and its driver far from experienced. As the race drew to a close Macklin made a last-minute attempt to bring the Austin-Healey through into the lead, but, after nearly 12 hours of racing, this final spurt proved too much for the '100S' and a rocker arm fractured. With the Austin-Healey running unsteadily on three cylinders, Macklin was forced to drop back and be content with a secure third place.

Despite this last-minute disappointment, it had been a fine achievement for the marque. Macklin and Huntoon finished easy class winners, averaging 70·5 mile/h for the 12 hours. The disc-braked prototype had performed well and, when the time came to decide upon a type designation for the new competition version of the Austin-Healey, there was no hesitation in naming it the '100S' in honour of this successful Sebring outing.

Macklin's Mille Miglia

Encouraged by the performance of the '100S' prototype at Sebring, the Warwick company prepared three similar cars for the 1954 Mille Miglia in May. Lance Macklin was to lead the Austin-Healey team, with Louis Chiron in the second car and Tom Wisdom with 'Mort' Morris-Goodall sharing the third entry. It was originally intended that the Austin-Healeys would run in the Grand Touring category with coupé hardtops, but the cars were excluded from this category due to an oversight in forwarding the necessary homologation declarations to the organizers. Rather than withdraw the team, Donald Healey had the cars hastily stripped of their G.T. equipment and transferred to the sports/racing class.

British entries in the 1954 event included a team of works-entered Triumph TR 2s, Aston Martins and a Jaguar-engined HWM. From the start at Brescia an immediate tussle began between the works Austin-Healeys and the Triumphs. On the first 180-mile stage to Ravenna the leading Triumph held a slender advantage over Macklin in the best-placed '100S', but as the cars set out on the second stage the Warwick team suffered their first setback when Chiron's car was forced to retire with a fractured brake-pipe. On the first crossing of the mountains Macklin turned the tables on the Triumph team, making 18th fastest time overall to lead all the British contingent, except one of the works Aston Martins. Near Rome it seemed that Macklin might have to drop out with clutch trouble, but fortunately he was not far from one of the Austin-Healey service depots. After some minutes' delay, he was back in the race.

Meanwhile the third '100S' of Wisdom and Morris-Goodall had been retired with a broken valve-spring, so now all hopes rested with Macklin. Along the fast coast route to Siena, Macklin made up for lost time, the '100S' climbing from 35th to 31st place. After the second crossing of the mountains the Austin-Healey had gained a further eight places. Covering the last 83-mile stage in a mere 56 minutes (an average of 89 mile/h), Macklin brought the '100S' across the finishing line at Brescia to be placed 23rd overall out of 380 starters. The '100S' was fifth in its class behind the winning Lancia and a trio of Ferraris, and the first British car to finish. Macklin's average speed over the 1,000-mile course had been 73 mile/h, a fine drive in this his first Mille Miglia, an event which he recalls with some pleasure.

'From my own point of view it was one of the races I used to look forward to a lot. I used to enjoy it thoroughly. I had a different attitude, I think, towards it from most people. I remember that before the start of the Mille Miglia – which was a rather frightening thing in the early morning, and you hadn't had very much sleep; it was usually cold and wet and rainy – the only person I ever found I could talk to was George Abecassis, as he was the only person who wasn't in a terrible dither.

'Most of the drivers you went up to and started talking to weren't even listening to what you were saying, they were much too intent waiting for their time to come up to start. George was a very phlegmatic sort of person, and didn't worry about it. I must say I didn't worry too much, because I used to think to myself before I started, suppose someone said that this wasn't the Mille Miglia, but you were in Paris and they said, "Look, Lance, here's a nice sports car, we're closing the road from Paris down to Nice, then from Nice across the mountains to Grenoble, then from Grenoble back to Paris again – we'll have police all the way so there'll be nobody in the way, no speed limits or anything – just have a go and enjoy yourself with this sports car and see how you like it." This is how I reckoned to drive the thing.

'I used to drive only as fast as I considered was safe, although looking at my times after the race proved that I used to go as fast as anybody else did in the same sort of cars, but I certainly never allowed myself to get frightened by it, because if I frightened myself, or looked like getting wound up and going too fast, I just used to say, "For Pete's sake, relax," and I'd do just that.

'In fact, one of the most difficult things on the Mille Miglia was not going too fast, it was a question of not going fast enough. You'd be down in the south, Pescara way, a lovely sunny day, the sea would be sort of sparkling, you'd be miles out in the countryside, not seeing another car for half an hour, and you'd suddenly think, oh my gosh – I'm supposed to be in a race, and you'd look at the speedo and find that you were only doing about 80 when you should have been touching 110. I think that was the hardest part, keeping the concentration going.'

Withdrawal from racing

Returning to the European racing scene, the trend in sports car racing continued to turn further towards the specialist-built sports/

racing machinery. In protest against this state of affairs, Donald Healey
in conjunction with the Austin Motor Company, issued a public
statement to the effect that no works-entered Austin-Healeys would
appear in international events until there was a change in sports car
regulations to cater for the series-production vehicle.

The statement was made in the belief that sports car racing had lost
its value to both the manufacturer and the buying public because
basically production cars, such as the Austin-Healeys, had to compete
against vehicles which bore not the slightest resemblance to production models. Furthermore, the manufacturers of this specialized
machinery showed little intention of producing similar models for
future sale, or making available to the private owner modifications
which would bring their standard production models up to a similar
level of performance.

The news of the Austin-Healey's withdrawal from international
racing received a mixed reception in the motoring Press, perhaps
because it was ill-timed – it came on the eve of the 24-hour race at
Le Mans, where a team of three '100S' cars had been entered. Nevertheless there were many British manufacturers who supported the
Company in taking this courageous action.

192 mile/h at Utah

The decision to withdraw from international sports car racing did
not prevent the Austin-Healeys from making further record attempts,
and in August 1954 Donald Healey led a team to the Bonneville Salt
Flats at Utah to attack American National and International Class 'D'
records.

Two cars were taken over, the 1953 record-breaking Austin-
Healey '100' (now fitted with the complete '100S' modifications) and
a second car which was a special supercharged streamliner. This car
used a standard chassis and body to which were attached aerodynamic
nose and tail sections, a bubble-domed cockpit cover, and a large
stabilizing fin upon the driver's head fairing. The engine incorporated
the full '100S' modifications but the power output was raised to
224 b h p with the addition of a Shorrock supercharger. Other
interesting features of this car were the five-speed gearbox with
built-in overdrive, non-standard 16 in. disc-type wheels, a built-in
automatic fire-extinguishing system mounted in both the engine and
fuel compartments, a self-jettisoning device for the bubble-domed

cockpit cover, and an automatic fuel cut-off control which came into operation if the oil pressure dropped low enough to cause an engine blow-up.

Unlike the 1953 record attempts at Utah, the 1954 runs were made in ideal conditions. Using the 'IOOS' prototype, the 6-hour and 12-hour records were claimed at almost exactly 10 mile/h over the 1953 figures with the stock Austin-Healey '100'. The 12-hour record was taken at 132·47 mile/h (as opposed to 122·91 mile/h in 1953) and the 'IOOS' went on to capture the 24-hour record at 132·29 mile/h. Altogether the 'IOOS', driven by Donald Healey and Carroll Shelby, claimed 53 American National and International 3 litre records.

The supercharged streamliner was primarily intended for the shorter sprint runs, and to find out just how fast the Austin-Healey would go. Both American National and International records were taken with this car, and Donald Healey gained a special American certificate of performance for covering the flying mile at the very impressive speed of 192·62 mile/h. It is interesting to note that, before these record attempts were made, the Austin technicians at Longbridge had estimated the potential speed of the streamliner to within 0·6 mile/h of the speed actually attained at Utah!

'IOOS' in production

These successful record-breaking runs at Utah, and the past trials at Sebring and in the Mille Miglia, had fully proved the 'IOOS' modifications. Just before the London Motor Show in 1954, the specification of the 'IOOS' was officially announced and the new model put into limited production, the cars being assembled at the Warwick premises of the Donald Healey Motor Company.

The final 'IOOS' specification included significant modifications to the body, engine, transmission, suspension and braking over the production Austin-Healey '100'. Outwardly the 'IOOS' could be distinguished by its light-alloy two-tone bodywork with a smaller oval-shaped radiator grille, louvred bonnet top, competition Lucas 'Le Mans' headlight units, a low one-piece Perspex windscreen and a centrally-placed filler-cap leading to a 20-gallon fuel tank. In the interest of weight saving there were no bumpers or similar embellishments, the 'IOOS' being some 220 lb lighter than the production '100'. The standard BN 2 suspension was modified by using stiffer spring settings with double-acting shockabsorbers. Dunlop disc brakes were fitted on all four wheels, making the '100S' the first British production car to be fitted with disc brakes as standard equipment.

But the most significant feature of the '100S' specification was the engine modifications. An entirely new light-alloy Weslake cylinder head was fitted. This had modified porting with the induction and exhaust ports on the opposite side to that of the standard '100' head. Twin $1\frac{3}{4}$ in. SU carburetters were fitted, with twin petrol pumps. A twin exhaust system was also used. Flat-topped, solid-skirt, high-compression pistons were used with a modified camshaft. A combined oil filter and cooler was fitted close by the radiator. With the raised compression ratio of 8·3 to 1, the '100S' produced 132 b h p at 4,700 rev/min – an increase of no less than 42 b h p over the production Austin-Healey '100'. The transmission utilized a lightened flywheel with competition clutch, and the four-speed BN 2 gearbox, without overdrive, was fitted with a modified remote-control lever. Standard axle ratio for the '100S' was listed as an astonishingly high 2·92 to 1, but a host of alternative ratios were made available.

All these modifications combined to give the '100S' a startling performance for a four-cylinder machine of that period. A mere 9·8 secs. would see it accelerate from 0 to 60 mile/h, the standing $\frac{1}{4}$-mile took only 16·8 secs., and the top speed was around the 125 mile/h mark. The '100S' holds the honour of being the fastest production Austin-Healey model.

The '100M'

The performance of the '100S' naturally interested the owners of BN 1 and 2 models who wanted to bring their own cars up to a similar specification, even if they could not enjoy the benefit of the lightened '100S' bodywork. To cater for these owners the 'Le Mans' engine conversion kit was introduced, and later the Austin-Healey '100M' was put into limited production at Warwick. As its name suggests, the 'Le Mans' conversion was developed from the modifications used on the Austin-Healey '100' at Le Mans in 1953, when a pair of BN 1s made their racing debut and put up a fine demonstration of high-speed reliability for the 24 hours.

The 'Le Mans' conversion consisted mainly of engine modifications. Twin $1\frac{3}{4}$ in. SU carburetters were supplied with a cold-air box, special inlet manifolds, a special advance curve distributor, a high-lift camshaft, and 8·1 to 1 high compression pistons. A steel cylinder-

Sir Leonard Lord with Donald Healey and the prototype Healey '100' (wearing its original Healey and not Austin–Healey badge) at the London Motor Show in 1952

The production Austin–Healey '100', a truly classical sports car body design that remains undated even today

Racing debut for the Austin–Healey '100' was at Le Mans in 1953 when the two-car team finished 12th and 14th overall. This is the car driven by Gordon Wilkins and Marcel Becquart

All the Austin–Healey '100s' and the early '100-Sixes' were built at Longbridge before the B.M.C. sports car production was centralized at Abingdon in 1957. This is the original '100' production line

The Austin-Healey '100S' distinguished from the '100' by its two-tone bodywork, oval radiator grill, louvred bonnet and light alloy body, provided the clubman with a comparatively inexpensive, fast and safe sports racing car. It was mainly built for export

The late Ron Flockhart is flagged away by Peter Cavanagh on the 1955 Scorpion Rally, the first competitive event run by the Healey Drivers' Club (later to become the Austin-Healey Club) of which they were both founder members

Lance Macklin and Stirling Moss with the '100S' before leaving for Sebring in 1955, when they finished sixth overall

Lance Macklin at the start of the 1955 Mille Miglia in which he finished 36th overall

The '100S' team await the start of the 1955 Mille Miglia. Below, Donald Healey and Jim Cashmore on the starting ramp at Brescia

The '100S' powered record breaker which, at Utah in 1954, captured American and International records and covered the flying mile at 192·62 mile/h

The same car with improved streamlining and using the '100-Six' engine was driven by Donald Healey at Utah in 1956 to achieve 203·6 mile/h

The first of the six-cylinder 'big Healey' models, the Austin-Healey '100-Six', was announced in September 1956. Two models were available, a two-seater and a two-four-seater with 'occasional' seats in the rear

The rally winning potential of the 'big Healey' was demonstrated for the first time in the 1958 Tulip Rally when Jack Sears put up some outstanding performances in the circuit tests and hill climbs

The '3000' Mark I, introduced in June 1959. Externally indistinguishable from the '100-Six'

The '3000' Mark II, introduced in May 1961, had the three-carburetter engine and a bolder radiator grille with vertical bars

Last of the line, the '3000' Mark III, introduced in March 1962, returned to twin-carburetter engine. The body had wind-up windows and a convertible hood

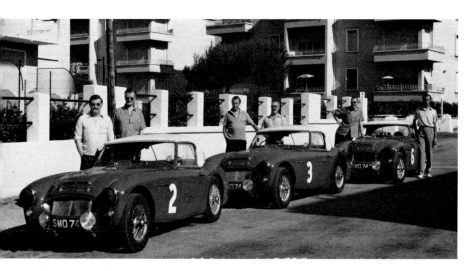

Alpine baptism for the '3000' was in 1959 when a team of three cars was entered for Bill Shepherd/John Williamson, Jack Sears/Sam Moore, John Gott/Chris Tooley

This team of Warwick-prepared '3000s' ran at Sebring in 1960

The first big-time success for the Abingdon team came in the Alpine Rally of 1960. *Above* Pat Moss and Ann Wisdom storming through to finish second overall and class winners. *Below* The girls are joined by the winning Austin-Healey team of John Gott/Bill Shepherd, along with Don and Erle Morley

Don Morley urges the '3000' on to his first Alpine Rally win in 1961

Pat Moss and Ann Wisdom concentrate hard on their way to outright victory in the 1960 Liège-Rome-Liège Rally

David Seigle-Morris has the distinction of having finished three consecutive Liège-Rome-Liège Rallies in 'big Healeys'. Here he storms along with Tony Ambrose to finish sixth overall and win his class in the 1961 event

Pat Moss and Pauline Mayman, Coupe des Dames winners on the 1962 R.A.C. Rally

Don and Erle Morley set off for their second Alpine Rally victory in 1962

The Morley twins on their way to their customary class win in the 1964 Alpine Rally. This was the car later driven by Timo Makinen on the Spa-Sofia-Liège Rally of that year, then sold to Peter Browning and rebuilt as the last of the works rally Healeys for the ill-fated R.A.C. Rally of 1967

Undoubtedly the most dominating victory in rallying history and the Healeys' finest hour – Rauno Aaltonen and Tony Ambrose, winners of the last of the great Spa-Sofia-Liège Rallies run in 1964

Timo Makinen's name will always be associated with the 'big Healey', particularly his performance in the forestry stages of the R.A.C. and Scottish Rallies. *Above* He finishes second overall on the 1964 R.A.C. with Don Barrow. *Below* Sideways as always, this time with Paul Easter on the 1965 Scottish Rally

Two famous competition '3000s' that continue to give a good account of themselves in club racing. *Above* John Chatham in the much rebuilt 1962 Le Mans car. *Below* John Gott in his faithful ex-works car of 1959, probably the most successful Healey or Austin-Healey of all times

THE AUSTIN-HEALEY 'IOOS' AND 'IOOM'   IOI

head gasket was used and the complete engine conversion raised the power output to 110 b h p. Suspension improvements incorporated a racing type anti-roll bar with special front shockabsorbers. Coachwork modifications included a louvred bonnet top, and the 'IOOM' was available with the same distinctive two-tone paint finish as the 'IOOS'.

The 'IOOM' could be purchased from Warwick as a factory-modified BN 2, or owners could buy the 'Le Mans' engine conversion kit and have it fitted to their own cars. It says much for the sturdiness of the original A90 engine that, today, some early BN 1s and BN 2s are still responding gallantly to being brought up to 'Le Mans' specification and giving their younger (but heavier) 'IOO-Six' and '3000' sisters a run for their money in club racing.

Pan-American Road Race

Soon after the official announcement of the 'IOOS', two cars were entered for that most unusual event, the Pan-American Road Race. This five-day event was one of the toughest and most dangerous in the international calendar, covering some 2,000 miles up the centre of Mexico and embracing the widest variety of motoring conditions. The two 'IOOS' entries were to be driven by Lance Macklin and Carroll Shelby, with Roy Jackson-Moore and Donald Healey as reserves. The Austin-Healeys were the sole British entries and the team did not have a very happy outing. Firstly the cars were delayed by a dock strike in Southampton, then, when they were flown to Cherbourg for shipment to the States, the boat was delayed between New York and Mexico. Thus the Austin-Healey team arrived at the start with little time for practising or final testing. On the first 330-mile leg, Shelby put up a promising show to be placed fourth overall, but he was later to crash on the second stage, the 'IOOS' being a write-off and Shelby breaking an arm. Macklin had an equally disappointing run, as he tells here:

'I was unlucky, because about halfway through the mountain section, when the car had been going quite well, it suddenly started to misfire badly. I got out and made sure a plug lead hadn't come adrift, or anything – these seemed O.K., so I changed over to a spare coil, but this didn't seem to make any difference. In the end I decided that if I was going to make the end of the stage, within the time limit allowed there wasn't any point in wasting more time trying to find the fault,

H.A.H.—8

LIBRARY
LOS ANGELES COUNTY MUSEUM OF NATURAL HISTORY

but just to keep going and try and finish the stage. Well, this I did, but the car was firing very intermittently, wouldn't do more than about 30–40 mile/h, and I still had 60–70 miles to go, so when I finally got to the end of the stage I was, I think, about 40 secs. over the time allowed, and I was disqualified.

'It was a pity, because the car, apart from this miss, was going very well, and I had been faster than the Porsche that came third on maximum speed and also on the first twisty bit, so we might have come third if we'd finished.

'The "100S" was generally a tough, reliable motor-car, and was about the only car that you could start off in something like the Mille Miglia or Pan-American and be pretty sure to finish. In fact in the Mille Miglia, although I had troubles, I think I finished every time I was driving a Healey. It was a frightening car to drive in the wet – it certainly oversteered rather violently – and it was difficult to keep on the road at 130–140 mile/h on those slippery Italian roads, probably more so than contemporary cars such as the Aston Martin. It was a car that always amazed me; considering that it was only an old taxi engine it was remarkable how fast it could be made to go.'

Return to Sebring

With the opening of the new season at Sebring, in March 1955, came more attractive opportunities for production sports cars in international racing. Categories for series-production cars had now been introduced, so the Austin-Healeys were back in competition and no fewer than seven '100S' cars were entered at Sebring. Leading the Austin-Healey team came the forceful combination of Stirling Moss and Lance Macklin, Moss having been released from the Mercedes team for this event.

Moss, master of the Le Mans start, gave the team a good getaway in the 12-hour race, and during the initial laps the '100S' was well up with the leading Jaguar and Ferrari opposition. Jackie Cooper was also well placed among the first dozen cars with the second '100S'. Lapping at 81 mile/h, Moss and Macklin held on to a secure ninth place during the first half of the race, and, although the Fergus/Watts and Allen/Ehrman cars were retired, the five other '100S' entries continued to circulate in impressive style.

After eight hours' racing, Moss and Macklin had brought the Austin-Healey up to sixth place behind the leading 'D'-type Jaguar two Ferraris and two Maseratis. Brewster/Rutan and Cook/Rand were placed ninth and tenth at this stage. Electrical troubles and an excursion into a sandbank delayed the Cooper/Jackson-Moore 'IOOS', so they trailed several laps in arrears. The race drew to a close with no change amongst the leaders, Moss and Macklin maintaining their very creditable sixth place overall. More significant was the fact that the Austin-Healeys had made it a 1–2–3 victory in the series-production class, Brewster/Rutan and Cook/Rand playing the supporting roles. With five out of the seven cars finishing to dominate their class, the 'IOOS' had put up a convincing demonstration on the doorstep of the American market.

First British cars in Mille Miglia

Sebring was followed by a memorable Mille Miglia for the Austin-Healey marque. Four 'IOOS' cars were entered for Lance Macklin, George Abecassis, Ron Flockhart and Donald Healey. As in the 1954 event, the Austin-Healeys enjoyed their own private battle with the British works entries of Triumphs, Aston Martins and Jaguars.

Lance Macklin remembers his personal battle with the late Ron Flockhart:

'He started one minute behind me, and there was a lot of discussion who would be quicker, Ron or myself. Ron was driving the Austin-Healey with the B R M-tuned engine. I wasn't particularly worried and I was quite prepared for him to catch me up, but I'd been going about two hours, I suppose, and I came into a small town, with a right-hand corner, and straw bales on the left. A slow corner but not a dangerous one – 30 or 40 mile/h I suppose – and as I came into the corner, I suddenly realized that there was something on the road – I don't know if it was oil or sand – but anyway the car started sliding a bit, slid across the road and hit the straw bales, and ended up perched on top of them.

'The heat from the exhaust set fire to the straw so, of course, all the Italians who were near by went belting off in the opposite direction, and I was frantically trying to get the car off the straw bales before they caught fire too much. In the end I got a few Italians, by shouting at them, to come and give me a hand, got the car off the bales, and backed down the road. There wasn't any damage or anything, so as soon as I got off the bales, I jumped in and drove off.

'Just as I drove off – I got about 100 yards up the road, and I suddenly saw a white Austin-Healey come up behind, and realized it was Flockhart. Well, I'd lost a good couple of minutes on the bales, but he must have thought he'd caught me because he'd been going faster. Soon after this there was a control, and we both went in together. I think they stamped our books at the same time, we both went out one behind the other, and for the next half an hour or so he was darting hither and thither behind me.

'I thought he was sitting rather close to my tail, so I thought that if he really wants to go all that much faster than I was going, I don't want to go any faster myself, I'd let him go ahead, and I waved him past. Of course, it's always much easier if you're following another car than if you're in front, so I had no trouble in sitting behind him and relaxing, whilst he had the trouble of being pathfinder.

'He was obviously trying pretty hard, and I reckoned he was pushing his chance a bit. In one or two places he was going round corners he couldn't obviously see round at motor racing speeds. Anyway, we came down a hill and at the bottom there was a left-hand bend on to a bridge. As I followed him down the hill, I put the brakes on when I thought I was coming on to the bridge a bit too fast, and rather to my surprise, he didn't; he pulled away from me on the braking. Well, I thought, I don't know; I was rather interested to see whether he was going to get round, going on to the bridge at that speed. When he got half-way on to the bridge I saw he wasn't going to make it; he got the car sideways, it shot across into the inside of the bridge, the front wheels hit the inside curb or something and this spun the car round, then it went backwards across to the other side, hit the wall of the bridge going backwards – I suppose he was still doing 60–70 mile/h – hit the parapet of the bridge, and a most incredible thing, the car literally reared up on its end, the front of the car lifted off the ground, did a complete backward somersault, knocked down the parapet and disappeared!

'I shot up alongside the hole he'd made, drove to within six inches of the hole and leant out of the car and looked over the edge into the water. All I could see was bubbles coming up from the river underneath and steam rising. So I put the car into first gear and shot down to the end of the bridge as fast as I could. It was quite a long bridge, but I got to the end, pulled off and jumped out and ran down to the river.

'When I got there, there were already three or four Italians in the water up to their armpits, and I was just going in to see if I could give them a hand and I suddenly heard someone say "Lance". I turned round and there was Ron, sitting on the bank. He'd got out of the car as it went over and had swum ashore.

'The Italians, for some reason or other, thought there was another person in the car, and were trying to get the co-driver out, so I shouted to them that it was all right, there was only one person. Anyway, Ron was perfectly all right, he hadn't hurt himself at all. I asked him if he wanted me to stay around a bit, but he told me to get on and not waste any more time, so I told him that someone would be coming round after the race, who would pick him up, and that was that.'

Macklin's efforts to retrieve his team mate had, of course, cost him valuable time – a pity when he was leading the entire British contingent and had averaged 94 mile/h for the first 390 miles. Now Abecassis took over the lead in the 'IOOS' team with Donald Healey in pursuit.

From Pescara, Abecassis (who had never raced an Austin-Healey before) began a truly outstanding drive. Over the first 450 miles his average speed had not dropped below 92 mile/h, and over the mountain stages he lost only 7 minutes to the works Mercedes of Moss and Fangio. At Rome, Abecassis lay in 26th place, the 'IOOS' holding more than an hour's advantage over the entire Triumph team. Meanwhile Macklin had the misfortune to have the throttle linkage come adrift, and he was forced to complete the race juggling with the ignition switch, while Donald Healey was later to retire with the fourth 'IOOS' entry. Along the coast to Siena, Abecassis recorded 15th fastest time overall, and by the time Bologna was reached the 'IOOS' was in 14th position. Through the final stages to the finish at Brescia, Abecassis must have driven the 'IOOS' just as fast as a 'IOOS' (or any other Austin-Healey, for that matter) has ever been driven, for his *average* speed over those last 83 miles was 100·5 mile/h. This brought the 'IOOS' up a further three places, so that Abecassis was finally placed 11th in general classification and fifth in the over 2 litre class behind the winning Mercedes and Ferraris. He and Macklin were placed first and second in their price classification, Macklin finishing in 36th position overall despite his throttle linkage troubles. Once again the Austin-Healeys were the first British cars to finish. Abecassis' drive will be remembered as a truly great performance and one of the highlights in Healey history.

New competitions department

Early in 1955 it was announced that the British Motor Corporation would be re-entering the field of active participation in international racing and rallying. Up till then the newly combined Austin and Nuffield groups had been inactive in this sphere, the Warwick-entered Austin-Healeys being the only B.M.C. works teams in international events. At this time a new Competitions Department was set up at Abingdon with Marcus Chambers in charge of operations, supported by a new Competitions Committee representative of all interested parties within the Corporation, and led by the MG Car Company's Director and General Manager, John Thornley. From now on it was clear that the Austin-Healeys would be playing a leading role in the B.M.C. competitions programme, along with entries of MG and other B.M.C. models.

Le Mans and TT disasters

Unhappily this announcement coincided with the beginnings of a series of disastrous outings for the '100S'. Prestige for a manufacturer earned through hard-fought competition successes can so quickly be dashed to naught by the association of the marque with widely-publicized accidents in motor racing, particularly if these involve loss of life to drivers or spectators. Nothing could have been more damaging in this respect than to have the name Austin-Healey coupled so closely with the tragedy of the 1955 Le Mans disaster. As is well known, the ill-fated Mercedes of Levegh collided with Macklin's '100S' opposite the pits, this accident causing the death of some 80 spectators, the worst tragedy in the history of the sport. It was miraculous that Macklin should step unscathed from such a disaster.

After Le Mans came the Tourist Trophy, run upon the dangerous Dundrod circuit in Northern Ireland, and again there was an accident involving a melee of cars in which two drivers lost their lives. Macklin was again involved, though only because he arrived on the scene of the accident seconds after the collision and was forced to ditch the '100S' to avoid further disaster. Once more Macklin was unhurt, but again the name of Austin-Healey was closely associated with a widely-publicized tragedy in the more sensational press. So, after the '100S' successes at Sebring and in the Mille Miglia earlier in the year, the 1955 season ended with these sad memories.

1956 brings '100-Six'

In the international field the '100S' achieved little more prestige for the marque in 1956, for by now the four-cylinder A90 engine was sadly outdated. For the clubman, however, the '100S' continued to be a most desirable machine, and those fortunate few who were able to take delivery of this basically export-only model enjoyed many miles of reliable and high-speed motor sport. Particular mention should be made of some private owners who put up noteworthy performances: John Dalton and David Shale, who were placed first and second in their class in the *Autosport* sports car championship in 1956; Raymond Flower, who was a regular supporter of both international and club racing; and the late Dickie Protheroe, who ran a '100S' well into the 1958 season, scoring many successes.

Very few original '100S' models are still around today but those that are will be treasured as collectors' items for a very long time.

CHAPTER 8

THE AUSTIN-HEALEY '100-SIX'

During a successful four-year production run, the Austin-Healey '100' and its two competition versions, the '100S' and '100M', had used the four-cylinder Austin A90 engine. This faithful 2,660 cc unit, first introduced away back in 1949, had truly served the marque well, but now the time had come for the Austin-Healey to receive a modern power unit, and the B.M.C. six-cylinder 'C'-type 2,639 cc engine, then used in the Austin Westminster, was the obvious choice. Along with this engine change, the Austin Motor Company took this opportunity to up-date the original Austin-Healey '100' specification in terms of improved styling, driver and passenger accommodation, weather-proofing and general appointments. Thus in September 1956 a new Austin-Healey model was introduced, to be named the '100-Six'.

Although the six-cylinder 'C'-type engine produced some 12 b h p more than the earlier A90 unit, an increase in the weight of the '100-Six' meant that the new model was little faster than its predecessor. However, the new power unit did offer the welcome flexibility and smoothness associated with a six-cylinder motor, and better low-speed torque on the '100-Six', coupled with smoother acceleration throughout, made the new model a more restful car to drive. Apart from the engine change, there was little alteration to the rest of the mechanical specification. The four-speed gearbox from the 'BN 2' was retained with the Laycock overdrive unit (operating on third and top gears) available as an optional extra. Because of the revised weight distribution, some adjustments were made to the settings of the front and rear springs.

To cater for the needs of the family man, the cockpit of the '100-Six' was enlarged to accommodate two occasional rear seats upon which two small children or one adult could travel in reasonable comfort. Inevitably this meant some sacrifice in the luggage-carrying capacity of the Austin-Healey, for the spare wheel was now housed in the boot. These cockpit alterations, with a slight increase in the wheelbase, generally improved driver and passenger comfort, one noteworthy feature being the wider doors now fitted with exterior handles. To achieve better weather-proofing, the folding windscreen fitted on the original '100' model was replaced with a fixed screen, and a much improved hood and sliding sidescreens were fitted.

Externally the '100-Six' was instantly distinguishable from its predecessor, for the new oval-shaped radiator grille now replaced the traditional Warwick grille design worn by all Healeys (except for the '100S') from the first 1946 saloon. The bonnet line on the new car was slightly lowered, and there was a fresh-air grille upon the bonnet lid allowing a little more under-bonnet room and improving engine ventilation. Re-styling at the rear of the car incorporated reflectors faired into the body panels, and an external fuel filler was fitted. Although wire wheels were fitted on all previous Austin-Healey models, these became optional on the '100-Six', disc wheels being fitted as standard wear.

Production of the '100-Six' commenced at the Austin Motor Company's works at Longbridge in August 1956, the new model being dubbed 'BN 4'. Then in late 1957 the Austin-Healey found a new home when all B.M.C. sports car production was centralized at Abingdon. Soon after this the 'C'-type engine received significant modifications, a further 15 b h p being produced with the use of a new six-inlet-port cylinder head, detachable aluminium alloy inlet manifold, twin HD 6 ($1\frac{3}{4}$ in.) SU carburetters and a modified distributor. On the raised compression ratio of 8·5 to 1, power output of the '100-Six' was now 117 b h p at 5,000 rev/min. A glance at the performance figures in the Appendices will indicate how these modifications gave added pace to the earlier '100-Six'. Production of the six-inlet port '100-Six' ran until March 1959.

Although the '100-Six' had been purposely designed as a 2/4-seater, there still existed a market for a two-seater version of the Austin-Healey for those who preferred greater luggage accommodation. Thus, from June 1958, both two and 2/4-seater versions of the '100-Six' were available.

A 200 mile/h Austin-Healey

The official announcement of the '100-Six' in September 1956 was heralded with the news of fresh Austin-Healey record-breaking achievements at Utah with a pair of six-cylinder 'C'-type powered cars. The first of these record-breakers was a conventional 'BN 2' fitted with streamlined body extensions at the front and rear, the

150 b h p six-cylinder power unit running on 9 to 1 compression ratio and using a pre-production prototype of the six-port head fitted with triple twin-choke Weber carburetters.

Carroll Shelby and Roy Jackson-Moore drove this car for the long-distance runs, claiming a healthy score of International and American Class 'D' records, including the 500 miles at 153·14 mile/h and the six hours at 145·96 mile/h. The second car was the 1954 streamliner further developed by Austins and now powered by a 250 b h p supercharged version of the 'C'-type engine. Unfortunately supercharger troubles delayed all record runs with this car, but Donald Healey managed to achieve one timed run, recording the incredible speed of 203·06 mile/h. This performance earned him membership of the exclusive 'Over 200 m.p.h. Club', whilst '200 mile/h with an Austin-Healey' became a much-used publicity line to head the announcement of the new '100-Six'.

Early competitions

First competition outing for the new model was in the Italian Sestrière Rally, held in March 1957. Tommy Wisdom was to drive the lone '100-Six'. Having her first ride in the passenger seat of an Austin-Healey was daughter Ann Wisdom (now of course Ann Riley), who was later to join Pat Moss and form one of the most consistently successful 'big Healey' rally crews of all time. The 1957 Sestrière placed the full emphasis on circuit speed tests and, with a dominating Italian entry, the '100-Six' met the strongest opposition in the G T category. Along with the majority of the British crews, the Wisdoms did not fare too well against the locals.

The international racing début for the '100-Six' was in the 12 Hour Race at Sebring later in March, when three Warwick-prepared cars were entered by the American distributors, Hambro Inc., and piloted by local drivers. All three cars wore the extended streamlined nose and tail sections as used on the Bonneville record car, but the Austin-Healey team did not enjoy much success at Sebring that year. Two of the cars retired with engine trouble, the third '100-Six' finishing second in its class after delays following an off-course excursion.

For the 1957 Mille Miglia – as things turned out, the last of the classic 1,000-mile road races in the series – a single car was made available to Tommy Wisdom and Cecil Winby. This car was the original Warwick competition 'BN 4' (as used on the Sestrière) now fitted with a prototype six-port head and engine modications to 'BN 6' specification. The '100-Six' completed the course without incident, winning its class in the limited price category and finishing 37th overall. Wisdom and Winby averaged 76 mile/h for the 1,000 miles, thus completing the course faster than any Healey had done before, except for that remarkable drive in 1955 by George Abecassis with the '100S'.

The 1958 season opened with the Monte Carlo Rally and a less fortunate outing for Tommy Wisdom, who, partnered by Cyril Smith, was eliminated in the early stages, along with almost all their fellow Paris starters, in impossible icebound conditions.

Soon it was Sebring time again, and once more a team of three '100-Sixes' was entered by Hambros and driven by local drivers. This year the cars ran with standard bodies and hardtops and they put up a better showing, all three cars finishing the 12 Hours to win the Manufacturers' Team Prize.

The potential of the 'big Healey' as a class-winning G T machine in the field of international rallying was demonstrated for the first time in the 1958 Tulip Rally, when the '100-Six' of Jack Sears and Peter Garnier put up superb performances on the timed climbs and circuit tests to cause a major upset amongst the leading G T teams of the day. Although the '100-Six' was unhappily retired from the event with a fractured distributor drive, the performance of this lone entry had clearly indicated that in future the marque Austin-Healey was to play a leading role in B.M.C.'s increasingly active participation in international rallying.

Up to this time the international competition programme for the marque had been looked after by the Donald Healey Motor Company at Warwick, Donald Healey and his son Geoffrey being responsible for the preparation of both race and rally cars. In the spring of 1958, however, the preparation of all works-entered B.M.C. rally cars was centralized at the Competitions Department at Abingdon. Thus Austin-Healey rally cars now came under the direction of Marcus Chambers (and later of Stuart Turner and myself) at Abingdon, whilst Geoff Healey concentrated solely on the racing side at Warwick.

The start of an era

The '100-Six' had its first full-scale international rally sortie in the 1958 Alpine Rally, no fewer than five cars forming the spearhead of the B.M.C. works entries. Leading the team was the B.M.C. rally captain, John Gott, partnered by Chris Tooley. Jack Sears/Sam Moore and Bill Shepherd/John Williamson completed the male contingent, for the remaining two cars were crewed by Mrs Nancy Mitchell/Mrs G. Wilton-Clark and the new partnership of Pat Moss/Ann Wisdom, appearing for the first time together with the Austin-Healey team.

From the traditional start at Marseilles the 56 starters, almost half of them in the same class as the '100-Sixes', set out on the 2,360-mile, five-day journey covering some two dozen of the most difficult passes in the Alps and the Dolomites and incorporating eight special tests, four of these being speed hill climbs and circuit tests and four regularity climbs over the Allos, Stelvio, Izoard and Soubeyrand passes.

Over the first 600-mile run to Brescia all went well for the team, Jack Sears in particular performing well in the speed tests at Monza to put up second fastest time behind the favoured Mercedes. At Brescia, four of the five '100-Sixes' were amongst the 16 unpenalized cars, Nancy Mitchell having lost her chance of the coveted 'Coupe' due to a timing miscalculation on the part of her co-driver. From Brescia a further 680-mile stage took the crews over the rugged passes of the Croche Domini, Vivione, Giovo, Stelvio, and the Gavia, then back across the Vivione from the opposite direction. On the Croche Domini, Jack Sears/Sam Moore were involved in a minor collision with another competitor when both cars took a wrong turn. The Healey's steering was damaged, and the crew lost some time before they could reach the B.M.C. service depot, where Marcus Chambers and his men soon had the '100-Six' roadworthy again.

On to Megève and Gap for the final run down to the finish at Marseilles, and things still looked rosy for the Austin-Healeys with the Gott/Tooley and Shepherd/Williamson cars still unpenalized, the former crew leading their class and lying in fourth place overall.

But as John Gott recalls, his Healey was soon to be retired:

'We were descending the Cayole and were over the worst of it, going quite briskly, although we had quite a bit of time in hand and there was nothing to worry about. It was just coming up to dawn and I remember admiring the beautiful silver and blue of the mountains in the early morning light. Then quite unexpectedly the whole panorama started to revolve around. Chris nearly fell out of the car and immediately blamed me for clouting a bridge. I was very in-dignant about this because I certainly had not hit anything – I just lost it probably, I thought at the time, through lack of concentration.

'We sat by the roadside having a little argument about it when something suddenly crashed down on to the hardtop, bounced on to the bonnet and bowled off down the road. I thought that perhaps there was an avalanche coming down the mountain but when we got out of the car we realized that there was no avalanche and the big lump that had fallen on the car was the rear wheel.

'What had happened was the wheel had come off, overtaken us without us seeing it, bowled its way up the mountain side in front of us, then fallen back on to the road again and hit the car. Closer examination revealed that the hub spline had fractured right off and we were left sitting on the brake disc.

'This was a complete tragedy for us because we afterwards discovered that at this stage of the event we were the only car left in the rally, unpenalized. In those days we were scratching around for success and to lose a Coupe and a class win was very sad indeed.

'But at least we had proved that there was a weakness in the hub design. Terry Mitchell of the Development Department was with us on this event; he flew home with the damaged parts and, as a result of further tests, stronger hub assemblies were fitted as standard equipment on the cars.'

That final leg from Megève to Marseilles was also to cause troubles for Pat Moss:

'Our Healey was still sound and intact but after a few hours of this last stretch, the engine started missing. The mechanics, who were leap-frogging the competitors by easier routes and setting up service points, decided that it was caused by blocked air filters and told me not to worry for the moment because we were on a tight section and could not spare any time. If we stopped for repair, and lost even one minute, we would lose our Coupe, and it is this servicing difficulty which makes the Alpine so hard on the cars.

'We hurried on and in the next section I managed to save three minutes and got out the tools and started to whip off the filters. I left the breather pipe hanging, which the mechanics had told me to do, and by then there was only 20 seconds left. A journalist from one of the motoring magazines was standing by the car watching and I asked him to close the bonnet while I threw the tools back in the boot, which he did, and we went on the few yards to the control and checked in.

'Soon afterwards the clutch started slipping and was very bad as we reached Mont Revard. Apart from the fact that the sections around Mont Revard were unbelievably tight they also had one of the special speed sections here. These sections are absolute races against the clock and the times on these sort out the final placings in the rally. We did badly there and lost time on the other Revard bits, so our Coupe was gone and so was a lot of our interest.

'The clutch was slipping really badly now and the oil pressure began to fall. We were over the Col Lusital by now and heading towards Gap and the oil pressure was so low that we stopped at the first garage that we could find and bought some. There was no point in hurrying any more, because we were out of the rally to all intents and purposes and we thought that we would have to retire at Gap.

'We trundled into Gap five minutes late and the mechanics had a look at the car. They had taken quick looks once or twice before, around Revard, but now they had a good look. They found that the breather pipe was tied in a knot and, of course, not being able to breathe the oil from the sump was forced back through the clutch. It turned out that this motoring magazine journalist – who was supposed to be a technical expert – had tied the pipe in a knot "because it looked untidy".

'Then we heard that all the Mont Revard sections were scrubbed because they were so difficult that not a single car was clean. This meant that the only time we had lost was the five minutes taken up buying oil before Gap.

'Once the breathing was sorted out, the car was fit to finish and we went to Marseilles without losing any more time and completed a race circuit test at Marseilles.

'There were 25 finishers and only the first seven won Coupes. We were eighth and would have won a Coupe but for that knotted breather pipe.

'However, we did win the Ladies', which gave us another five points towards the Championship, and we were fourth in the class.'

Despite these disappointments, the Austin-Healey team had enjoyed a magnificent outing in this, their first full-scale event under the B.M.C. rally banner. Shepherd/Williamson collected an Alpine Cup for an unpenalized run to be amongst the four British winners of the seven Coupes awarded; they also finished second in their class and seventh overall. To Pat Moss/Ann Wisdom went the Coupe des Dames, with Nancy Mitchell/Gillian Wilton-Clark as runners-up. Jack Sears/Sam Moore finished the rally with a rousing drive in the final circuit test,

making fastest time. The success of the 'big Healeys' in their first
Alpine endorsed the performance of the lone '100-Six' which had
shown such promise in the 1958 Tulip, and everyone expected further
successes in the next event on their calendar, the Liège-Rome-Liège
Rally. And they were not to be disappointed.

Liège Team Prize

Of all the international rallies, the 'Marathon de la Route' was the
supreme challenge to car and crew. More than 3,000 miles had to be
covered in a non-stop four-day run over the roughest mountain passes
in France, Germany, Austria, Italy and Yugoslavia. The organization
was the most sporting of any event, probably because the event was
really a straightforward road race involving no handicapping, complicated formulae or special speed tests. Only the finest cars and crews
completed the course; it was an honour to finish the Liège at all, let
alone gain a class award or the overall victory.

The 1958 Liège was one of the toughest events in the series, and again
a team of '100-Sixes' was chosen to lead the official B.M.C. works
entry. The four cars, crewed by Gerry Burgess/Sam Croft-Pearson,
Pat Moss/Ann Wisdom, Nancy Mitchell/Anne Hall and Joan Johns/
Sam Moore, were also entered for the Manufacturers' Team Prize and
in company with the 'MGA' of John Gott/Ray Brookes, they formed
the official British team entry.

The first 730 miles took the 98 starters out of Belgium across Germany, Austria and Italy to the Yugoslavian border, where the first
of the truly competitive stages were to begin. Here Pat Moss and
Ann Wisdom exhibited the brilliant form which they were to display
throughout the event, for they brought their '100-Six' up amongst
the 11 unpenalized crews at this stage.

Pat Moss continues the story:

'Night came again while we were on the next section to Rijeka and,
apart from darkness and bad roads, we had patches of mist which
made things very tricky before dawn when there were a lot of horse-
drawn carts, without lights, on their way to market. After Rijeka we
turned north to Zagreb and 100 miles of fine, beautiful road which
led us to the most staggering 200 miles in Europe.

'It was like driving over an enormous washboard with a loose
gravel surface, clouds of dust, mountains with twisty roads and almost
tropical heat. There were already more than a dozen cars out of the

rally before we reached that stretch, but those 200 miles put out another 10. Yugoslavia always shatters hopes and cars.

'The Healey is a low car with not much ground clearance and the underpart had a terrible bashing on the rough. But they are strong, those Healeys, built like tanks, and nothing broke. It is incredible how tough they are, when they look so sporty. But apart from that, and the speed, it was a bad car to be in from every other point of view.

'The August sun was blazing and the heat poured in through the roof. The engine was like a furnace and more heat came backwards into the car. The exhaust pipe was under the navigator's seat so there was heat burning upwards as well. The only way to get any air or breeze was to take out the sidescreens and then the dust poured in so that we could hardly breathe. Dust went everywhere. Our eyelashes became so heavy with it that we could hardly see. It got into our hair and through our clothes and still we were burning hot.

'Soon after crossing the border into Italy there was another special stage over the very rough and tough little Passo Duran, and only three cars cleaned this, a Porsche, an Alfa and a Volvo. We missed by 18 seconds, but that was good enough to put us in the lead of the big-banger class and we moved further ahead in the Ladies'. The road sections, supposed to be easy, were now getting so tight that the organizers decided cars should not be excluded for lateness unless they were more than 30 minutes behind schedule on any section. Nobody had, in fact, been excluded for lateness because those who were late and fit to go on kept going anyway.

'We went across by night to the Stelvio and the Gavia, once again, and they were both taken as one speed section at dawn. Eleven crews cleaned this and our time was the fourth fastest. On the previous two, we were fifth fastest.

'I have mentioned how tight the times are on the Alpine, and you can imagine the shock when we got to the Vivione – which is as nasty as the Gavia – and discovered that the time for it in this rally was three minutes less than allowed in the Alpine! Nevertheless, eight cars cleaned it and I was thrilled when we were second fastest, which gave us a very strong lead in the class and an even bigger one in the Ladies'. We were also fifth overall in the rally behind three Porsches and an Alfa.

'There was a long, fast, flat stretch after the Vivione, and Wiz took over while I rested. I was incredibly tired and must have been a bit delirious with the heat and at one control I woke up and thought I saw people putting up signs. I asked Wiz: "Why are Gerry Burgess and Nancy Mitchell putting up those horse show signs?"

'Wiz told me to go back to sleep and I did.

'I had to wake again for the French Alps, for this was the toughest part of the rally from the speed point of view and we had to average 50 miles an hour, including a crossing of the Izoard. Seventy of the 98 cars were out by now and not one of the remainder managed this section on time, although the fastest was only 2 minutes 44 seconds out and the slowest was just 10 minutes late. Ahead of us, the lead was changing between a Porsche and an Alfa by seconds. The Strahle/Buchet Porsche was just 38 seconds ahead of the Hebert/Consten Alfa and the third car, another Porsche, was only 1 minute 17 seconds behind the Alfa. Another Porsche was still fourth, just over three and a half minutes behind. And all this after more than 70 hours of driving.

'We were fifth, but trailing by about another five minutes, which was too much to worry those ahead and we were happy anyway. The order remained the same over the Col St Jean, where the loose gravel was six inches deep at times and the wheels spun like mad when I accelerated. This was followed by the Soubeyrand, and here Buchet in the leading Porsche ran out of road on the rather dangerous descent and the Alfa of Hebert/Consten took the lead by nine seconds, with the damaged Porsche second. This mountain road was so rough that the Reiss/Wencher Porsche in third place holed its sump and was retired, so we moved up to fourth. The Alfa moved farther ahead over Chaudiere and at the last special stage, the Col de la Echarasson, I decided to have a real go and see if I could move up one. I thought the damaged Porsche of Buchet and Strahle might be very slow. I was absolutely worn out and burning with heat, but just managed the second fastest time over the tarmac surface of the Col road, but we were still only fourth.

'The last part of the rally was a long, 500-mile trek back to Spa, with no tests to give us a stimulus. It was difficult only because we were so tired the driver might fall asleep, and the heat was still burning us up.

'The order did not change, so at Spa we were fourth overall and first in the Ladies', which gave us a lead of seven points in the Championship.'

Of the remaining members of the team, Joan Johns and Sam Moore had an accident in their Healey which was too badly damaged to continue. Gerry Burgess/Sam Croft-Pearson brought their '100-Six'

into 10th place with Nancy Mitchell/Anne Hall in 15th place. The
Austin-Healeys won the Manufacturers' Team Prize and, in company
with the Gott/Brookes 'MGA', Moss/Wisdom and Burgess/Croft-
Pearson gained the Club Team Prize. It had been a most fruitful outing
for the marque – but the coveted outright victory in the world's
toughest trial remained out of reach. Despite their brilliant showing,
few would have believed that in two years' time the fabulous Moss/
Wisdom combination, with the more powerful Austin-Healey '3000',
would achieve even this – outright victory in the Marathon de la
Route.

Montlhéry records

Shortly after the 1958 Liège came a very different entry in the list
of achievements for the '100-Six', a four-day record-breaking venture
at Montlhéry. This was a semi-works-supported outing, but the
organization and running of the whole affair was managed by a team
of undergraduates from Cambridge University Car Club led by a
cheery individual named Glyde Horrocks. In the previous year this
team had claimed an excellent bag of international records at Montlhéry
with an Austin A35, and they now proposed to do the same with
the '100-Six'. The venture proved very successful, for the '100-Six'
gained seven international class 'D' records, including four days and
10,000 miles at fractionally over 97 mile/h.

Final sorties

Back to the '100-Six' rally sorties and to the 1959 Tulip Rally,
where the Moss/Wisdom partnership began the event in their brilliant
Liège style until an accident forced their retirement. This left the Jack
Sears/Peter Garnier '100-Six' to carry the Austin-Healey flag, which
they accomplished in no mean terms by disposing of formidable
Mercedes, Ferrari and Aston Martin opposition to win the G T category
and finish eighth overall. Jack Sears also carried off the premier award
for the circuit races at Zandvoort.

For their first sortie on the rugged Acropolis Rally, B.M.C. sent
Pat and Ann in a '100-Six'. As Pat recalls, it was not a very successful
début in Greece.

'In the very early part of the rally we arrived at a control at night –
the first night – where we had an hour or two and I slept in the car.

After we were due to start again, I wanted some more sleep so Wiz drove.

'A funny movement of the car woke me up and I saw Wiz with her arms crossed up on the wheel; the car was going sideways. We started to spin towards a bank and, having had a look, I ducked down again because I believe it is the best thing to do when all is not good.

'The car turned over and we rolled down the bank, about 15 or 20 feet and stopped. The hardtop was cracked and loose and I could see the sky and Wiz was groaning and holding her side. I was all right so I got out and helped her. Her side was hurting so much she thought one or two ribs must be broken and she was badly winded. A lot of other rally cars stopped and men came running down the bank and took charge of Wiz while I examined the car, which was badly bent but still looked like a runner. I tried the starter and it worked and the engine fired, so these men manhandled it back to the road so we could go on with the rally. But on the road it would not restart, so I had to make another phone call saying: "Marcus, we've done it again".'

The summer of 1959 saw the introduction of the new 2·9 litre 'C'-type engine and the Austin-Healey was the first model to be introduced with this new power unit. The engine change was also the occasion for further improvements to the car's specification and the announcement of a new model – the Austin-Healey '3000'.

CHAPTER 9

THE AUSTIN-HEALEY '3000'

In June 1959 there came a new version of the B.M.C. six-cylinder 'C'-type engine enlarged from 2·6 to 2·9 litres, and this was shortly followed by the announcement of a successor to the '100-Six', the Austin-Healey '3000'. By increasing the engine capacity to 2,912 cc and raising the compression ratio to a little over 9 to 1, power output of the new model was rated at 124 b h p compared with 117 b h p of the '100-Six'. The '3000' thus offered greater pulling power and improved all-round performance. For the competition driver, the 2·9 litre engine obviously made better use of the International 3 litre class limit. The larger engine capacity, achieved by enlarging the cylinder bores, meant the use of an entirely new cylinder block and crankcase casting and, in line with the increased power output, there was a larger diameter clutch and stronger transmission gears. Improved braking was achieved with the use of Girling discs at the front. Apart from these mechanical improvements the '3000' was externally distinguished from its predecessor only by the flash on the radiator grille. As with the '100-Six' both two-seater and occasional four-seater versions of the '3000' were available.

Just as the use of disc brakes on the works-entered competition '100-Sixes' had led to the fitting of front discs as standard equipment on the '3000', so the use of a triple-carburetter layout on certain competition cars during the 1960 season prompted the announcement of the triple-carburetter '3000' Mark II in May 1961. With three 1½ in. SU carburetters installed on a new inlet manifold, and the use of modified valve springs and a redesigned camshaft, the power output of the '3000' was now quoted at 132 b h p. The additional power of the Mark II was most evident in the middle and upper ranges of engine speed. Most surprisingly, the fuel consumption of the triple-carburetter Mark II was slightly *better* than that of the twin-carburetter Mark I. The availability of servo-assisted brakes as an optional extra was a welcome feature. Later production models of the Mark II were fitted with a short, vertical, remote-control gear-lever, and a glass-fibre gearbox cover, which helped to improve cockpit cooling and reduce transmission noise. Externally the Mark II wore a bolder radiator grille, vertical bars replacing the horizontal styling on the Mark I.

But the triple-carburetter Mark II proved, perhaps, just too much of a delicate essay in tuning for many owners, so in March 1962 came a return to twin carburetters with the announcement of the restyled '3000' Convertible. This, the most refined and luxurious production Austin-Healey, presented the first major styling changes to the model since the introduction of the Healey '100' almost exactly 10 years previously. The '3000' was now brought into line with the present-day demand for a grand touring car offering saloon car comforts and appointments. A wrap-around windscreen was fitted and the doors had wind-down windows and quarter-lights. There was a new-styled quick-action one-piece hood complete with removable rear window panel. The Convertible was available only in occasional four-seater form. The return to twin carburetters represented a loss of 2 b h p, but the styling changes had improved the aerodynamics to compensate for this and the Convertible was the fastest production Austin-Healey, excluding the '100S' as a strictly competition machine. Handling of the latest '3000' was improved by fitting a stiffer anti-roll bar at the front and by using modified damper settings.

All the '3000' models proved worthy successors to the '100-Six', both through sales in world markets and in the field of international rallying. Although the styling remained basically unchanged for 11 years, in looks alone the '3000' compared favourably with the current G T models from rival marques and no other production model offered better value for money in high-performance sports car motoring.

Alpine baptism

International competition début for the new '3000' was in the 1959 Alpine Rally, a classic event later to become closely associated with Austin-Healey successes, rather as the Mille Miglia had been the happy hunting ground of the Warwick-built Healeys. The three works-entered cars for the Alpine ran in standard twin-carburetter form, the only modifications being the side exhaust system to improve ground clearance. Although the somewhat optimistically set average speeds meant that the larger G T cars were out of the running for the coveted Coupe des Alpes, the new 3 litre cars certainly proved that they now had the power to conquer such class opposition as the works Mercedes.

John Gott tells the story of the '3000's Alpine baptism:

'The "Alpine" is a very considerable test of a car and is often used to sort out the bugs in a new model. For this reason, the B.M.C. works team for 1959 was originally intended to be five of the then completely new Austin-Healey '3000' models. However, our recce party, returning from the Acropolis Rally via Austria, reported that there was a gap of some seven minutes between the time the A.C. de Marseille et Provence allowed for one sticky section and the actual time taken in practice by the redoubtable Pat Moss driving a 2·6 litre Austin-Healey '100-Six'. Even allowing for the extra urge of the 2·9 litre engine, and the fact that one can usually knock off a couple of minutes in the rally from the practice times, this seemed a bad class to put all the works cars in, especially as further research showed that the organizers had badly under-estimated the potentialities of the saloons, particularly the small saloons, and given them a very easy target speed. Our plans were therefore hastily altered. European Champions Pat Moss and Ann Wisdom were given their usual car, an Austin A40, John Milne and Stuart Turner were mounted in a Twin-Cam MG and three of the new Austin-Healeys were driven by Bill Shepherd/John Williamson (Healey winners of a Coupe in 1958), Jack Sears/Sam Moore (Jack was a Healey class winner in the 1959 Tulip Rally), Chris Tooley and myself, backed up by Tommy Wisdom/Jack Hay in an Austin-Healey "Sprite".

'The opening stage, just over 800 miles to Cortina d'Ampezzo, in the Dolomites, was a run of amazing contrasts – blazing heat from the Mediterranean up to the foothills of the Alps, bitter cold and violent thunderstorms on the high passes, and steady, driving rain across the plains of Northern Italy. In the stage were two speed tests, a 10-mile climb on the 7,000-foot Col d'Allos, taken at dusk, and three timed laps at Monza, taken at what seemed just after dawn. The Austin-Healeys were in the first group of 10 cars on to the track, when conditions were at their worst with lashing rain and a strong side-wind. The co-drivers (privately thankful that *they* did not have to try and average around 84 mile/h in that sort of weather) encouraged their drivers, but without much success, for it was a very dispirited little group that gathered round the Clerk of the Course to hear what ambulance facilities were available. Only Walter Schock, who knows Monza like the back of his hand, and Jack Sears, who loves track

racing, looked at all cheerful, and I expect that I looked as lugubrious
as the rest. When the spray had died down, it was the turn of the
co-drivers to look dispirited, for only Schock, Jack and I had managed
to do our time, Schock being the fastest. That one test spoilt four
chances of a Coupe des Alpes in our class alone.

'On the run from Monza to Cortina, another Coupe went west, for
Jack Sears hit a gulley on the Passo Vivione at speed, which caused
the fan to carve through the radiator, and the "big Healey" was out.
When we arrived at Cortina, we heard that Johnnie Milne had shot
off the road in a rainstorm, his Twin Cam being too damaged to
continue. To compensate, Pat and Ann were leading the ladies and
were sixth in the Touring Category, whilst Tommy Wisdom/Jack
Hay and Chris and I were still unpenalized, second in our classes and
respectively fifth and sixth in the Grand Touring Category.

'The key Austrian section, over loose-surfaced, narrow roads with
no straights for a big car to use its power, just wasn't on for the large
G T cars. In our class, Annie Soisbault put in a wonderful drive to
finish only a minute late, making the second-best performance in the
G T category and being 2 minutes faster than any other Triumph,
but Bill Shepherd and Bill Bennett were 3 minutes late and the Aston
Martin retired. The works Mercedes, and Chris and I, were 2 minutes
late, the margins actually being 1 min. 32 secs and 1 min. 21 secs
respectively, which pleased us immensely but meant little, as penalty
times were taken to the whole minute. Only one G T car did the
section "clean", the DB of Rey/Guilhaudin, which had two minutes
longer allowed than its larger rivals.

'So now we had no hope of a Coupe and it was to be a bitter battle
for class and category placings. Soon after the section, the Mercedes
retired with a split tank and Chris and I took over the class lead – but
it was to be of short duration.

'After one particularly hectic section we pulled into the control in
a cloud of steam, and had just enough time to fill the radiator and
quickly check the hoses before bellowing off to the first timed test.
Here we met our Water (literally) loo. The timekeepers were not in
position, which meant that the cars were impounded in *parc fermé* and
could not be touched. We waited for 19 minutes before tackling the
test, during which time a steady drip from our radiator showed that
something was seriously wrong. The drain-tap had been hit by a
stone and almost torn out. We started the climb with an almost empty
radiator, but had to drive on until we found a space wide enough to

pull off without blocking the pass, by which time the temperature needle did almost two laps of the dial! Stopping in a test meant a double penalty: once for stopping, at one mark per second; and again at the far control, for the lateness we could not make up. But now all we were concerned about was to finish. This was a humble ambition, but to achieve it the Austin-Healey probably took a bigger beating than if it had been leading the rally. We drove absolutely flat to get enough time in hand to try and check the leak; gum, soap and Radweld were useless, for the flow through the break was too fast. We could do only 30 miles without refilling, and when that dropped to 20 miles we had no option but to try to get the radiator brazed up.

'Do not believe that a blacksmith "can do anything, old boy"; we wasted quite a lot of time proving otherwise. Finally we found an intelligent garage, where the tap was ripped off and a plate brazed across the hole. We were now in business again with a leak-free car, but a "billiard score" of penalty points and a determination to finish if we had to push the car all the way.

'In general it had not been a good day for B.M.C. The Moss/Wisdom A40 was still leading the ladies and lying fifth in the Touring Category, but was showing signs of the gearbox malady which was to lead to its retirement on the following stage. The Triumphs were now first and second in our class, and threatened to draw still further ahead. The only bright spot was that the "Sprite" was still second in class and category. Besides, in the Alpine, as in the Mille Miglia, he who leads at half-distance rarely leads at the finish.

'I was therefore not surprised that the next stage of 400 miles to St Gervais, over that most spectacular of all climbs, the 9,000-foot Stelvio, brought disaster for the Triumphs. On the Stelvio, the big Austin-Healeys put it across them well and truly, which possibly worried Bill Bennett into trying too hard on the Vivione and hitting the rocks, with dire results both to his time and the Triumph's coachwork. The same test saw the end of Annie Soisbault, who had a puncture but mislaid a vital part of her jack! The three survivors in our class accordingly arrived at St Gervais with Bill Bennett as the meat in an Austin-Healey "sandwich", 19 points behind Bill Shepherd and John Williamson.

'Piquancy was added to the situation by the fact that Bill Bennett had blown the exhaust manifold gasket on his Triumph. This was obvious to anyone with ears, but what wasn't obvious was whether Bill krew that if he pressed on like that the exhaust gases would play on to the dynamo, which would assuredly melt the shellac on the windings and leave him without electrics. Assuming he knew this, how long would a repair take and could he manage it without losing more time? Each camp, of course, went to great pains to disguise from the other their knowledge and their plans.

'The final stage to Cannes was the hardest of all – 750 miles in 26 hours over the Aravis, Allos, Croix de Fer, Cayolle, Galibier and Vars – passes which have seen the blighting of many a hope in the past and which were to live up to their reputation in 1959. With such a run ahead it was a relief to have a 24-hour break, which I personally spent mostly in bed.

'At sunset our class led off, and Bill Bennett's strategy was disclosed. He drew straight into a garage. Wisely he had decided to risk losing time and repair his car at a point where it was cool and assistance could be organized well in advance. This was the correct decision, but it cost him two minutes' lateness, which gave Bill Shepherd a comfortable lead of $2\frac{1}{4}$ minutes over him.

'Chris and I settled down to play a waiting game – waiting for the Triumph to give trouble or its crew to make a mistake. But the most serious mistake did not come from the Triumph boys. On the Col d'Ornon are two deep gullies, cut to allow flood water to escape in winter. On the far side of one we could see the ominous black marks where a car had hit it at speed. Within another few yards came the signs of bad trouble – black marks of oil in the dust. Ahead were the rear lights of the Shepherd/Williamson Healey and those of the Triumph. One was slowing. Which? Alas, it was the Healey, out with a cracked sump and ruined bearings. Only one of the three new 3 litre cars was left.

'So now it was a war of attrition between Bill Bennett and Chris and me. Through the bitter night to a blazing dawn over the Col d'Allos we chased the Triumph, but though we cut its lead, Bill was driving with his head and never made the error which would allow us to take it over. Slashing South through Provence and the lavender fields, the sun grew even stronger and the dust began to rise and hang in the air – to my mind the most unpleasant driving conditions of all. Our last chance for the class lead was the final test on Mt Ventoux but, though the Austin-Healey bellowed up the 13-mile climb to return second fastest time of the day, Bill just made his set time and dropped no more points.

'Now the rough stuff was over, but we still had to cover 250 miles to the Côte d'Azur. These were perhaps the most worrying of all, for every little creak (and there were many after that gruelling run) could signify a last-minute failure. But the Austin-Healey and the Triumph ran on tirelessly, and soon we caught glimpses of the Mediterranean from the tops of the passes. As a final touch of *panache*, Chris and I made up enough time to wash and polish our car, which was unscratched. We may not have been the leaders (actually we finished fifth in category and second in class), but we were certainly the most immaculate of the 27 survivors from the 58 cars whose crews had left Marseille with such high hopes five days before.

'Also amongst those survivors was the Wisdom/Hay Austin-Healey "Sprite", which had gone magnificently to finish second in category and class.

'Our only regret was that the schedule had made it impossible for large G T cars to win a Coupe des Alpes. We had, however, found very few bugs in the new Austin-Healey "3000".'

First Liège class win

As the Alpine prompted the need for better underbody protection against the pounding of rough rally roads, so the next outing for the '3000', the Liège, emphasized the importance of a thorough pre-rally recce. Of the four works '3000's entered, navigational errors caused the retirement of two crews whilst a third entry was eliminated after a minor accident.

John Gott recalls the episode which put him and Ken James out of the rally:

'This was the first time that Ken had taken part in an event quite as long as the Liège and, by the time we came out of Yugoslavia, I reckon he was just about whacked. However, he had been asleep for quite a few hours when we arrived at the Italian border and, as he had driven up to this point on the way down, we agreed that he should take over the wheel. I asked him whether he felt fit and he said that he was fine after the rest. So I settled down in the co-driver's seat and went fast asleep.

'Now there was a right-hand fork about 10 km down the road and I never thought to warn Ken about this, thinking that he would probably remember it from the trip down. But I had not quite made allowances for his tiredness.

'I woke up after about 30 minutes, did not immediately recognize the road ahead but thought that perhaps I was still a little sleepy. A few minutes later we came to a village which I was sure was not on our route so I got out the maps and found that we had overshot the fork by about 30 km.

'I told Ken to stop and get out and that he was now going to have to pay for his error by being frightened out of his mind as I tried to make up the lost time back to the fork and to the control.

'We had to average 75 mile/h I think to make it on time. I missed it by 1 minute 45 seconds and we were excluded on overall lateness.'

Fortunately for the Abingdon team, Peter Riley and Rupert Jones saved the day by bringing their '3000' its first international class victory.

The rest of 1959

After a class win by Jack Sears in the Gold Cup meeting at Oulton Park (sadly one of only two international class victories for the '3000' upon the race track) came the German Rally, when the Pat Moss/Ann Wisdom partnership tried the new '3000' for the first time and came second overall, which at that time was the highest placing ever achieved by a ladies' team.

Results of the 1959 R.A.C. Rally were somewhat overshadowed by delays in hearing protests, and the event was almost forgotten when it was confirmed that the works '3000's had taken first and second places in their class, the twins Don and Erle Morley winning the class honours in their first drive with the Austin-Healey team. The results might have been different had gearbox trouble not retired the John Williamson/John Milne car when it was leading the rally by a handsome margin.

The 1959 season closed with the Portuguese Rally, when Pat Moss/ Ann Wisdom entered a lone '3000' in search of points for the European Ladies' Championship. Although the girls gained their ladies' award, a somewhat unsporting gesture by a fellow competitor in withdrawing from the event meant that there were insufficient lady crews for the rally to count for the Championship. Pat and Ann were to have their revenge the following year!

1960 – mixed fortunes

First international outing for the marque in 1960 was to Sebring for the 12 Hour Race. Here a pair of '3000's entered by B.M.C. North America finished second and third in their class behind a Ferrari.

Shortly after this came the Circuit of Ireland Rally, which brought Bobby Parkes/G. Howarth in a privately-entered '3000' a class win after the works car of Pat Moss/Ann Wisdom had retired with gearbox troubles.

Pat was decidedly unhappy about her Healey for the Circuit:

'SMO 744 was a pig of a car. Everybody crashed this one and I do not think it ever finished a rally. It was already getting a reputation by then and I added to it. The Healey was a most unsuitable car for a driving-test type of rally, because it had a stiff gearbox and heavy steering, and it was altogether a bit big for manoeuvring; in addition to that, this particular car gave us every sort of trouble. The clutch was slipping from the start and to get up steep hills we had to keep going under the car with the fire extinguisher to spray the clutch in the hope that this would blow out the oil causing the trouble.

'And in the end, the gearbox packed up and we retired; nobody was surprised because it was that particular jinx car. Nobody in the team wanted to drive that one; after every rally it had to be practically rebuilt—either because of a host of mechanical troubles or because of a crash. In the end B.M.C. sold it to Bobby Parkes and he had no trouble with it at all – typical!'

Pat and Ann had a better Healey, SMO 746, for the Lyon-Char-bonnières Rally but they were again out of luck and Pat experienced the most dramatic accident of her career:

'The rally ran around France and Germany and one of the speed tests was on the Solitude circuit, near Stuttgart. I had never driven on Solitude before and this was not the best day to get to know it because it was raining hard. The circuit was 7·1 miles long, with quite a few corners and kinks, and we were allowed one practice lap, which was never finished because, just as we reached the last couple of corners, marshals started signalling us to slow down ready for the start so we had to take the last part slowly.

'We were in a very mixed class with ACs, TRs and Porsches, including one driven by Hans Walter, who was very quick. We needed a fast time on this test so I planned to have a go in spite of the greasy track. We started at 5 second intervals and it was still teeming down so Wiz watched from the restaurant. My Healey was last to go.

'The car was good so I was able to go fast and after some real dicing I managed to pass all the other cars in the class. The last one, a Porsche, I took about a mile from the end of the lap, which was fairly close to the corner we had not been able to practise and I thought: Well that's nice, I'm in the lead so I'll be careful.

'I changed from overdrive top to overdrive third, which would do over 90 mile/h anyway, and went into the last corner, which looped round like a long hairpin and led to the short straight of the start and finish.

'A big Healey is a handful on a slippery surface and I was going far too fast for this corner. I think maybe the car aquaplaned as well but without a doubt I was going too fast. The car started to snake and with a Healey if you do not catch it after a couple of snakes it is a case of Good-bye and Good Luck.

'Luckily I was well ahead of the nearest car so there was nothing to hit me while I fought for control. I was on the straight by now and the car started to spin and I could see I was going to crash, so I ducked down out of the way and crouched close to my door.

'The safety barrier was made of railway sleepers and the car hit them sideways. A sleeper broke and tore through the wheel and the wheel arch like a lance and went through the car, ripped through the passenger seat and went out again through the boot, which opened. It missed me!

'The Healey is a heavy car and it was going fast; you cannot stop a car dead from 90 mile/h, so it shot into the air. The other end of the sleeper snapped from the upright and the whole of it stuck in the car.

'It went incredibly high and started to somersault. Wiz, sitting in the restaurant, saw it over the top of the timing box and thought to herself: "Thank God it can't be Pat. She's at the back."

'There were red ACs with black roofs in the class and she thought it was one of those. Then she saw my white roof and nearly passed out. Inside the car I was fairly calm because I was sure I was going to be killed. I knew I was about to die and said to myself: "You bloody nit."

'The car sailed over the bank behind the barrier. It somersaulted completely and then miraculously landed right way up on its wheels. There was a terrible jolt and a bang but I barely noticed it because I could hardly believe I was alive. I sat up and I seemed to be all right, so I switched off the ignition. The spare wheel had come out of the boot and flown even higher than the car and I saw it land a long way off. Then I tried to open my door, but it was jammed. I could not get to the other door because of the sleeper so I started to undo the sidescreen to get out that way.

'The way I set about it was not very bright; it sounds so silly now

but there was a reason. Healeys had sidescreens with sliding windows
and they used to work themselves open, so we always had to stuff
them with paper to keep them closed. This Healey had super sidescreens which did not come open and Wiz and I had decided long ago
that we would take them with us to our next Healey. The roof was
not damaged in the crash because the car turned over in the air; the
sidescreens were perfect, so I thought: I'm not going to ruin these
by breaking them to get out. I'll take them off.

'I was sitting there undoing them when people started to arrive,
all running and crossing themselves. Erik Carlsson and Wolfgang
Levy, the German DKW and Auto-Union driver, were first to reach
me and Erik grabbed my sidescreen and yanked it off, then they both
dragged me out. They thought I must be half dead at least but I was
perfectly all right and most indignant about my beautiful sidescreens.
So I shouted at them: "What the hell do you think you're doing?
Leave me alone."

'They, of course, were worried about fire, as drivers always are
after a bad crash, but I thought of nothing but my screens. Nobody
could believe I was uninjured yet all I had was a knock on the leg
and a bloody nose; after a couple of minutes I trotted off to see Wiz
and tell her I was all right.

'I met her on the way and she was walking with her head down and
looking terrible because she was sure I must be dead. She had run out
of the restaurant and kept running until she could run no more and
now she was walking towards where she knew I would have landed.
I think she did not really want to arrive there and see the awful mess
I must be in after flying so high in the air. As soon as I saw her I
went: "Ann – Yoo-hoo!"

'Her face when she saw me was a study. There was absolute dis-
belief – she must have thought I was a ghost – and then she completely
lit up with joy, although there were tears in her eyes.'

Not surprisingly Pat started her next event, the Geneva Rally, with
some apprehension:

'This was a fast, tight rally over the usual twisty and mountainous
roads and in all the sections we had to average 60 km/h – or about
40 mile/h – so we would have to motor. I was really twitched and
worried and nervous and for the first time I was a bit frightened of the
big fast car. Wiz must have known and it must have been a tense time
for her, but she was very good and did nothing to make me feel
worse – like letting me know how worried she felt.

'The first half of the rally was reasonably easy but we could see from the route and the regulations that the second would be difficult as a lot of it lay over the Cols de Savoie and Dauphine. Even on the first bit I had to force myself to drive competitively and I was much slower in corners than ever before, but I improved steadily and grew more confident as I realized again how well the car handled and how safe it was on dry roads.

'I felt all right by the halfway stage where we prepared to start on the most difficult part, but soon I felt edgy again as we passed car after car which had crashed. There were lots of crashes that year and on one twisty bit we came round a corner and found a DKW on its roof spinning like a top and with the wheels still turning. It was too tight a rally to stop for a crash and we could see the team inside were all right, so we pressed on.

'There were special stages on the rally and my times, in comparison with the other cars, kept on improving and on the difficult Chamrousse we had the fastest time in the rally. This gave us a good lead in our class and we were among the top three or four in the rally until another stage which should have been 8 km long. We kept going for 10 km and then decided that we had gone wrong somewhere and went back. In fact, they had stretched that stage to make it faster and if we had gone another few hundred yards we would have reached the control in good time. As it was we lost several minutes and dropped several places. In the end we finished eighth but won the class and the Ladies!

'Even more important than that, I had won my personal struggle against the nervousness I had been feeling ever since the crash.'

The girls' new confidence was proved again on the Tulip Rally when they finished eighth overall, class winners, and gained yet further points towards the Ladies' European Rally Championship with another Coupe des Dames. They were less fortunate on the Acropolis Rally when rough roads literally smashed the chassis.

Tony Ambrose remembers that he and Peter Riley had an even more dramatic experience on this event in the second of the works Healeys:

'This was my first event with the big Healey and my first outing with Peter Riley. We elected to start from Trieste and there were no problems to Belgrade, but from here on we got on to the old rough road, now the autoput, and things began to get a bit tough. I remember that we reached Skopje with only something like 11 minutes in hand which was a bit desperate. Half of the time we did not really know where we were and in which direction we were travelling and I recall navigating by the stars on one occasion.

'The next day we came to the first of the special stages in Northern Greece which began with a long flat-out stretch along fairly straight dirt roads before climbing into the mountains. I think we were the third car away with a couple of Corvettes in front of us. Peter soon wound the Healey up, then after about 7 km, when we were howling along at peak revs in overdrive top, we had a tyre blow out on the rear. We were running on Durabands at the time and these were not really cleared for speeds in excess of 100 mile/h. I shudder to think how fast we were going at that particular moment.

'It was a diabolical spot to have a blow out, the road had deep ditches on either side, and Peter only just about managed to keep the car on the road. We were shattered when we stopped and jumped out to survey the damage. The stripped tread had gone right through the wing and we were motoring on little more than the inner tube, a shattered rim, a few bent spokes and a hunk of molten rubber.

'We hurriedly jacked the car up and, with the aid of a pair of gloves, managed to tear what was left of the wheel off and fit the spare.

'We were well placed in the rally at that time, having done a couple of important stages; I think we must have been in the top three places. We had not been beside the road for very long before we were passed by the two leading Porsches so we set off again with a vengeance, determined to make up lost time.

'Peter caught the second of the Porsches as we approached the start of the mountain climb and after a fabulous dice he finally passed him on the treacherous bends, lubricated with fine chalk that blows off the mountains. And then we came to a dreaded right hander with the usual rock face on one side and nothing on the other. Peter was going far too fast, he lost the Healey in the biggest possible way and we went straight over the edge, backwards first.

'With a deafening crunch we landed on the tail of the car, the hardtop flew off and Peter and I flew out. We did not, of course, wear seat belts in those days. We landed in a bed of rocks and rubble, looked up and saw to our horror that the Healey was about to topple down on top of us. Peter dived one way and I went the other as the car crashed down between us, landed on its wheels and started to roll off again down the hill.

'I clambered after it, hobbling over the rocks with one shoe missing and managed to grab the steering wheel. I was about to try and get my foot into the car and on to the brake pedal when Peter, leaning on one elbow from his bed of rocks, cried out: "Let the bloody thing go."

'Being a very young and keen works driver, I thought that perhaps Peter's counsel was wise, so reluctantly I let go of the wheel, rolled away from the car and let the Healey continue on its way. Slowly it gathered speed, charged some 500 yards down the mountain, slewed over a little outcrop of rocks, bounced over a low stone wall and finally stopped, right side up, but completely wrecked.

'Peter and I looked at each other and a sorry sight we must have been. I had bruises all over, Peter had more serious abrasions on his back. The Greek Army were policing this stage and they came bounding down the mountainside to treat us with evil-smelling swabs and lotions which was far more painful than the accident itself.

'A somewhat alarming and unhappy first sortie in a big Healey.'

A dominating Alpine

Returning to the Alpine Rally, the stage was now set for the works Austin-Healeys to enjoy an unprecedented run of dominating class victories in Championship rallies. The incredible Pat and Ann, on the peak of their form, finished the Alpine second overall, gaining a Coupe des Alpes, winning the class and yet another Coupe des Dames.

Pat tells the story of that incredible Alpine:

'Fifty miles from the end, the Alfa Romeo of Henri Oreiller was just ahead of us on points and then we started the speed test over Les Quatre Chemins, which was 34 km of narrow D-roads in the mountains behind Grasse. Oreiller spun on this section and failed to clean it, so we had a big chance to take first place.

'The road had just been resurfaced with tar and gravel. The tar was still wet and the stones loose which made the surface slippery and so far only one car had cleaned it, Jose Behra – a brother of Jean Behra, the Grand Prix driver – driving with Richard in a 3·8 Jaguar, which was running as a standard car and so was allowed an extra minute. We knew it was going to be tough so I set off like a rocket, full speed ahead. I caught up with Edward Harrison in a fully modified Zephyr, who was good and let us pass straight away without the slightest hold-up. After another kilometre we came to a bend with no stones at all on the apex, just liquid tar. We spun.

H.A.H.—10

'There was a fair-sized drop although a lot of conifers growing out of the mountainside would stop a car falling too far, but we did not go over. The road was only about two feet wider than the length of the car, yet we spun without going over or touching the rough wall of mountain on the other side. We finished up round the corner, but across the road diagonally and with my door nearest to the bend.

'I jumped out and ran back to stop Edward Harrison, because he would not be able to see us and was not too far behind. He was just coming into the bend as I got there and I waved my arms like mad until his car was nearly on me and then I jumped over the edge and clung to a tree.

'Even on that narrow road he managed to sling the Zephyr sideways and stopped before touching our car. I came up again and raced to the Healey to get it out of the way, which meant going back the way we had come. As Edward set off again he shouted to me: "I didn't know you did things like that!" He went off laughing.

'We had to go back about half a kilometre before we found a piece of road wide enough to turn and I really put my foot down after that. We caught and passed Edward again and finished the stage with just 9 seconds to spare.

'We were not certain that we had cleaned it when I pulled up at the control and Wiz, who is very quick, was out of the car like a flash and ran to the clock to push in our time card. But she was shaking so much she could not press the knob. She just stood, trembling with agitation, until one of the marshals saw her and gave the knob a thump.

'The Alfa of de Laganeste did not spin on this stage and made a much better time than us, which gave him first place in the rally with us second. We also won the Ladies, of course, and the class. And a Coupe.'

A truly fantastic result, not only for the girls though, because the Austin-Healeys had made it a 1–2–3 class victory, runners-up John Gott and Bill Shepherd missing their Coupe by just 20 seconds after a spin, like Pat, on that same Quatre Chemins stage. Don and Erle Morley completed the Austin-Healey trio despite gearbox troubles which also caused the retirement of the fourth works car, driven by Ronnie Adams and John Williamson. In addition to these class successes, the Austin-Healeys, now running under the banner of 'Ecurie Safety Fast', collected all five team prizes.

And so to the Liège

After their performance on the Alpine, it was clear that outright victory in a Championship rally was within the grasp of the Moss/Wisdom/'3000' combination, but few would have prophesied that they would achieve this ambition in the gruelling Liège-Rome-Liège Rally, the next event for the Austin-Healeys. The four works cars, now running in three-carburetter form, came to the starting line with improved gearboxes and transmission, the standard design having been unable to cope with the immense torque of the engine in tuned form. The Austin-Healeys were destined to enjoy their most successful outing, though they had no easy rally.

Pat Moss takes up the Liège story:

'I now knew enough about cars and rallies to have my own ideas about preparation and tuning; that year I managed to persuade B.M.C. to do something rather special to the Healey. I wanted the top speed reduced, because I thought the Healeys were too fast for many of the roads we had to drive over. In competition tune and high gearing they could be made to do about 150 mile/h but on rally roads there was nowhere – except race circuits – where we could go that fast, so the usual rally car was geared to have a top speed of around 120 or 130 mile/h. I thought this was still too fast.

'I kept asking them to put in a lower-ratio back axle and for this Liège I persuaded them to use one from a London taxi, which is the lowest ratio axle made by B.M.C. It was so low that it cut our top speed in direct top to about 80 mile/h and gave us direct top cruising of only 70 mile/h, but the acceleration was fantastic. I could hardly change gear fast enough. It was like a kick in the back and we had a 0–60 mile/h time of about five seconds. It was incredible. B.M.C. were dead worried that the car would not stand up to it over the 3,300 miles of the Liège and when I first felt that explosive thrust I thought they might be right, but I was still determined to use the car that way. On mountain roads we never really needed more than about 70 mile/h with short bursts of 80 mile/h. We needed acceleration to get us there quickly and for ordinary road work we could cruise at more than 80 mile/h in overdrive top.

'The Liège was the usual tough rally, scheduled to last 96 hours without a stop, and on some sections anyone who was as much as one second late was penalized with exclusion. Lateness was allowed on other parts. The car went beautifully at the beginning and on some stages we had the fastest time. Then our overdrive packed up. There were 83 starters and the route was across Germany, Austria and Italy and into Yugoslavia. We went so well that we were tying for second place when the 65 survivors entered Yugoslavia for the really car-wrecking bits. The roads there were so cruel that year that only 30 of the 65 survived to leave Yugoslavia again.

'It was in Yugoslavia that our clutch started slipping. I was shattered. I thought the power of that big engine coupled with the low gearing had ripped it to pieces and that my gamble had failed. I was almost afraid to mention it to the mechanics, because I knew what they would tell me. But I did tell them, and they diagnosed a broken oil seal between the clutch and gearbox, which was a relief, except that there was not time to mend it. We had to go right through Yugoslavia like that, stopping when we could to squirt it with the fire extinguisher.

'It slowed us down so that we had trouble making our times and that meant that we never had anything in hand for the repair, because it was a big job. Marcus hoped to be able to do it on the way back across Italy, but there was still no time. The trouble also cut down the amount of rest I could have because I did not want to put Wiz in to drive the car with a dodgy clutch. It was not until we got to France that we could do anything about it. There were only 15 cars left running by then and we were leading in spite of our trouble. We had been hoping to be able to do some work on it during a long, five-hour section leading to Roverto, but our notes said that this would be five hours of damned hard motoring and the notes were dead right. We still held our lead and the mechanics got to work during a long easy section leading to Allos.

'They had found an oil seal from another car, I think a French one which could be fiddled to fit and that would be quicker than mending the broken seal, but it was still a ridiculously big job to do in the middle of a fast rally. The Healey has a big, big gearbox which is not easy to shift around in a hurry, yet they made the exchange in exactly one hour. We could not spend longer or we would have gone out of the rally on lateness. We did not have time even to replace the tunnel inside the car properly. It was just stuck on loosely and Wiz had to hold it down.

'This was a section where there was nothing to be gained by being early so we lost nothing by taking the full time allowed. However, the marshals at the next control did not expect anybody to be so slow that they would need all the time and when we did not show up early they assumed we were out of the rally and opened the road on the Allos.

'It was a hell of a trip. The people at the top who had been watching came pouring down towards us, not expecting any more rally cars, and we were expecting clear roads. It was a dangerous run, but we made it on time and the control was still there so we were able to check in and still led the rally.

'The last test before the easy run back to Spa was on the Granier and I was so tired by then that I could not hurry any more. I was limp and sleepy and so worn out that 50 kilometres an hour – about 31 miles an hour – seemed fast. I just could not force myself to go any quicker, although I was sure we could lose our first place in the rally because of it.

'This was supposed to be a speed test, a race against the clock, and I was driving a big, fast car with good road-holding and brakes, yet I was crawling like a snail. I was very cross with myself, yet I could do nothing about it.

'It turned out that everybody felt the same and all had pretty well the identical time over the course. So we were still in the lead and held it to the finish. That perked me up, for although I had driven for 90 of the 96 hours, the thought of winning the Liège, of all rallies, outright was the best tonic possible.'

The other Healeys in the team were less fortunate and troubles beset the car of Peter Riley and Tony Ambrose who takes up the story:

'We came to the Col Durand and were going very well, lying second to Trautman in the Citroën. The Liège win had always been my ambition and here we were well within striking distance. Halfway up the climb, Peter suddenly noticed that the water temperature guage was creeping up. Two kilometres farther on it had gone right off the clock. It was a very difficult section, desperately important, so it was all or nothing for us now. We decided to press on and hope that the engine would last – perhaps we could coast down the other side of the climb and not lose too much time.

'But when we reached the summit the engine was very sick indeed and we had no option but to coast down the other side. We arrived at the control losing 15 minutes which was disastrous and discovered that the fan had gone through the radiator.

'The engine was only just about running now as we poured everything we could lay our hands on into the radiator to try and save the ship. But it was to no avail and we finally decided that we would have to retire. There was no chance of taking the radiator out and having it repaired because there was only one hour's lateness allowed in those days.

'And so we retired and went to bed, two very dejected rally men.'

John Gott, driving with Rupert Jones, had troubles too with a puncture on the first stage in Yugoslavia, which cost him a lot of time penalties which he was forced to carry throughout the event.

Amongst the 13 survivors which returned to Liège – out of 81 starters – were three of the four Austin-Healeys, the incredible Pat and Ann achieving their greatest drive to be placed outright winners. Rallying history had truly been made. Never before had a British crew in a British car won the Marathon; never before had an all-ladies' crew won a Championship rally. The Austin-Healeys won the team prize for Britain for the second year running, Seigle-Morris/Elford and Gott/Jones completing the honours list by giving the '3000' another 1–2–3 class victory. Truly the marque's finest hour, and the first outright victory in a major international event for either a Healey or an Austin-Healey.

A run of class wins

The remaining events in 1960 underlined the Liège and Alpine successes, David Seigle-Morris and Stuart Turner leading the Austin-Healeys to yet another 1–2–3 class victory in the German Rally. Then came the R.A.C. Rally when it was the Morley brothers' turn to lead the '3000' class domination, the Abingdon cars again collecting the team prize. The year closed with the highest honours being showered on Pat Moss and Ann Wisdom as joint Ladies' European Rally Champions, coupled with their election by the Guild of Motoring Writers as 'Drivers of the Year'. The Austin-Healeys which had carried them to victory also received due praise, the run of international rally class wins totalling 10 out of 14 events since the '3000' was introduced in July 1959. The year had been the most successful season for B.M.C. to date.

By 1961 the works Austin-Healeys had established such a reputation in international rallying that it was almost unheard of for the team to return to Abingdon without at least a class victory. Pat and Ann opened the season with a brilliant drive on the Tulip, the performance of their '3000' on the timed climbs and circuit tests being a feature of the event. As the overall placings were assessed on the 'class improvement' basis, the '3000's did not feature high in the results. Nevertheless, the Austin-Healeys gained first and second places in the class, the girls winning the Coupe des Dames. In company with the Morleys '3000' and the 'Sprite' of Gold/Hughes, Austin-Healey again won the Manufacturers' Team Prize.

A thorough recce of the difficult terrain on the Acropolis rewarded Peter Riley/Tony Ambrose with a class win, their '3000' also being the highest placed British entry. Close runners-up to the works car, until a crash put them out of the event, were the privateers Bobby Parkes/John Sprinzel.

The Morleys first Alpine

Highlight of the year was the Alpine. The five Austin-Healey team cars, now at the peak of their development, must have been the most powerful entry with which B.M.C. ever attacked an international rally.

Team Captain John Gott takes up the story:

'This year we determined to add the "Alpine" win to the Ecurie's battle honours. The cars used were 1961 model Austin-Healey '3000's, crewed by last year's successful team of Pat Moss/Ann Wisdom, the Morley twins and John Gott/Bill Shepherd, and further strengthened by Peter Riley/Tony Ambrose and David Seigle-Morris/Vic Elford.

'As might be expected, the Alpine entry list included all the European rally cracks and we had a tough assignment in the face of such opposition, but it was a great boost to our morale to know that the big Austin-Healeys were reckoned by the experts as "the ones to beat".

'In this assessment, the experts were proved right. When it was all over, the Morley twins were the only crew to finish the rally without penalty, and so were the only crew to win the coveted Coupe des Alpes awarded for a penalty-free run. One has to go back in Alpine history to 1949 to find a year in which only one Coupe was awarded, and this magnificent "double" of an outright win and a Coupe was a fitting reward for a wonderful drive by the farming brothers from Suffolk.

'At one time it looked as though "Ecurie Safety Fast" would again take all the team honours for, at half distance at Chamonix, the big

Healeys were first and third overall in the rally, and leading for the premier team award, the Coupe des Alpes des Constructeurs.

'But one by one we blotted our copybook and it was on the dawn climb out of Chamonix that Bill Shepherd and I had our little moment. There were no excuses, I just lost it on a left hander and over the edge we sailed with the drop on Bill's side I remember. As always, we never knew whether the drop would be 20 feet, 200 feet or 2,000 feet, and as I set the Healey up into its flying attitude we just sat there in the dark wondering. Bill put his feet up on the dashboard, one arm through the grab handle and one arm round the back of my seat, and wedged himself firmly in waiting for the inevitable crunch. Time seemed to stand still and I shall always remember Bill saying quite quietly in his gorgeous Scots accent, "John lad, you know you did na do that wee bit very well".

'Flying through the air I also recall that I had time to glance out of the window and in the half light saw a fellow standing beneath the car as it flew over his head, his eyes standing out like chapel hat pegs, his mouth hanging open, scared rigid. He had been standing by the roadside and we had flown right over his head!

'After what seemed like an eternity the Healey landed fair and square in a soft meadow, only about 25 feet down. Bill and I looked at ourselves to see whether it was all a rather nasty dream and, realizing our good fortune, set about getting the car back on the road.

'This we finally accomplished but not until after the loss of a lot of time which put us right out of the running.'

Tony Ambrose takes up the story from here:

'We were amongst the first half-dozen cars over the Stelvio on a dry but misty early morning. Peter Riley was going great guns, the car was in perfect shape, and we were making good time.

'Then suddenly Peter yelled: "No brakes!" Before I had time to react, the Healey slewed across the road as Peter tried to put it sideways; we spun, the rear of the car clouted one of those concrete posts and snapped it off like a piece of barley sugar. We did one more spin in the opposite direction and then went straight over the apex of the bend and into space.

'Fortunately we fell only about 20 feet and landed in quite soft ground but I was very thankful that I was securely strapped in with a full harness. Peter was less fortunate for he was only wearing a lap strap. He had been thrown forward on to the steering wheel and then backwards hard against the sharp edges of his bucket seat which had broken his ribs.

'He crawled out of the car, obviously in some pain, and I laid him out as comfortably as I could beside the battered car. I then climbed back on to the road and after some time we were able to get a lift with one of the organizers to a local hospital where Peter was made more comfortable.

'That was the end of our Alpine Rally and the end of another fine Healey.'

Finally, Pat Moss tells of her misfortunes:

'We had the characterless Healey again for the Alpine, but it ran nicely. We were clean on the first few tests and, after one of them, were tootling along with our crash helmets off and going down a mountain reasonably quickly but not hurrying, say about 70 miles an hour. We came to some loose stones and I honestly think I was not paying enough attention and we spun. It was not in a dangerous part and I thought: "How stupid".

'The spin slowed us to practically no speed at all and we started going backwards towards the bank, terribly slowly and with the brakes on. Brakes are never very good in reverse and I could see we were going to hit the bank and I was annoyed that we would damage the tail of the car. It was all so slow that we were watching out of the rear window waiting for the bump. Unfortunately there was a big stone in the way which we did not see and one of the wheels went over it and the car rose up very slowly and turned over. The hardtop collapsed on top of us and forced us down – or up really since the car was upside down – into the foot-wells.

'We were all right, but trapped, and we had just put 20 gallons of fuel into the tank. It came pouring out and so did acid from the battery. I switched off and we did not catch fire, thank God. The windscreen was smashed but the pillars were not completely folded so there was a tiny gap, or hole between the top of the car and the ground. I could not move because the steering wheel had moved a bit and was pinning my legs to the seat. Needless to say, we could not make the doors open from the inside so Wiz tried to get through this little hole.

'I do not know how she did it and I am sure she never could again, but Wiz managed to struggle through. It was terribly tiny and although she is slim she is big-busted and really had to squeeze and kick about for a long time. No other cars came past so she had to do

it on her own and then she pulled open my door from the outside
and I managed to fall into the road.

'A couple of cars came then and we tried to right the Healey, but
it would not turn over for us and we pushed it yards and yards down
the road. Then it stuck against something and we got it righted.

'There was some petrol left in the tank and we had a can of oil in
the boot which we poured into the sump, because that had drained
away too. The hardtop was still attached at the back and we could
drive if it was held up at the front, so we went off like a rocket. On
that easy stage we were allowed to be half an hour late without
exclusion and we made it by two minutes.

'At the control we got rid of the hardtop, knocked the rest of the
glass out of the windscreen and took off the pillars, so it really looked
a very stripped-down car when we went on. We managed two more
special stages and then the gearbox seized solid. The oil had drained
out of that, too, and there was no service at that point; we had been
unable to get more oil anywhere. We had just hoped there would be
enough left to see us through, but there was not. So we went out of
the rally. It was very annoying to go as a result of a silly accident on
such an easy section.'

Ambrose on the Liège

The Liège brought hopes that perhaps Pat and Ann could repeat
their 1960 victory, but unhappily they were retired with a broken
chassis and it was left to Seigle Morris/Ambrose to win the class for
Austin-Healey.

Tony Ambrose, master of the Liège, has left us this report of the
1961 event:

'This year the B.M.C. works team consisted of four Austin-Healey
'3000's crewed by Pat Moss/Ann Wisdom (last year's winners), John
Gott/Bill Shepherd, Don Grimshaw/Rupert Jones, and David Seigle-
Morris and myself. At the start, although confident that the cars
were well prepared and among the strongest in the entry, we were
not at all certain that the course could be covered in the time allowed.
Our recce was responsible for these misgivings, since we had been
able to tell a tale only of the difficulties dreaded by all rally drivers:
we had encountered very heavy traffic in Germany, Austria and
Northern Italy; unco-operative officials when crossing the Bulgarian
border; and mile after mile of rough, dusty tracks covered in tem-

peratures as high as 105 degrees in the shade. Nevertheless, all our crews set off from Spa (where the real start took place) grimly determined to do battle with the cream of Europe's rally crews.

'The cars left Spa in groups of three, at three-minute intervals, starting at 10 p m on the night of Wednesday, 30 August. In order to create immediate interest, a test over closed roads was held within a few kilometres of the start, but we were quite sure that nobody would be fooled into straining either crew or car on this, when so much difficult motoring lay ahead. However, the Japanese entry, which had attracted much advance publicity and had reputedly spent a month practising beforehand, ended their rally at this early stage by hitting a rock face and damaging the car too badly to continue. We settled for being third fastest of the field, 20 seconds behind Oreiller's Alfa-Romeo.

'We wound our way through the Black Forest without much difficulty, and Thursday's dawn saw us making up time along the German autobahns. I should explain that, while this year's regulations did not inflict cumulative penalties for lateness, the time schedule was tightened by means of a peculiar twist. Competitors were in fact compelled to average much higher speeds than those required for zero penalty – simply by severely restricting the period for which each control was open. As the secretary of the organizing club gleefully pointed out to us, it was possible for a competitor to arrive with zero penalty at the halfway point, Sofia, only to be excluded because the control had already closed!

'So it was that Thursday found us threading our way through the traffic in Austria and Italy, trying hard to be polite without dropping any time. This is always a strain for British competitors; Europeans tend to show less consideration for tourists, and one has to resist the temptation to be sucked along at a speed which is a bit too high. Indeed, there were two nasty accidents involving rally cars and tourists. In one of these the tourist was certainly to blame, but the fact that a car with rally plates and numbers on its doors was involved does tend to aggravate an already delicate situation.

'Our aim while crossing Austria was to eat. We achieved this at Landeck, and, as we pushed down the last few mouthfuls of an early lunch, wondered where our next meal would be eaten. I think we both had a sneaking suspicion that it would be at Liège, some three and a half days later – and that suspicion proved to be well-founded.

'Some gentle motoring through the Dolomites followed, and then we reached Canazei, the last control in Italy. From here we made our first tactical effort to gain an advantage over our rivals. This entailed clocking in at Canazei at the earliest possible moment, and then going really hard for some 200 kilometres to the next control at the Yugoslav frontier. The effort was slightly complicated by the fact that we had a B.M.C. service crew waiting for us at Tarvisio, the last village before the frontier, where we thought it wise to call for some adjustments to a troublesome throttle linkage.

'After a brief servicing stop, we dashed to the frontier control and the first really difficult section of the rally. The reason for our haste was to ensure that we completed this tricky part in daylight, but unfortunately plenty of other competitors had the same idea, and our hectic journey over the passes of Predil and Moistrocca involved overtaking eight other cars. Admittedly, though, the joy of driving a car like the Austin-Healey, which is obviously very fast, is that other competitors respect its performance and quickly move to one side to let you by.

'Now, on a section like this, the navigator must not only keep his driver on the correct route, but tell him whether he can afford to slacken off and save his energy and his car for a subsequent tough section. I had calculated that we must be $6\frac{1}{2}$ minutes *ahead* of schedule *before* starting to ascend the Moistrocca Pass – and if you have ever been in that neck of the woods, you will understand why I am profoundly glad to have something to do other than watch the road and the speedometer on such occasions!

'Even in the midst of my calculations, though, I have time to look up and see a blind bend rushing towards us at an alarming rate. A glance at the speedometer shows that we are doing no less than 110 mile/h; I draw a quick breath, whisper "Gently . . .", and am relieved to feel my seat belt tighten as the powerful disc brakes of the Austin-Healey are applied. Two quick flicks of the tail as we go through the bend confirm my suspicion that we approached it a little faster than David intended, and the overdrive switch is snapped off as we accelerate towards the next bend with 100 mile/h again showing on the speedometer.

'David is driving superbly, making the very best use of a short stretch of narrow tarmac road up the valley between the two passes. But by half-distance we are only just over three minutes ahead. Should I tell David, who seems to be driving just about at the limit on such a road? I decide that he is sufficiently strong-minded not to attempt to exceed his limit, so I tell him. Just then the road becomes a little less twisty, and the loose grit which we have encountered on several bends is no longer apparent. We overtake three more cars and reach the beginning of the Moistrocca ascent – with exactly 6 minutes 32 seconds in hand. If our calculations are correct, we should make it!

'The tarmac has now given way to a loose, dusty surface. Hairpins come upon us one after another, and the gradient is about 1 in $4\frac{1}{2}$. It doesn't matter whether we use first or second gear – we can't accelerate quickly out of hairpins because of the loose surface, so as the wheels spin we joke about it and agree that tank-tracks should be offered as optional extras for Austin-Healeys. We try going into the hairpins more quickly, but again the loose surface takes command and we rush straight on towards the edge with full lock applied; that is obviously not a good idea. Anyway, we are now in a cloud of dust, so we are catching someone. The dust gets thicker – in the middle of it I see a kilometre stone straight ahead and yell "Hairpin". David copes with it, mutters "Thanks", and I glance across at him to see if he looks as frightened as I feel. If he is, he doesn't show it, as he is concentrating on catching whoever is responsible for this dust. The dust-cloud becomes thicker, but no longer blocks our vision completely, and we can see that the car in front is a Citroën; it is only 20 yards away now, and from the number we see that it is Roger de Lageneste, the French champion. We decide that we must be going quite well, for although the Citroën has less power its independent suspension gives it better traction. I sound the horn, using my special foot-operated switch, and de Lageneste moves over to let us through.

'A few more hairpins loom up, and I tell David that we are now only $2\frac{1}{4}$ minutes ahead of schedule; obviously we are rapidly losing our time in hand. As we approach the summit we enter another dust-cloud, this time made by a Porsche. We close on him. As we cross the brow the dust thickens, and, a bit hopefully, David ploughs straight on into it. Fortunately I remember from the recce that the road swings right just after the summit, and yell to David, who sees this for himself a moment later and locks hard over. The car slews and slows, stopping just a couple of feet from the edge. Mercifully, the dust-cloud is too thick for us to see just how far we might have fallen.

'We descend with rather more caution, but passing three more cars, including the Porsche. Two hairpins to go. I tell David we are only 10 seconds ahead of schedule. This is obviously "touch and go", and we rush down the last kilometre, which is on tarmac.

'Heavens above! The control is farther away than the road-book says – we must be late! My seat belt is already unfastened, the road-book in my hand. As the car slides to a halt at the control I bale out, yelling in both French and German the time at which I would like to be booked in (this is pure "rallymanship", in case the clock is just on the turn of the minute). The controller calmly consults his chronometer and enters in the time, which indicates zero penalty, while he congratulates me in faultless English. I run back to the car, which the experienced David has moved well past the control out of the way of other competitors – he knows they will be arriving in a panic. There is just time to take the covers off the lights and we are away on the next section, mentioning to each other the dangers of over-relaxing now that the going is easier. We are on good road, though, and likely to be for the whole of the night, so we spend a few minutes discussing how to divide the driving so that we can both get some rest.

'After that the tempo eased, and we both managed to get plenty of rest as we continued the long drive through Yugoslavia, passing the controls at Ljubljana and Zagreb. In the small hours of Friday morning, taking my second stint at the wheel, I was tempted to wake David (who is an architect) to show him the brilliantly-illuminated modern building used for meetings of the Non-Committed Nations at Belgrade. But I drove on south and east to Kragujevac (where Doug Hamblin was calmly welding up the chassis of Pat Moss's car, half an inch away from a petrol tank containing 20 gallons of fuel) and to Nis, where Marcus Chambers was waiting with hot soup.

'The road became rougher up to the Bulgarian border, which this time was crossed without delay. And so on to Sofia in the lightening dawn, with the inhabitants of many villages turning out in force to watch the rally cars go by. We had hoped that at Sofia we might learn our position in the rally, but we were disappointed (we were even more disappointed when we later discovered that we had, in fact, been leading the entire entry at that stage!).

'Four hours' rest in an arm-chair was the best we could manage in the Hotel Balkan, and then we were off again, with 20 cars leaving together at the drop of a flag. Can you imagine that happening in London or New York? But the populace loved it, and waved and cheered madly. The police didn't seem to mind either. Soon we were crossing back into Yugoslavia, but this time there was a little trouble at the frontier; somebody had been rude to a Customs officer, and he decided to "work to rule". Fortunately we were among the first cars through, so avoided any delay.

'At the next control, at Skopje, Marcus Chambers was again in attendance with his mechanics. Here we had our horns secured, since they had fallen off and refused to function. This repair was absolutely vital, as without horns it was quite impossible to overtake, for any driver looking in his mirror could see only his own cloud of dust. Off again the moment the control opened, and we found ourselves on a very rough section leading to Pec, close to the Albanian border. This section started with some of the roughest road which we were called upon to cover in the entire rally, but a short cut which we had found on the recce reduced the required average speed to 30mile/h.

'It was here that we passed a memorial stone which we treated as an ominous warning. On the parapet of a gorge, it featured a steering wheel and a gear-lever. The fact that the inscription was in a language we could not have understood, even if we had stopped to read it, was of no importance, for the bold figures '25' told of the magnitude of the disaster.

'Refuelling at Pec was primitive. It was effected at a cylindrical tank near the railway sidings, where we waited rather impatiently for a disinterested Yugoslav to pump in, by hand, a fuel of dubious quality, the quantity being calculated from the number of times he rocked the handle. The start from Pec was a desperate affair, with seven cars leaving together and each driver determined to be the first to exit from the tarmac square on to the dusty track that led over the mountains to the new town of Titograd. We didn't win this little race. In fact we were fourth in the procession, which was led by Trautmann in his Citroën, followed by Pat Moss's Austin-Healey and Oreiller's Alfa-Romeo Zagato. We knew that this was a really vital section and tried to better our position, but there was too much dust and very soon we were driving completely blind, just aiming at the centre of the dust-cloud. Remembering our lucky escape at the top of the Moistrocca, I suggested to David that we should hang back a bit, as Oreiller was likely to go almost as quickly as we could. No sooner had I spoken than the tail of the Alfa-Romeo appeared through the murk; the front was wedged firmly against a rock face! The fact that we were almost immediately at the tail of Pat's dust-cloud indicates that Oreiller was, in all probability, aiming for the centre of it when the cliff face intervened.

'The next 100 miles were a nightmare, for it took us just that distance

– 100 miles – to get close enough to Pat even to let her know that we would *like* to come past.

'Meanwhile, out of her dust-cloud appeared 'buses and lorries with locked wheels, mule trains with animals still frightened by Pat's meteoric arrival, and peasants to whom this track was the sole means of communication with the outside world – and who were justifiably irate. All this time the steering wheel kicked viciously in David's hands, the suspension bottomed, and sump and fuel tank, both heavily reinforced, crashed with deafening thunder against rock outcrops and loose boulders. Why the car did not just break in half I will never understand; we could not have complained had it done so in such appalling conditions.

'When we did eventually overtake Pat we knew that we were going to be late at the end of the section, but nevertheless reckoned that we must lose more time by refuelling at Titograd that night. This was a tactical error, as Pat managed to reach the next pump, 150 miles farther on, without stopping. While we were taking on fuel, Pat swept past, so that when we restarted we were determined to get past her again before the dust made this once more impossible. In striving too hard for this end, David entered a left-hand bend a bit too quickly and we ended up against the rock face, with both front and rear offside wheels in a steep-sided ditch. Our final impact had been quite gentle, so damage was slight, being confined to broken lamps and a dented wing, but try as we might we could not get the car out of the ditch. Fortunately, after about a quarter of an hour, team-mates Don Grimshaw and Ruper Jones arrived on the scene and very sportingly gave us a tow out I fear that our minor accident disheartened us greatly, for we were very tired, this being our third night out of bed, and we had been denied the "lift" of knowing how well placed we were at Sofia. Our progress was slow but sure, as it had to be, for our lights had suffered in the crash and our tired eyes were not able to compensate for this.

'At Dubrovnik we were again greeted by new "boss" Stuart Turner and Doug Hamblin, who had had a little rally of their own to get there from Kragujevac. Their practical and moral support did a great deal to hearten us, helped in my case by my first 'wakey-wakey' pill, and the information that we were only the sixth car through gave us fresh hopes. David and I were just able to summon the energy to discuss the situation as we bumped our way up the Adriatic coast on Saturday morning. From there on, our resolve was to finish rather than to win, for we were quite sure there would be very few survivors, and one could even visualize a tragic state of affairs in which the last remaining car in the rally finally ground itself to a standstill on the outskirts of Spa.

'With talk of such absurdities we amused ourselves through those last weary miles in Yugoslavia, from time to time passing competitors' cars abandoned by the road-side. The last of these to be encountered was the Healey of Pat Moss and Ann Wisdom, with a broken front suspension. We shed a silent tear for them.

'Across the frontier and into Italy, we came once more on to tarmac roads. These, after Yugoslavia, felt so unfamiliar that at first we imagined all kinds of odd things to be wrong with the steering and suspension of the car. We battled on, hardly able to keep awake, through the fourth night. We survived two punctures and a wheel reluctant to slide off the splines until, on the final testing section over the famed Gavia and Stelvio passes, a fearful screeching noise from the rear of the car and a strong smell of burning paint told us that the rear wheels were rubbing against the wings. It soon became apparent that the rear axle had moved and many of our spring leaves had broken into several pieces. Fate was kind to us, however, for at the foot of the Stelvio we were met by our Swedish friends, Erik Carlsson and Mario Pavoni, who had retired from the rally on the first night. They had spent two nights in bed since then, and it was their cheerful encouragement and practical help that enabled us to struggle to the finish – still some 600 miles away.

'When David Seigle-Morris and I reached the Spa final control that Sunday evening, we were filthy from head to foot, our eyes burned in their sockets, and we were tired beyond description. But we knew that, of 85 starters, only eight crews had completed the 5,500-kilometre course – and we were among them. We had won our class, we had been placed sixth overall, and we had finished, which gave each of us a greater sense of achievement than any previous rally result.'

Class wins on all fronts

Final 1961 Rally Championship round was the R.A.C. Rally. Here Pat and Ann found their past form to finish overall runners-up to Erik Carlsson's Saab, their '3000' of course winning its class and the girls taking home yet another Coupe des Dames, although Pat considers that they were, however, extremely lucky to finish.

To close the season, the girls took a lone '3000' to compete in the Tour of Corsica. But the event was abandoned after some 12 hours because of a freak snow storm which blanketed the Island. The results were announced according to the positions of the cars at the time the rally was stopped and thus Pat and Ann won their class and were placed 17th overall.

To keep pace with the consistent run of '3000' class wins in international rallies was by now becoming a task for the mathematicians. From 22 sorties, the '3000' had gained 16 class wins, had three times won the marque team prize, and on only three occasions finished lower than second in their class.

David Seigle-Morris/Tony Ambrose began the 1962 season by winning their class on the Monte Carlo Rally, the '3000' being runner-up to Lyndon Sims' Aston Martin on the Monaco circuit races. In April the privateers Bobby Parkes/G. Howarth repeated their 1960 effort by gaining a class win on the Circuit of Ireland. Then came the Tulip, when the Morley brothers, with Peter Riley/Derrick Astle in close company, defeated strong Jaguar and Mercedes opposition to be placed first and second in the large G T category.

Ann Wisdom having now become Mrs Peter Riley, the Moss/Wisdom partnership came to a close. A newcomer to the B.M.C. team, Pauline Mayman, joined forces with Pat, this new combination on their first outing collecting a class win on the Acropolis; their '3000' was also the highest placed British entry.

Soon after the Acropolis, John Gott came out of retirement with his ex-works '3000' to compete in the International Police Rally, the Austin-Healey recording the fastest time on all speed tests and winning the class just like old times!

The Alpine was again the highlight of the season when the Morleys brought their '3000' through to score outright victory for the second year running, a truly brilliant performance. Pat Moss/Pauline Mayman were third overall, collecting their usual Coupe des Dames. Despite a puncture on the Vivione, Seigle-Morris/Ambrose also finished and thus helped to bring the Austin-Healeys the team prize.

On the Polish Rally, Moss/Mayman brought the '3000' its seventh consecutive international rally class win, Pat finishing overall runner-up to Bohringer's Mercedes.

Hopes for another outright victory in the Liège were dashed when the leading '3000' of Seigle-Morris/Hercock suffered a cracked chassis, and the second team car of Logan Morrison/Rupert Jones had to

concede class victory to the flying Bohringer. Seigle-Morris brought
the crippled '3000' to the finish, achieving a personal triumph and a
gold Liège award for finishing in three consecutive years on an
Austin-Healey.

Paddy Hopkirk, in his first drive with the B.M.C. team, had to
drop out in the third of the works cars with damaged rear suspension
while the fourth car, crewed by Rauno Aaltonen and Tony Ambrose
was disqualified when their road book was stolen. Rauno recalls that
heartbreaking occasion:

'We arrived in Belgrade without penalty and had about 40 minutes
to spare before we were due to book out of the control. I parked
the Healey outside a cafe and Erik Carlsson came over and asked us
to join him for a cup of coffee. Tony went into the cafe to get a table
while I gave the car a quick check. Then I remember clearing up the
interior of the car, picking up the road book, making sure that it
was folded open at the right page and placing it in the special pocket
we had made in the navigator's door. I remember closing the sidescreens and closing the doors. You could not, of course, lock the
works Healeys.

'When we came back to the car some five minutes before we were
due out of the control, Tony got into the car, reached into the pocket
for the road book and found that it was missing. Clearly someone had
stolen it although I don't for one moment think that it was a fellow
competitor.

'We pressed on to the next control, all the way to Sofia, in the
hope that the organizers would be kind to us and let us finish with a
new road book, but, quite rightly, they had to abide by the regulations
and we were disqualified.

'It was a heartbreaking occasion and I think that it was from this
time onwards that all co-drivers carried their road books where ever
they went.'

Paddy Hopkirk/Jack Scott had their first success with the '3000' on
the R.A.C. Rally by winning the class and finishing runners-up to
Carlsson's Saab. Moss/Mayman followed Hopkirk into third place,
adding yet another Coupe des Dames to their collection.

The year 1962 had truly brought further impressive successes to
the marque, the works '3000's claiming eight international rally class
wins in nine events. Pat Moss and Pauline Mayman also clinched the
Ladies' European Rally Championship, this being Pat's third Championship victory.

With Makinen on the Monte

The new season began well with the partnership of Timo Makinen and Christabel Carlisle winning their class on the Monte Carlo Rally, the '3000' being runner-up again in the circuit races at Monaco.

Christabel recounts how this seemingly unlikely partnership survived the rigours of the Monte:

'Having taken part in the rally the previous year in a Sprite, I had very much wanted to do it again. However, nothing would induce me to drive. The thought of ice, snow, narrow roads and hairpin bends frightens me, so Stuart Turner entered the car without naming a driver. Not until after the R.A.C. Rally did he discover someone suitable – Timo Makinen, who had won his class with a Mini in that event. So I was to navigate for a Finn who could hardly speak any English!

'We met in Geneva to do a four-day "recce" of the route south of Chambéry. After three hours of motoring over a snow-covered mountain pass, I nearly took the first aeroplane back to England. I felt literally sick with fear. Previously, if there had ever been any snow on the roads, the person driving me never exceeded 30 mile/h and if I drove myself (which I only remember having done once) I certainly never went above 15 mile/h. This Finn was doing at least 80 mile/h and every corner was a vast slide with full opposite lock. The car seemed to get into the most incredible positions, skidding almost incessantly, even on a straight line, but somehow we never hit a bank or went over the edge, nor even spun. By the following day I had resigned myself to fate, but by the end of the rally I had so much confidence in Timo's ability that I was even able to shout to him to go faster in order to get to the controls on time. His technique and driving of that large car were quite fantastic, and it was obvious that he preferred snow to dry roads. Whenever we met those conditions, he used to start throwing the car about, playing with it as though it were a toy and whistling under his breath.

'I flew back to London to have a couple of days to recover from noise and hairpin bends before setting off again for Paris and the start.

'Reports of the ever-changing weather conditions did nothing to lessen my fears. I worked hard on my maps and notes, and made out a card system by which we could follow the road numbers on the easier sections for the first two days, thereby allowing the person not driving to sleep. Theoretically this should have worked, but in practice it was so cold, draughty and uncomfortable that I never slept for more than half an hour at a stretch. Also, I always had nagging dreams that we were off-route, so woke up automatically to check.

'The city as usual was gay, and I cannot understand why the members of the team did not start the rally with enormous hangovers! We spent one morning at the B.M.C. garage checking the spares and tool-kits. I was only too thankful that I had a man as a driver, who understood what all the spanners and vicious-looking tools were for. I prayed that we would never have to use chains, as the Healey wheels are rather large, and the thought of trying to fit those hulking bits of metal on to the wheels, in the middle of a howling blizzard, did not exactly enthral me. As a navigator, I was just shown how to work the watches and zero the trip recorder. I made a mental note of the good strong crash-bar, fitted my safety belt tightly, and reckoned that that was all I could do. Speaking truthfully, I only wished the rally were all over and finished.

'Saturday morning was bitterly cold. Some French friends had warned me that the road to Belgium was icy, so we fitted two spiked tyres on the front, and one Frenchman very sweetly said that he would lead us out of Paris. This was a great relief, as to navigate through Paris is a nightmare, and at least this would ensure that we would start off in the right direction. I must say it felt rather grand, rolling up to the starting line, sitting in the passenger's seat of a large, gleaming red sports car. If we had been going for a short drive, I would have felt super; as it was, the thought of the three days ahead sent butterflies to my tummy.

'The first two days of motoring are fused in my mind as two days of slow torture, of extreme cold and endless controls. At the first control at Entreaupont, we changed the two other plain tyres to spikes – or perhaps it is fairer to say that I looked on while a willing petrol-pump attendant did my share of the work! An hour and a half to spare at Liège, so we all made our way to an excellent restaurant, but only drank, alas, Coca Cola. Now it was beginning to get dark and a long slog followed to Arnhem. The wind was such that it had blown drifts across the road, and hitting these produced a dead muffling sound, treacherous to the unconcentrating driver. At Arnhem we heard reports of the Frankfurt starters. Only three crews had got through unpenalized, and to do this they had had to travel twice the set distance within the same time schedule.

'There were rumours of blocked roads near Boulogne and later at Rennes. At the Hague, fresh rumours of all the Glasgow starters being diverted and, with a force 10 gale imminent, being unable to cross the channel.

'Like a fool, I had never imagined it could be so cold, and I had not nearly enough clothes. I must have looked a bluish colour, because some kind person thrust a jersey upon me. At Ghent I acquired a super lined coat, and at Rennes the next day, a rug – all most welcome presents. Yet with all these I was still frozen. The works Healey is, of course, an excellent rally car, but I do wish there were not so many chinks in the bodywork, and a heater at least four times the size would have been more appropriate!

' "My Finn" had driven solidly to Boulogne from Paris (Paris starters begin their Monte by travelling northwards). I had offered to take the wheel previously and had been relieved when this had been refused. Now I thought I really must make an effort.

' "Wouldn't you like to have a rest now and let me drive this section?" proved too long a sentence for him to understand, so I just had to say, "You sleep, I drive!"

'From Chambéry the rally proper started. No longer was there time to feel bored or tired. It became a race against time, with the hands of the clock persistently moving on to zero hour. Each control was made with not more than the odd minute to spare, and sometimes I thought we would never even get there. The times and kilometres never seemed to get anywhere near each other and we found ourselves with an apparently impossible 5 minutes, 8 kilometres to do, on a road with endless bends. The thought of the Competitions Manager's wrath if we did not arrive in Monte Carlo with a clean road-book made me shout above the noise of the engine to Timo to go faster and faster. How he managed, on the snow and ice-covered roads, never ceases to amaze me.

'His times on the special stages were fantastic. We had pace notes whereby I reminded him of the hairpin bends, slow lefts and rights, and the fast sections. Because of language difficulties, navigation from Chambéry onwards was rather tiring, because I could not say, "In two kilometres there is a village, turn left." Instead I had to follow the road, see the village, find the turning and then say, "Left". One 3-hour section was through a blinding blizzard. Again I just do not know how we ever got to the control on time.

'Often we had to change tyres to long spikes, back to studs, to plain tyres for a dry special stage, back to studs and finally plain ones yet again for the final part.

'By far the most glorious feeling was eventually arriving in Monte Carlo. With engine switched off for the very last time, there came a wonderful sense of achievement, pride and relief at having actually got there. It was terrific.'

Racing with the '3000'

In the warmer climes of Sebring, the 12 Hour Race brought one of the all-too-few notable '3000' achievements on the race track when Bob Olthoff/Ronnie Bucknum finished fourth in class behind a trio of prototype Ferraris. The second '3000', driven by Paddy Hopkirk/Don Morley, finished sixth in the class.

In reviewing the racing achievements of the '3000', the marque has understandably been able to make little impression on the Ferrari domination of the 3 litre class. In three consecutive years mechanical troubles eliminated the '3000' entry at Le Mans, the Bob Olthoff/John Whitmore effort in 1962 being the most creditable attempt, for their '3000' had reached eighth place overall before retiring only six hours from the finish. In less ambitious races, however, the efforts of private owners should be recorded here. Bob Olthoff, Mike Bond, David Dixon, Elizabeth Jones, John Gott, John Harris, Clive Baker, John Chatham and Stewart Hands are amongst those who have made '3000's perform exceptionally well on the track outside the field of international events. Particularly notable performances were Bob Olthoff's win in the 1962 Leinster Trophy and second place in the Rand Six Hours in South Africa.

A luckless Alpine and Liège

Returning to the 1963 rally scene, the Morley brothers brought the '3000' its fourth consecutive class win on the Tulip, and when the Alpine Rally came around again there were high hopes that the popular twins would win this summer classic for the third consecutive year to gain the highest Alpine honour of all, the Coupe d'Or. The Alpine, however, turned out to be a disastrous outing for the marque and one of the almost unprecedented occasions when not one of the Austin-Healey team completed the course. The Morleys seemed assured of their third consecutive victory when, on the final night, failure of an experimental rear axle caused their retirement. The other members of the Austin-Healey team enjoyed equally bad fortune, crashes eliminating Paddy Hopkirk/Jack Scott and Logan Morrison/Ross Finlay, and a smashed hub putting Timo Makinen/Mike Wood out of the event.

The team's luck certainly did not change for the Liège. Firstly, Geoff Mabbs tells us how he and Timo Makinen retired:

'As we had an early number, I suppose it was inevitable that we should have ended the rally as we did – buried deep into the tail end of a very solid Yugoslavian truck.

'I think I probably made a mistake by reading to Timo before we set out on this particular section, the instructions at the top of our pace notes. This said quite simply: "Unless you are absolutely mad this section is quite impossible." That was enough for my man Makinen!

'He set off from the start of that stage as though he was trying to set a new world record for the standing quarter mile and I pleaded with him to ease up a bit. "Slow down, Timo," I cried. "There's a long way to go yet and after all it does not really matter whether we do lose a few minutes at this early stage." But the great man was not listening.

'It was about 20 km farther on that we went slap into the back of this lorry. We were screaming through this corner in a full-bore drift, the Healey sideways as usual, and there she was, right in the middle of the road. Not even Timo could miss it. How both of us are still alive I really don't know because we must have been doing about 50 mile/h on impact. I suppose that says something for the strength of the old Healey. What a fantastic mess it was.

'Timo sat back in his seat, looked at me, reached in his pocket for a cigarette and said quietly: "I think we stop here, Geoff."

'I'm sure if that truck had not been there we would have done that stage on time, although when we got out and had a close look at the car we found that the rear tyres were already down to the canvas and we had not done more than 50 km since they were changed.

'I remember another incident during our recce for this event. I had not been to Yugoslavia before, neither had Timo, so I picked him up in Brussels for the recce and I drove down to the Italian border. As the roads deteriorated and we got on to the loose, I began to hang the tail out a bit which immediately set Timo leaping up and down in his seat like a wild thing saying that he must drive. But I replied that it was quite safe, I was not really trying and that he had nothing to worry about.

'Then we came to the Yugoslavian border and, of course, I had to get out and deal with all the paperwork. No sooner had I turned my back than Timo leaped out of the car and ran round to jump into the driving seat. When I returned, there he was behind the wheel with a frightening grin on his face. I had hardly had time to get one foot into the car before the Healey roared into life, Timo let in the clutch and we were away along the dirt road.

' "Hang on," I yelled. "Let me get the pace notes out." But by now the Healey was in overdrive top, howling along this little 10-foot-wide track and heading towards the mountains.

'Again I pleaded with the maestro to take it easy because we had a long way to go with this car and we would never be able to complete our recce of the whole route if we went on at this pace. But Timo just turned to me and smiled saying: "Fantastic good car."

'By the time we had reached the foot of the mountain road I was absolutely terrified. The speedo hovered continuously around the 100 mile/h mark with the rev-counter needle soaring higher and higher. Then we came to the dodgy bits with the rock face on one side and nothing on the other. Now I was really sweating. I have been upside down in cars, I've been over the edge in cars, I've been trapped in burning cars but I've never been in anything like that. I was saturated in perspiration and I kept trying to talk to Timo quietly now so that I would not disturb him but perhaps make him slow down a little so that he could hear what I was saying. I was terrified that he might take his eyes off the road for one second to look at me. It was terrible.

'As the Healey roared on I began to picture the terrible accident that was about to happen and the thought came to me that if I damaged my head I was bound to end up as a jibbering idiot. My past did not go through my mind but my future did, and I had visions of being a mental idiot in a wheel chair. It was then that I thought that I must try and get my crash helmet on which was lying on the floor behind the seats. So I began to slowly thread my hand down between the seats, all the time muttering to Timo and trying not to disturb him. I located the helmet, grabbed hold of the strap and slowly inched it up between the seats hoping all the time that Timo would not see me. I was sure that if he saw that I was about to put my helmet on he would go even faster.

'Now the Healey was approaching the really tight bits with hairpin corners, blind bends and big drops. Timo was obviously preparing himself for what lay ahead, as he shifted in his seat and tugged at his seat belt. Ahead I saw this right-hand bend coming and I was sure that this was going to be the big moment. The Healey pounded along, closer and closer to the bend until I was convinced that no human being could possibly get that car round the corner. With 100 yards to go I could stand it no longer and in one lightning move I slammed the helmet over my head, put my feet up on to the dash panel, took a firm hold of the grab handle and took a mighty deep breath.

'I then witnessed a truly incredible performance of slides and counter slides and arm-crossed motoring of which Timo is master and, of course, we sailed round that corner without so much as a flicker of apprehension on Timo's face. It was an incredible experience and he did the same on every bend, time and time again without ever over-playing it. And we went back and forth over that pass, faster and faster every time until he had mastered every move.

'From that moment on I had complete faith in Timo and realized why he is rated as the fastest rally driver in the world.'

Rauno Aaltonen and Tony Ambrose were equally unfortunate on that Liège and for the second year running they dropped out when in the lead, this time, as Tony Ambrose recalls, through an unaccountable driving error.

'I will never know what caused that accident on the Vivione, certainly it was not a mechanical failure. Both Ranno and I were in good spirits, fully awake, and very much aware of the situation that we held a one-minute lead over Bohringer. All we had to do was to return a reasonable time over the Vivione to hold on to that minute and we would have achieved our greatest rallying ambition.

'The Vivione starts with fairly fast tarmac for four or five kilometres, then it goes on to the loose for about the same distance and then it starts to tighten up as you come to the mountain ranges. It is not particularly rough but when you start to reach the summit, you are motoring between the rock face and those rather nasty steel railings on the other side.

'We did the climb in the dark on this occasion and everything was going to plan; we were well up on schedule and certainly Rauno was not trying very hard. The car was in perfect shape. And then we came to this right-hander, where Rauno slid the car just a little bit wide, over-corrected and clouted the rock face. Rauno again over-corrected, the Healey gave a vicious swerve, hit the rocks again and then spun away across the road and crashed head first through the railings.

'Why we never went right over the edge I will never know.

Neither did I know how far the drop was. I do know, indeed I will never forget, that when I opened my door to step out there was nothing but fresh air and the car was balanced on the brink. We sat still, hardly daring to breath, then Rauno slowly opened his door, found that he was over the road and gingerly stepped out, the Healey giving a little sway as he did so. I clambered across his seat, hardly daring to move less the whole thing lost its balance. I slithered out on to the road beside him.

'I then realized that my brief case was in the back with our passports and all our money inside and, with a natural co-driver's instinct, rescued these with baited breath.

'Paddy Hopkirk then arrived on the scene with the other works Healey and tried to pull us back on to the road but it was quite useless. The car was also in such a position that it was quite impossible for him to get by so we had to tip the Healey up about six inches to let him pass underneath. She was perfectly balanced like a see-saw.

'It took two jeeps with chains to get that car back on to the road the next day and then I got an even bigger shock when I saw just how far we would have fallen had we lost our balance the night before.'

Into 1964

As usual, the year ended with the R.A.C., where Makinen and the Morleys finished first and second in their class respectively. Aaltonen, however, shortened the chassis of his car when he went exploring in the forest of Bin. Timo had a moment on the slippery Tulloch stage and took 12 minutes to regain the road, and Don Morley on a later stage spent some four or five minutes persuading his electrics to operate again after a particularly deep mud-splash. So ended a relatively disappointing year, although another five class wins were added to the records, bringing the tally in international events to 29.

By 1964, the major effort of the Competitions Department had swung over to the ubiquitous Mini, which proceeded to pile up a fantastic record of competition successes. The '3000' was not completely ignored, however, and during its two-year swan song, the odd singleton entries continued to uphold the Austin-Healey honour.

To start the season, Donald Healey entered a car in the annual 12 Hour Race at Sebring, to be driven by Paddy Hopkirk and Grant Clark, the Canadian champion driver. Quite early on, Paddy ran over a piece of metal wreckage, bursting a tyre and having to limp back to the pits on the rim. The damage was soon repaired and the car resumed, well down the field. After some 30 laps, the Healey was back into 33rd place, but shortly after Clark took over, he lost it in a big way just after the pits, somersaulting on to his roof.

The Morleys, making their first appearance in the new Mark III '3000', once again put up the best overall performance in the Tulip Rally, but as usual had to be content with a class award, the winner being Makinen/Ambrose in a Cooper 'S', which was also making its competition debut. Paddy Hopkirk/Henry Liddon had a go at the Austrian Alpine and put up fastest times on all the tests to win outright, although hard pushed by a little Steyr-Puch of all things!

The French Alpine followed, and the Morleys had a trouble-free run, collecting their class, and a Coupe d'Argent for three non-consecutive penalty-free trips, some small consolation for missing their Gold Cup the previous year.

Aaltonen and Ambrose win Liège

Three works Healeys were entered for the Liège, the last of the classic 94-hour events. This time Rauno Aaltonen and Tony Ambrose made no mistakes and completely dominated the event to win outright by nearly 30 minutes from their nearest rival. Tony Ambrose has provided us with this graphic account of his outstanding drive with Rauno Aaltonen:

'Every year the Liège is described as the toughest yet. This year the 3,100 mile route was very similar to that of the 1963 Marathon and the condition of many of the toughest and roughest roads was unchanged. But this year the average speeds were raised considerably. For instance, last year six hours were allowed between Perast and Stolac in Yugoslavia, but this year the time was cut to $4\frac{1}{4}$ hours. That's a *tremendous* step-up in average speed over a really vital part of the route. And the fact that 21 of the 98 starters finished the course (many more than in past years) is no reflection on the severity of the event. During the rally the organizers were forced to amend the route due to local road works in Yugoslavia and they extended a far too generous lateness allowance. Had the original route and time schedule stood, there would probably have been no more than six or eight finishers – in the best traditions of the Liège!

'The Liège demands just about *everything* from the co-driver: navigation, stamina, car management (most important this), but above all driving ability. A crew with a co-driver who is not a really proficient driver stands little chance of finishing the Liège. It's very much a co-driver's rally.

'I drove just about 50 per cent and much of it on the tough sections. Rauno is unusual in this respect. He needs a good eight hours' sleep a day, he takes no "keep-awake" drugs and calls upon his co-driver to drive more than most Number Ones do. On an event like the Liège he has to be preserved to the maximum possible extent.

'Rauno's smoothness is unbelievable. These Finnish drivers have the ability to put a car sideways on the loose stuff and yet maintain complete control; whereas some of the Finns tend to overplay this and may have one wheel in the scenery at times, Rauno does it with complete control and precision *all* the time. Within the past few seasons Rauno's performances have become more balanced. He used to be just as hairy as the next man and determined to put up the fastest time on *every* stage. This is not the way to win rallies; certainly not the Liège.

'We had an early number and were a little concerned about this before the start because last year another of our team cars had a very early number and everyone said he would end up by hitting a lorry. He did just that! This year, however, the rally was rather better planned in that most of the really difficult stuff on loose mountain roads was at night and therefore the chances of meeting oncoming traffic in unexpected places were less. We were in fact able to exploit the advantages of an early number by not having to follow in someone else's dust cloud, which is a very real menace on the Liège. Actually, we did not see another rally car from the moment we entered Yugoslavia until we got to Bulgaria and we only saw one car between leaving Sofia and entering Italy. It was a very lonely journey!

'The really vital sections were in north Yugoslavia on the second night of the rally, the southern Yugoslavian stages on the third night and the Italian Alps on the last night. The first crossing of the Alps I don't really rate very tough. It wears down the car and crew but it should not worry the top crews.

'Right from Bled, the start of the first Yugoslav stages, Rauno drove beautifully. He drove intelligently, he drove safely and yet almost as fast as I have ever known him drive. I was quite convinced that nobody would do Bled to Col on time, I thought that it was just possible to do Col to Ogulin on time and again just possible to do Ogulin to Novi on time – because we managed this section on time in the opposite direction the previous year. I was certainly correct about Bled to Col because we were 12 minutes late. This included driving the last 2 km on a flat tyre; in fact the tyre almost disintegrated as we tore into the control on the wheel rim! Five minutes were taken out of the next section as we changed both rear wheels and refuelled and we still just managed to reach Ogulin on time, literally arriving with the last ten seconds. That meant refuelling within the next section and we ended up at Novi just four minutes late. We really began to feel then that things were going our way!

'It was on this next stage that the controversial route change was made. I think the Yugoslav authorities got a bee in their bonnet about some road works. The organizer didn't have time to work out whether there was need for a scare or not and had to take the Yugoslavs' word that the road was in fact blocked. They therefore issued these alternative route instructions which put approximately 70 km, for which they gave a very generous extra two hours' lateness allowance.

'We set off from Novi expecting things to be fairly easy after the thrash from Bled. Rauno was very tired now, so I took over and I set off hoping to make up some of our lost time so that we could have a bit of a rest and get some servicing done. Bombing over the brow of a hill I came to a junction where I knew I had to fork left, only to find a control banner across the road. The Yugoslav officials appeared, thrust a piece of paper through the window which said that the road was blocked on the route we intended to take and that we must take the alternative route *via* five place names. Rauno, who was now a little rested, immediately took over, and I began to sort out the navigation for we were now running over unknown roads and I didn't even have a local map out at the time. It was a diabolical little track and for some 30 km I had no confidence that we were on the right road and of course we were the first car through. Eventually we came to a signpost which listed two of the place names for which we were looking; the road then became tarmac and matters improved. But it was not long before we were back on the rough stuff again, the weather deteriorated and with patchy fog, the road became patchy damp and driving conditions were now really foul. It was here that Rauno made his only mistake of the rally, spinning the Healey on a right-hander at round 70 mile/h. We side-swiped a large pile of gravel; I thought the Healey was going to flip but fortunately she bounced back on the road. Two kilos up the road a tyre went flat;

we made a hasty wheel change and set off once again. I noticed now that Rauno was not going at his maximum and when I glanced at him I saw that his eyes were closing from time to time. "Rauno, wake up," I yelled. "I am very tired. Can you drive?" he said. I told him that this was a desperate section and we were going to be late. "I know," he replied, "but you will drive quicker than I." And so I took over, having made a calculation that we had 123 km (77 miles) left and 37 minutes to run; a truly ridiculous average!

'By now it was dawn; I remember after the first few kilos feeling that I was going better than I thought I could. Rauno went immediately to sleep leaving me alone on the job. A co-driver, of course, should never really be called upon to make up time on a critical section but the possibility is always there, however organized a crew may be and this was one of those occasions. Now I really had to get going.

'There were all sorts of hazards at that time of the morning. Bullock carts, peasants, cyclists off to work, and still we were travelling on roads which I had never seen in my life, groping for the signposts and trying to maintain an impossible average speed. I recall on one occasion seeing 200 km/h (124 mile/h) register on the speedo as I fled down the main street of a little village. I knew that if I did not maintain this pace then certainly Carlsson and Bohringer would do so! The fact that Rauno did not wake from his sleep perhaps indicates that we did not have too many near squeaks! At last we screamed into the Zagreb control just 15 minutes late (having *averaged* 89 mile/h!) beaten in fact only by Erik Carlsson, which did a lot to boost our morale.

'On these really rough sections where almost any speed above a mere crawl would normally be ludicrous, you compromise between acceptable car strain and lateness penalties. This is a tremendously difficult compromise to achieve, and the mark of the finest rally drivers. The trouble is that you do not know how the other drivers are treating these sections at the time. For example, one of the roughest sections was from Perast to Stolac and we lost 20 minutes. Now at that time we only had a lead of eight minutes, so we could have found ourselves arriving at Stolac having lost our lead. In fact we didn't, because it turned out that other people had gone just as slowly.

'After the excitement of the rerouting we got involved with a little rock blasting. This occurred on the section between Belgrade and Belogradcik as we headed into Bulgaria; it's a very long section of

about 330 km (205 miles). The first 150 km were over very fast
autoput and then we turned off eastwards on a truly diabolical track
where we were delayed by roadworks. By flashing a few Dinars
around we were able to get past and maintain a fair average. Suddenly
we came over a brow and were forced to a halt by a fellow with a
red flag standing in the middle of the road. Rauno stopped, we
peered up the road and could not understand what the hold-up was
all about. Then we saw that blasting operations were about to take
place, but as several fellows were still running around the cliff I
reckoned that they would not start blasting immediately so I said to
Rauno that we should press on as time was running short. Rauno
was not at all keen to move on but I prodded him again and he edged
the Healey forwards. Three more chaps then came down into our
path forming a barrier so we had to stop again; in fact, Rauno
reversed back to the first bloke with the red flag. The minutes ticked
slowly by, the three chaps up the road disappeared, still there was no
sign of the blasting operations beginning so I again pleaded with
Rauno to get going. After some hesitation he let in the clutch and the
Healey surged forwards, the fellow with the red flag giving us a
hearty whack on the top of the bonnet as we flew past. Just as we
passed the cliff face there was a deafening explosion as the charges
were set off.

'Rauno accelerated like mad as the Healey was pelted with stones.
We roared away thankful that we had not ended up with a boulder
in the cockpit!

'Being the first car through we naturally attracted a great deal of
attention; besides, a big red sports car is a pretty rare sight in these
parts! At many places we were shaken by the hand by many Com-
munist party officials and welcomed to their country with due
ceremony.

'It was soon after this, by the way, that Rauno had a 'moment',
tearing down a little cobbled street into a little village. We flew over
a brow and should have turned sharp left. Rauno could not get the
Healey round and had to bring the car to a dramatic sideways stop in
a gravelled courtyard which lay straight ahead. There were two old
Bulgarian peasant women sitting up against the far wall of the courtyard who must have thought this the latest *bourgeois* method of
extermination!

'In the latter stages of the event the time schedules did ease a little
and we were able to make up enough time to have a few minutes

here and there; to get out of the car, snatch a bite to eat, put our heads under a cold tap and lie down for a few moments. Our longest break was at Vittoria Veneto where we were able to have about an hour out of the car.

'We existed almost entirely on lemon glucose drinks, the odd sandwich, some fruit that we were able to pick up at the service points, and we also carried tins of Shippam's tinned food. I found that I did not really *want* any solid food; I certainly had no longing for a hot meal as the temperature was so high. Just lots and lots to drink. We carried liquid in a Thermos bottle mounted up behind the seats with suck tubes leading forward. The amount of liquid we consumed was quite fantastic. At the Novi control for example I sank well over half a gallon of liquid and was quite ready for another half gallon at the next control! You lose nearly all of it again in perspiration.

'Although we wore crash-hats on all these flat-out sections we did not use the "intercom" telephone used on some rallies because really we speak very little to each other. On these desperate sections it's Rauno's job to drive at his maximum and mine to see that we are going the right way and to see that Rauno is performing within his limits yet not going too slowly. On the Liège we do not use the very detailed "pace notes" as on the shorter events; the Marathon is too long and too complicated and the crew would wear themselves out "talking" each other over so many miles.

'By the time we had battled our way up the Dalmatian coast and got to Novi, Rauno had had a terribly long session at the wheel. I had done an equally tiring stint and, quite frankly, we were both pretty exhausted as we pressed on into Italy. I certainly have never felt so whacked on a rally in all my life. I could not get to sleep in the car, it was intolerably hot and when I got out of the car at the Adjovscina control and went to pour myself a drink I just did not have the strength and literally fell down in the gravel under some shade. Rauno's wrists and hands were just aching pieces of flesh at the ends of his arms which virtually had no feeling at all after some eight hours at the wheel.

'After this we pressed on to the final Italian Alps section, in the lead as we were last year when Rauno crashed on the Vivione Pass, losing the rally. I think we both felt pretty twitchy as we set off up the Vivione. Usually the organizers assure you that these roads are closed to traffic but this year as we approached the spot of our 1963 disaster we swung around a bend to be faced with the headlights of a couple of cars and a few motor bikes; this made us really glad that we were not pressing on quite as fast as we might have been, for we now had a lot of time in hand.'

And so Aaltonen and Ambrose won what will go down in motor sport history as the last of the great classic road rallies. It was a dominating victory and the marque's greatest competition achievement. Aaltonen, however, was the only member of the Abingdon team to finish, Paddy Hopkirk retiring in Yugoslavia with gearbox troubles and Timo Makinen running out of tyres when plagued with a series of punctures.

Makinen's fortunes

The R.A.C. Rally saw two cars entered for the Morleys, for Timo and Don Barrow; the former lost a lot of time after running out of road on one of the Welsh stages, but Timo and Don drove the big car into second place overall and best GT car. At one stage they were leading the rally, but slippery conditions in Scotland favoured the smaller cars, and they were unable to maintain their early lead.

The final appearances of the works cars in 1965 came with the Morleys collecting class awards in the Tulip, Geneva and Alpine. This latter event was particularly tough on the G T cars, not one of which was able to win one of the coveted Coupes. Timo had a go at the Scottish and R.A.C. Rallies, failing to finish in the former, but coming second overall again on the latter. This was an unlucky event for him, as, with Paul Easter as his co-driver, he led for most of the rally only to be literally overtaken on an icy Welsh hill by Rauno (Mini) who went on to the outright win! Timo reckons that this was his best-ever effort in a '3000'.

Timo had an outing of a different type early in the year, when he was paired with Paul Hawkins for the Targa Florio race in Sicily. Despite using tyres and wheels at a phenomenal rate (it required a tyre change every two laps – approximately 88 miles), the 'big Healey' was leading its class when a rotor arm broke at the start of the eighth lap (10-lap race). Paul Hawkins walked back to the pits for a replacement, and the gallant pair went on to finish second in class to a Ferrari GTO. Paul Hawkins also drove the '3000' at Sebring, this time with Warwick Banks as his partner, and came 17th overall, winning the class.

The unsung Swan Song

There were no works '3000's entered in international events in 1966 but when the R.A.C. Rally came around again at the end of 1967 it was announced that this event would be open to prototype sports cars running in the group 6 category. (The past R.A.C. Rallies had only been open to series production cars.) Thus the 'big Healey' in fully modified form was eligible and, as I was then B.M.C. Competitions Manager, I decided that this should be the swan song for the 'big Healey'. I was determined to break the run of bad luck that had robbed the Healey of outright victory in its 'home' event.

As there were no new cars available, I was persuaded to hand over my own car for the project, the ex-Morley Alpine car of 1964, formerly registered ARX 92B, but now re-registered with my personal plates, PWB 57. It was originally intended that Timo Makinen would drive the car, but Timo later opted for a group 6 Mini-Cooper 'S' with fuel injection, so Rauno Aaltonen and Henry Liddon were to be the 'big Healey' crew.

The car was probably the most powerful road-going '3000' ever built. An all-aluminium engine was fitted, bored out to 2,968 cc, with three 45 DCOE Weber carburetters, giving a power output of nearly 200 b h p *at the wheels*! Despite extensive lightening, the additional load of rally gear, sump and underside guards, etc., brought the weight up to just 24 cwt, which was carried on four sturdy Minilite mag.-alloy wheels shod with Dunlop 185–15 SP44 radial Weathermaster tyres.

But alas, all these preparations were in vain for at the very last moment the Rally had to be cancelled because of the disastrous foot-and-mouth disease which threatened to cripple the country's farming community. My own disappointment was shared with everyone who had put so much work into the car, and particularly Rauno Aaltonen who was wildly enthusiastic about its performance and potential:

'I am sure that if a development programme had continued with the "big Healey" and it had been eligible for events in the fully modified form in which we rallied it, it could still be competitive in international events today.

'I was really very disappointed that I did not have the chance to prove the point on the R.A.C. Rally because a tremendous amount of hard work and thought had gone into the preparation of this car.

Indeed, it was probably the most developed car ever to come out of the Competitions Department at Abingdon.

'From my impressions of testing the car before the event, the handling was quite superb and unlike any other Healey I have driven. The use of light alloy panels all round and the alloy engine revolutionized the handling and it made all the difference to get the weight off the front end of the car.

'The latest SP44 radial tyres also made a lot of difference and they were so much better than the Weathermasters of five years ago. For the first time, too, on a "big Healey", we had been able to get the balance of the brakes right and with the use of twin servo units we were able to achieve the correct balance in favour of more braking on the rear than previously. This made the car so much safer for driving fast on the loose because it meant that you could use all four wheels for stopping the car in a straight line instead of having to drift it sideways all the time. Sometimes, particularly on the R.A.C. Rally, there is not always room to drive the car in this manner, and you need a lot of room to do it with a Healey.

'With the known reliability and the immense strength of this car, I am sure that we would have done very well indeed on the R.A.C. We may not have been able to put up the fastest times on all the stages but I was confident that we could have won by returning consistently fast times throughout the event, always expecting other people to lose time with mechanical troubles.

'It was really incredible that the Healey, of all cars, never won the R.A.C. Rally, the event for which it was best suited. I would dearly have liked to have had the honour of having the final attempt to break the "big Healey's" run of bad luck on this event.'

Almost coincident with this, the last appearance of the works Healeys, came news of the British Leyland merger and the inevitable rationalization of sports car marques and models. While it was quite clear that the Austin-Healey marque would be phased out in favour of MG, Triumph and Jaguar, the '3000' also fell victim of the American Safety and Air Polution Regulations. In the light of declining sales, it was quite uneconomical to consider a major redesign of the car.

And so the last of the 'big Healeys' left the Abingdon works in December 1967 and, sadly without any ceremony, one of this country's great classic sports cars came to the end of the line.

CHAPTER 10

THE AUSTIN-HEALEY SPRITE

After the phenomenal success in 1952 of Donald Healey's design for the Austin-Healey '100' it was not surprising that the Austin Motor Company showed the keenest interest when, five years later, Healey produced plans for a smaller and less-expensive sports model to be a little sister for the then established Austin-Healey '100-Six'. Just as Healey's design for the '100' utilized major components from the larger saloon in the Austin range, so the new small Austin-Healey employed the use of parts from Austin's baby saloon, the popular and well-proven Austin A35. The conception of the 'Sprite' – as the new model was named – was for a compact two-seater sports car possessing individual character, acceptable performance, excellent road holding, economy of operation and, above all, low initial cost.

The sturdy 948 cc B.M.C. 'A' series engine and gearbox from the A35 formed the ideal basis for the Sprite's specification. Although the compression ratio remained unchanged, the Sprite engine differed from the A35 unit in being fitted with special valve springs, improved exhaust valves, modified crankshaft bearings and twin $1\frac{1}{8}$ in. SU carburetters. Thus the Sprite had a well-proven and reliable power unit, tuned to give a happy compromise between economy and performance. The front suspension was also taken from the A35, using the standard coil spring and wishbone assembly, the lever-type Armstrong hydraulic damper arm providing the upper suspension link. The rack-and-pinion steering owed its origin to the Morris Minor '1000'. The rear suspension was a break with tradition, using quarter-elliptic leaf springs and torque links, but the rear axle was basically from the Minor '1000', as were the 7 in. Lockheed brakes.

Perhaps the most unconventional and controversial feature of the Sprite was the bodywork, particularly the frontal bonnet design with its twin headlamps mounted on top of the bonnet and the small radiator grille giving the Sprite a happy 'frog-like' appearance. It was originally planned to make the headlights retractable (as on the first Healey roadster of 1946) but this plan was later abandoned and the lamps were left in their distinctive position to comply with the American vehicle lighting regulations. At least this front body assembly was a practical design, the whole front section being hinged at the scuttle to give access to the engine compartment and front suspension. The rest of the Sprite was clothed in a simple but neat body shape, the tail and rear wing panels forming a shell braced by the rear wheel arches. Since the Sprite was intended for the less wealthy sports car enthusiasts, the price was kept as low as possible. Only the basic essentials of equipment were fitted to the 'standard' car, but the list of optional extras was very comprehensive and the owner could add to the original specification as his pocket allowed.

On the road, the Sprite showed a lively turn of speed matched with excellent road manners. Top speed and acceleration were adequate, if not dazzling by sports car standards. For those requiring improved performance there was plenty of scope for tuning the 'A' series engine. The works offered various tuning stages in a Special Tuning Manual and there was no shortage of tuning equipment available from other well-known specialists.

Production of the Sprite commenced at the B.M.C. sports car factory at Abingdon in early 1958 and in May the covers were lifted and the new model introduced to the world's sports car enthusiasts. The Sprite created a new concept in sports car motoring in terms of superior and economical performance at a cost comparable to many standard family saloons. The enthusiast could now buy a true sports car which would give a good account of itself in competition at the week-end, yet could be used quite comfortably for business travel during the week. It had remarkable luggage accommodation for a small sports car, although access to the luggage compartment on the original model was a little restricted. The Sprite was comfortable and weatherproof (especially in hardtop form), the good handling qualities made it a joy to drive and it was both economical to run and easy to service. Not the least of the qualities which endeared the Sprite to so many enthusiasts was its refreshingly different appearance, the controversial frontal styling soon being accepted as the characteristic of the model.

Sprite Mark II

After a production run of only one car short of the 49,000, and almost exactly three years after the announcements of the original

Sprite, the restyled Sprite Mark II was announced in May 1961. Using the original chassis-body platform, the Mark II carried re-designed front and rear body stylings. At the front the original one-piece bonnet section was replaced with fixed wings, convention-ally placed headlights, a wider radiator grille and top-opening bonnet. The rear of the car was almost completely redesigned with a lockable boot lid and restrained tail fins with a new rear light cluster. Com-pensating for the slight increase in weight, the engine performance was stepped up by fitting a high-overlap camshaft, larger inlet valves, double valve springs and a modified exhaust manifold. The com-pression ratio was also raised, improved larger ($1\frac{1}{4}$ in.) versions of the SU carburetters with paper-element air cleaners were fitted. As a direct result of competition experience, the gearbox was much improved with a closer set of ratios.

Despite inevitable cries of protest from many Mark I owners at the loss of the original Sprite's identity (plus the fact that one month later an almost identical model was introduced as the MG Midget!) the restyled Mark II was soon accepted as a popular and worthy successor to the Mark I.

'1100' Sprite

The London Motor Show in October 1962 brought news of an improved version of the Mark II Sprite. Significant improvements included the enlargement of the engine capacity from 948 cc to 1,098 cc effected by a slight increase in the bore size and by the use of a new longer-stroke crankshaft. Power output was raised to 55 b h p and there was a larger diameter clutch; an improved baulk-ring synchromesh gearbox was fitted and front disc brakes were now provided as standard equipment. The new '1100' offered more luxurious cockpit comforts, a welcome improvement over the somewhat spartan trim of the earlier models, and wire wheels were offered soon afterwards as a standard option.

Sprite Mark III

Introduced in March 1964, the Mark III brought the Sprite up to date with the modern trend for the sports car with saloon car com-forts; a trend very much dictated by the export markets (particularly the U.S.A.) which accounted for some 84% of all Abingdon-built sports car production. Major improvements on the Mark III included wind-up windows with swivelling quarter-lights, a redesigned fascia and further improvements in interior trim. Engine performance was stepped up to 59 b h p; this was achieved by improved manifolding and the use of the MG '1100' cylinder head. The characteristic 'twitchy' ride of the former Sprites on rough going was cured with the fitting of half-elliptic rear springs in place of the quarter-elliptics.

'1300' Sprite

The Motor Show of 1966 brought the announcement of the Mark VI Sprite which used a de-tuned 65 b h p version of the 1,275 cc Mini Cooper 'S' power unit. This engine provided a useful increase in both tractability and acceleration while the fuel consumption was comparable to the 1,098 cc Mark III. Another attractive feature of the new Sprite was the one-piece fold-away hood which was very much easier to operate than the removable button-down style on the earlier models.

'Sebring' Sprite

Before reviewing the international race and rally record for the Sprite, the 'Sebring' competition version deserves mention almost as a separate model as sufficient numbers were built for the car to be recognized by the F.I.A. as a separate G T model.

The Sebring was first introduced by Donald Healey at Warwick and offered as a lightweight version of the standard Mark I bodywork, using engine modifications in line with the then current range of Healey Speed Equipment. John Sprinzel, at one time working for Healeys in London (along with his chief mechanic Paul Hawkins), later introduced the more attractive Sebring bodywork made by Williams and Pritchard.

The very comprehensive Sebring modifications gave the owner a choice of many stages of tune; given below is the full competition specification as this is more likely the form in which the Sebring race and rally cars were running in the international events described later in this Chapter.

Initial preparations for Sebring tune began with the boring of the standard Mark I 948 cc engine to 995 cc and careful balancing of all moving parts. A sports camshaft with special bearings was fitted, also a matching distributor. High compression solid-skirt pistons were used and the cylinder head had modified inlet ports and combustion chambers. Compression ratio was raised to 11 to 1, giving 80 b h p at 7,000 rev/min. Twin $1\frac{1}{2}$ in. SU carburetters were used with twin SU electric fuel pumps. There were special inlet and exhaust manifolds with a sports exhaust system and silencer. Lubrication was by a full pressure-fed wet-sump system with a full-flow filter and an oil cooler. The standard 'Sprite' clutch was replaced by a 9-spring competition version; a close-ratio needle-roller gearbox, special halfshafts and sealed wheel bearings were used. The Sebring suspension remained basically as on the standard Sprite but stiffer front coil springs were used with an anti-roll bar. At the rear there were adjustable Armstrong shockabsorbers with stiffer leaf springs. Centre-lock 60-spoke wire wheels offered a useful increase in track; $8\frac{1}{2}$ in. Girling disc brakes were fitted at the front with 8 in. drums at the rear. The very attractive Sebring fixed-head G T bodywork was in alloy with a fibreglass front-hinged bonnet; steel bulkhead and wheel arches were retained for rally use but for ultra-lightness the additional use of alloy and fibreglass brought the weight down to close on 11 cwt. Performance of the full Sebring was, to say the least, exhilarating, the standing $\frac{1}{4}$-mile being covered in a mere 17 secs; 3rd gear performance was around the 80 mile/h mark and (with the 4·8 axle) the Sebring would reach 105 mile/h.

The Sebring theme was carried on by Warwick with the production of a series of special-bodied lightweight coupé cars, primarily designed for Le Mans. These works racing Sprites were, however, strictly competition cars, built expressly for the purpose of taking part in long distance international motor races which they did with unqualified success.

The sleek and purposeful bodywork of the works Sprites was designed by Geoff Healey although use was made of the wind tunnel at Longbridge to determine the contours of the 1965 Le Mans cars. The first coupé was built for the 1961 Le Mans race and is probably best identified as the car with which Mike Garton later scored so many successes. Quite a few bodies were built in this style including two cars for the Targa Florio (one closed car and one an open version) and one car which ran at Le Mans in 1963. The first of the sleeker Le Mans cars appeared in 1964 and these Mark II versions had the big wrap-around rear window and a modified front end with fixed wings

and a top-opening bonnet. The Mark III version was built for Sebring
in 1965 and can be identified by its dual iodine-vapour headlight
system and the adjustable air scoop in the nose.

Under the skin, most people are very surprised to find how near
standard the works Sprites are compared with the production model.
In their international sports/racing class the Sprites are certainly one
of the very few cars that utilized basically standard components. True
enough, the excitingly different body shape bears little resemblance
to the standard Sprite, but these bodies were specifically designed to
improve the top speed of the car down the long, long straight at
Le Mans but at most other circuits they would perform equally well
with standard coachwork.

The backbone of the car was a completely standard Sprite chassis/
platform, the only modifications being to the floor panels beneath
the seats which were lowered at the rear so that the lowest possible
seating level could be achieved which in turn permitted a low roof
line. The suspension too was basically standard Sprite, slightly stronger
coil springs being fitted at the front while the Armstrong shockabsorbers were fitted with competition valves. An anti-roll bar of $\frac{5}{8}$in.
diameter was fitted. At the rear, softer leaf springs were used with
Armstrong lever-arm hydraulic dampers. To provide better axle
location on the rougher international circuits like the Targa Florio,
Healeys employed an unorthodox rear suspension set-up comprising
angled telescopic dampers and an anti-tramp bracket.

The brakes were Lockheed, standard $8\frac{1}{4}$ in. disc (Mintex XM48
pads) being used at the front with 8 in. drums at the rear. To comply
with the international sports car regulations a dual-line braking
system with tandem master cylinders was fitted. Four-stud hubs
carried special bolt-on Healey 13 in. × 5 in. rim magnesium alloy
wheels. Dunlop 500L–13 R7 green or yellow spot tyres were used.

The power pack for the works Sprites has been a special 1,293 cc
version of the 'A' series engine. When the 1,098 cc engines were
standard wear in the Sprite, these 1,275 cc in-line units were extremely
hard to come by, mainly because of the non-availability of the special
crankshaft. With the arrival of the 1,275 cc Mark IV Sprite, and the
supply of nitrided crankshafts for these engines, the Sprite owner
could carry out fuller engine tuning in line with the well-proven
tuning recommendations for the Mini Cooper 'S'.

Healeys' engine modifications for their works cars included boring
out the 1275 block by 0·020 in. to give a 2·80 in. bore and 3·20 in.

stroke (1,293 cc). The balanced, nitrided crankshaft used standard Mini Cooper 'S' bearing shells; standard 'S' type connecting rod bearings were also used. The competition high-lift camshaft (0·394 in.) had a 95 degree overlap. The standard 'S' type pistons were replaced by forged ones, the compression ratio being raised to 11·9:1 by machining the cylinder head and the block. The standard 1275 cylinder head was gas-flowed, the combustion chambers and the ports being carefully matched. Standard 'S' type valves were used with matched push-rods and lightened rockers. The static ignition timing was 2 degrees b t d c. Champion N-60Y plugs were used. Lubrication was by a dry-sump system, oil being circulated by a gear-type concentric pump, driven off the camshaft, to all working parts. There was a separate scavenger pump, the oil capacity being $2\frac{1}{2}$ gallons including the oil cooler.

Carburation was by a single twin-choke 45 DCOE Weber carburetter upon a short manifold. There were twin SU electric fuel pumps and the tank capacity was 16 gallons. Healeys built their own three-branch exhaust manifold which terminated into a single big-bore pipe.

For most events the standard Sprite gearbox was used with close-ratio gears, competition linings being fitted to a $7\frac{1}{2}$ in. diaphragm-spring clutch. In search of more top speed at Le Mans an 'MGB' close-ratio gearbox was tried, coupled to a 0·8:1 overdrive operating on third and top gears. With a 4·2 rear axle, this gave the Sprite a top speed of around the 140 mile/h mark on the Mulsanne straight. At Sebring in 1963, a special five-speed version of the 'MGB' gearbox was used, the fifth speed being incorporated in the box to overcome the additional weight of the overdrive unit. The power output of the fully race-tuned 1,293 cc engine was 110 b h p at 7,000 rev/min, the maximum torque being 88 lb ft at 3,000 rev/min.

Two years ago Geoff Healey was kind enough to let me road test the 1966 Targa Florio car and I must say I found a fully race-tuned 1,275 cc Sprite quite exhilarating to say the least! Apart from the almost unbearable exhaust noise, this car was in complete contrast to some of the tuned cars that I have driven; it was a joy to drive on any sort of journey and was just as happy chugging along at low revs in top gear in traffic as howling along the open road.

My immediate road impressions were of the 'tautness' one comes to associate with works cars, the whole car (although being so very light) felt so safe and solid. The steering was firm, nicely balanced, and with little kick-back. The combination of rock-steady suspension and the racing tyres gave that characteristic 'weavy' feeling at low speeds, but once you got your foot down, the handling gave immense confidence. In fact I found it almost impossible to evaluate the road-holding of the car properly on the road and I had to retire to the seclusion of a local airfield to find out what really happened when the little Sprite was driven on the limit. When the car did break away it did so pretty quickly, but a flick of the small steering-wheel was all that was necessary to keep the car under complete control.

Weighing just about 12 cwt (that's 2 cwt lighter than the standard Mark IV) the performance of the 1275 race Sprites is really quite breath-taking, particularly when you realize that one of these cars could go straight out today and better the performance of the record-breaking Sprites which ran at Utah in 1959. The body shape is an important factor here, of course, and it's worth revealing that only 50 b h p is required to propel the Le Mans body shape along at 100 mile/h.

On the road the beautifully balanced motor just revs on and on and it is very easy to exceed the 7,000 rev/min maximum. The easy-revving engine, coupled with the close-ratio gearbox and quick, precise gear change, means that the car accelerates away through the gears so fast that, if you're making a quick getaway, you really have not got time to take your hand off the gear lever! Maximum in the gears (7,000 rev/min) gives 63 mile/h in second and a shattering 92 mile/h in third. There's no doubt that the little 'flier' would have gone on happily into the 120 mile/h mark despite the fact that the Targa body is not particularly streamlined. A remarkable little car indeed!

Rallying with the Sprite

Turning now to the Sprite's competition activities, only two months after the announcement of the new model, a team of three Sprites was entered for the Alpine Rally. Of the 56 cars which started the tough 2,360-mile route across the classic French, Italian and Swiss Alpine passes only 25 completed the course. Three of these were the Sprites which took the first three places in their class. John Sprinzel, former keen racing and rally exponent with an Austin A35, led the team to victory; the first of many successful sorties in international events for the Sprinzel/Sprite combination.

On the same week-end as Sprinzel and his co-driver, Willy Cave, were winning the Sprite's first international rally honours on the Alpine, John Anstice-Brown was recording the Sprite's first racing success, a thousand miles away in Ireland. Anstice-Brown had entered a Sprite in the Leinster Trophy Race, a handicap event run in two 72-mile heats over the famous 4-mile Dunboyne circuit. The Sprite beat all comers with a race speed of a little under 65 mile/h. Such was the successful competition début for the Sprite one eventful week-end in July 1958.

Although the Sprite's impressive début in the 1958 Alpine has not been equalled, the model's record of achievement in subsequent Alpine trials is not disappointing. Motoring journalists Tommy Wisdom and Jack Hay finished second in their class in the 1959 Alpine; they were also placed second in the general classification for G T cars. Sprinzel and Cave suffered gearbox troubles in the 1960 event, but had better fortune in the following year when they finished runners-up in the class. John Williamson and David Hiam were similarly placed in the 1962 Alpine.

The Sprite can claim a pretty fair record of success in the Liège-Rome-Liège Rally, the 3,000-mile Marathon upon spine-shattering tracks over which a careful Sprite owner would hesitate to crawl at a snail's pace let alone press on at racing speeds, for 5 days and nights. After being eliminated with a smashed stub axle in the 1958 Liège, John Sprinzel, partnered by Stuart Turner, brought a privately entered Sprite to win the class in 1959 and finish eighth amongst the 14 finishers out of the 104 which started! Surpassing even this performance, the tireless Sprinzel returned the following year and, with co-driver John Patten, won the class again. This time the privately entered Sprite, which was the smallest car to finish, was placed third overall amongst the 13 finishers. A truly remarkable achievement somewhat overshadowed perhaps by the sensational outright win by Pat Moss/Ann Wisdom in the 'big Healey'.

In early R.A.C. Rallies there was always a strong Sprite entry, and since 1959 Sprites have twice been placed second overall and twice won the class. Tommy Gold and Mike Hughes were overall runners-up and class winners in 1959. John Sprinzel and Dick Bensted-Smith repeated this performance in the following year. Behind Sprinzel in 1960, taking second and third places in the class, came Pat Moss/Ann Wisdom and Roy Kirkham/Peter Baldham.

The Sprite has always had a strong following in Ireland, where it is a very popular driving-test car, and the combination of the Sprite plus local driver talent has produced many class wins on the Circuit of Ireland. On two occasions Sprites have won the Circuit outright, Adrian Boyd in 1960 and Ian Woodside in 1963.

Because the Sprite arrived on the scene at the heyday of the 'big Healey' domination of international rallies, the model has sadly never had the benefit of extensive rally development from the Competitions Department at Abingdon, thus all of the Sprites' rallying successes have been achieved by the private owners.

Deserving special mention in this sphere are Horace Appleby/Robert McGhie who enjoyed three very active seasons rallying a Sprite; Tommy Gold/Mike Hughes who have made several international sorties; Mr and Mrs Ian Miller who were regular Monte Carlo Rally competitors with a Mark I Sprite; and Barry Shawzin who had an ambitious season in 1961. But Douglas Wilson-Spratt must head the list of successful private owners with 10 international rallies to his credit.

Sprite record breaking

In September 1959 the Development Department at Abingdon built a special record-breaking Sprite, Ex. 219. This had a low-drag streamlined body designed on the lines of the famous Goldie Gardiner and George Eyston record cars. The Sprite engine was modified, using catalogue parts available from the Competitions Department and a Shorrock supercharger was fitted. The object of these preparations was to attack International Class G records (750–1,100 cc). The trip across the Atlantic to the world's favourite high-speed record ground at Utah's Bonneville Salt Flats was well worth while, as John Thornley tells:

'Conditions in the morning were well-nigh ideal and a gentle breeze blew from the north at about 4 mile/h, keeping everything pleasantly cool. Tommy Wisdom took first stint and started just after 6.30 a m. It took him rather less than two laps to get settled down and to "find his way round", and thereafter he covered a further 42 laps with quite exemplary regularity. Gus Ehrman then took over, followed by Ed Leavens and then Tommy again, each taking roughly a 3-hour stint. It is significant that throughout the 12 hours, during which 168 laps were covered, with the exception of those laps which were interrupted by pit stops, no more than 10 secs separated fastest and slowest laps, a variation of plus and minus 2 per cent of the mean running speed.

'Driving round and round this circle is a monotonous occupation, even at 140 mile/h, and so to keep the driver amused the pit flew a wide variety of signals. The lap speed achieved on the lap next but one preceding was shown in large numerals each time round, with "Faster", "Slower" and "O.K." signals as occasions warranted. As each record fell the news was conveyed on a blackboard and, as the end of each stint approached, illustrations of mugs of beer and rows of bottles arranged on the top of a crate also appeared by way of encouragement.

'So the 12-hour record was safely wrapped up at 138·75 mile/h, over 3 mile/h faster than our target, taking eight other International Class "G" records on the way. At the conclusion of the 12 hours, an extra lap was covered in order to bring in that American National 12-hour record which rates from a flying start.

'We have never previously run on the Salt so late in the year, and this meant that there was barely 14 hours of daylight, which not only gave small enough margin for a 12-hour run, but also meant that at the beginning and the end the driver was certain to have the sun straight in his face on some part of the circle.

'With the 12-hour completed, the car was towed away to Wendover for the engine to be changed to the sprint version in readiness for an attack on the hour record the following afternoon. The boys worked in shifts through the night and the car was out on the Salt just after mid-day. Gus Ehrman was to make this run and, as soon as everything was ready, he moved off, with the soft plugs in, for his warming-up laps. As he left the pit area and changed into second gear, the engine went up to something above 6,000 rev/min, sounding as if it was fitted with an hydraulic torque converter. Nobody said anything, but I am sure we all thought, "The clot! He can change gear better than that!" Before he had gone a quarter of a lap it was obvious to the intent listeners at the pit that all was not well. The engine speed rose and fell while the speed of the car was obviously substantially constant. Clutch slip – no two ways about it.

'Mental apologies to Gus for being so hasty.

'Now this clutch had stood full torque on the test-bed back at Abingdon, and there was no known reason why it should slip. The inference was therefore that there was some defect in the hydraulic operating mechanism which was obstructing its full engagement. The car was brought back, put up on its ramp, and Alec Hounslow and Bill Pringle crawled underneath for a look-see, intent on disconnecting the hydraulic operating cylinder so that with a push-start we could check the clutch operation again.

'This occasion provoked the greatest possible regret that I had not got the tape recorder with me. With the car fitted with an undertray, the operating cylinder was sandwiched in between the bell-housing and the tray, and there was not enough room to get the set bolts out. Bill Pringle is an Australian and Alec Hounslow is – well, Alec Hounslow, and a record of the running fire of dead-pan cross-talk which went on between these two would have got itself into the Top Ten in no time at all! Never have so many exquisite lines been thrown away.

'Never has the parentage of slave cylinders, set bolts, undertrays and Sprites in general been so much in doubt.

'In the end, with the aid of a portable generating set and a pistol drill, a flap was cut in the undertray in order to get the bolts out, but on a re-run the clutch still let go at maximum torque, so the inference was that the previous slipping had "cooked it", and it was evident that the engine would have to come out. So, back to Wendover.

'Crises of this kind invariably ensure that the Abingdon boys will be seen at their splendid best, and this was to be no exception. Asked how long it would take to do the job, Alec said he expected to be finished the following afternoon. "So we can plan to run tomorrow evening?" "Well, you know how these things are – better say Sunday morning."

'The boys were divided into two shifts, one of which went straight off to bed, while the other set about removing the engine, cheerfully facing the prospect of a second consecutive all-night session. The means adopted to check the torque capacity of the clutch would make a story in itself, were there time and space here. Suffice it to say that with an odd piece of iron bar welded to a socket wrench, and a spring balance borrowed from the local Post Office, sufficiently accurate indications were obtained to enable a satisfactory clutch to be built, using some bits off the spare engine and some washers under the springs. The important feature of the night's work was, however, that by 5 a m the boys were ready to put the body shell back on, and by 9 a m (Saturday) we were all out on the Salt again ready to go.

'Twelve hours' pounding on the circle had caused the Salt to break up in a couple of places, such that Tommy Wisdom had reported in

The car that started a new era of small sports car motoring – the Mark I Sprite announced in May 1958. Easy access to the engine and front suspension was provided by the one-piece hinged bonnet

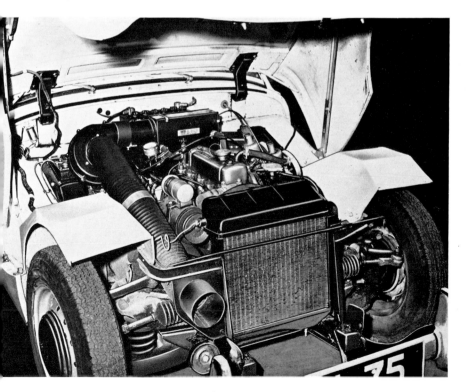

The restyled Sprite Mark II offered improved cockpit comforts and a lockable boot. The later 1098 cc engine brought an increase in performance and front disc brakes were also fitted.

The Sprite Mark III had wind-up windows and quarter-lights.

The Sprite Mark IV had the 1275 cc engine and a one-piece convertible-type hood

Awaiting their turn to clock out on the Mountain Circuit test on the 1959 Monte Carlo Rally, Tommy Wisdom and the late Douglas Johns in one of only two works rallying Sprites ever built

John Sprinzel with his famous 'Sebring' Sprite PMO 200, a combination associated with so many outstanding competition successes

Tommy Wisdom and Alec Hounslow of Abingdon's Development Department with the Sprite record-breaker which established the 12 Hours record at Utah in 1959 at a speed of 138·75 mile/h

Functional cockpit of EX 219, the Utah Sprite record breaker

One of the most successful Sprite privateers was Doug Wilson-Spratt who has ten international rallies to his credit, many of them driven in his own special-bodied coupés

Amongst the most successful club racing drivers with the Sprite was Mike Garton, who commenced his racing career with this car and later went on to achieve many successes with an ex-Le Mans car

This special-bodied Sprite won its class at Le Mans in 1960, driven by John Dalton and John Colgate, averaging 85·6 mile/h. The strange bodywork was to take full advantage of the sports car regulations of the day

The well-known supercharged Sprite of Paddy Gaston that gained countless club racing successes in the early 1960s

Sprites at Sebring in 1961, with Walt Hangsen being hard pressed by Stirling Moss

Le Mans start at Sebring in the following year, with the familiar figure of Stirling Moss level-pegging with film star Steve McQueen, who also drove in the works Sprite team

Pit stop for the works Sprite in the 1965 Targa Florio, an event in which Clive Baker and Rauno Aaltonen have performed with regular distinction

Built for the 1967 Racing Car Show, this road-going version of the works racing coupés was one of the most attractive bodies produced at Warwick

Two Le Mans Sprites in the 1966 race

On their way to winning the 'Motor' Trophy for highest placed British car at Le Mans in 1967, Clive Baker and Andrew Hedges. The same car, driven by Alec Poole and Roger Enever, won the same trophy in the following year

Richard Groves bought a pair of ex-works Sprites and gained several international successes with drivers Clive Baker and John Moore. This is the team with their class-winning laurels after the 1965 Nurburgring 1000 kms

Sprites have, of course, been tremendously popular in S.C.C.A. racing. This is 1967 National Class 'G' Champion Jerry Truitt in the car prepared by Hank Thorpe

Eight years separate these pictures which illustrate the continued popularity of the Sprite in club racing. *Above* Mark Is at Mallory Park in 1959, running in very standard form with road tyres. *Below* The start of a more recent marque sports car race at Brands Hatch, with all models of Sprite represented

Above An early BN 1 engine with cold air box instead of the more normal twin air cleaners

Left The very much more complex under-bonnet layout of the later '3000' Mark II

Left and below
The three-carburetter 132 b h p engine of the '3000' Mark II

Concours example of the very accessible Mark I Sprite engine

Plain but perfectly functional driving compartment of the Sprite Mark I and II

Luxurious interior of the last of the production 'big Healeys' – the '3000'
Mark III

Typical cockpit modifications on the later works Healey '3000s' included stop
watches, Halda twin master, fuses mounted on the centre console, overdrive
switch on the gearlever and a host of light switches

Above The 2-litre Healey-Climax built for Le Mans in 1968 being tested at Silverstone by John Harris

Below Power-house of the last of the works rally '3000s' built for the ill-fated R.A.C. Rally of 1967. This engine, with the rare aluminium block and triple Weber carburetters, produced 200 b h p

the last hours of the run that going through the rough knocked some five to six hundred revs off the speed. It was therefore decided that, for the hour, Gus should swing wide outside the rough patches on to fresh, reasonably firm salt. Furthermore, in view of the high speeds involved, tyres were fitted which had had the majority of the tread buffed off in advance to reduce the risk of tread throwing. The combination of these two factors was to cause some excitement.

'After the preliminary warming-up laps Gus took off at the drop of the flag, and his second lap was at a speed of 153 mile/h. Out went the slow sign. On Lap 5, when swinging out to miss the first patch of rough stuff, he lost adhesion and spun away into the middle distance. He kept the engine going and got back on course, but this lap had taken 45 secs longer than it should have done, and altered the whole picture.

'Quick calculation showed, however, that, barring further incidents, if speed were maintained at just over 150 mile/h for the lap, the record could still be taken fairly comfortably. However, on Lap 13 it happened again. This time, having been outside the second patch of rough, Gus "dropped it" when pulling in to resume station close up against the marking stakes. This time he spun inside the circle and in the bewildering excitement of the gyrations forgot the necessity to rejoin the course at the point of leaving it. This meant that he travelled for about a mile inside the circle and was promptly disqualified. Back to Square One. . . .

'In view of the fact that the car had been lapping satisfactorily at 143 mile/h and over during the 12-hour run, and that a steady lap speed of 147 would be sufficient for the hour, the treaded 12-hour tyres were put back on the car, and a fresh start made. This done, the laps ticked off with splendid regularity and 146·95 miles were covered in the hour, five other International records falling on the way.'

Speedwell-modified Sprites have enjoyed many competition successes, one of the best known being the car owned and driven by John Venner-Pack. To find out how fast this particular car would go, in 1960 Speedwell took Venner-Pack's G T coupé and a special-bodied streamlined Sprite to Belgium for timed runs. The drivers were Graham Hill and George Hulbert. Despite poor weather conditions, the G T coupé recorded 110·9 mile/h over the flying kilometre, whilst the stream-lined car reached 132·2 mile/h. Both cars collected respective Belgium National Class 'G' records.

Racing with the Sprite

The 12 Hour Race at Sebring and the 24 Hour Race at Le Mans
have witnessed the Sprite's principle entries in the sphere of international racing, 'works' cars being entered by the Donald Healey
Motor Company along with 'Sebrings' by John Sprinzel.

For the 1959 Sebring 12 Hour Race, three 'works' cars were
prepared by Donald Healey to be driven by Canadian and American
amateurs. The Sprites put up a commendable high-speed demonstration to take the first three places in their class and carry off the
manufacturers' team prize. The class winning car, driven by Hugh
Sutherland/Phil Stiles, averaged 64 mile/h for the 12 hours. In the
following year at Sebring, Stirling Moss was engaged to drive a
Sprite in the 4 Hour Race. Stirling finished second overall to a Fiat-
Abarth but won the class averaging 71 mile/h. Donald Healey and
John Sprinzel headed rival Sprite teams for the 1961 Sebring races,
both the 4 and 12 Hour events. For the 4 Hour Race, Donald Healey
signed up such notables as Bruce McLaren, Walt Hangsen, Ed Leavens
and Briggs Cunningham. John Sprinzel's 'Sebrings' were in the hands
of Pat and Stirling Moss.

Pat Moss recalls the only occasion that she has driven against her
brother:

'I was invited to drive in a race at Sebring and, although I do not
like racing, I did like the idea of going to Florida in March, so I
accepted the offer.

'It came through John Sprinzel who was competing with and
selling Sebring Sprites like mad, and it was a Sprite that I was to drive.
Stirling was in the same race in another Sprite and again the offer came
through John, although the car belonged to another man called Cyril
Simson.

'In practice my car ran perfectly, although it was not nearly as
fast as the Fiat-Abarths. Stirling's car had a dicky clutch which slowed
him down a lot, so being a nice little sister, I offered to let him have
my car, and the owners agreed to the swop.

'I was pretty twitched as we stood there at the Le Mans start, but
Stirling and Dan Gurney, next in line, were very nice. They both told
me just to relax and then run like mad across the track when the flag
fell. They managed to convince me I was not going to be killed by
other cars before I reached mine.

'And when the flag fell I sprinted like mad, got the car door open quickly and stabbed my foot on the clutch and started the engine before I even closed the door again. The car was already in gear, of course, so once the engine fired I was off and had the biggest thrill of my life. I beat Stirling away on a Le Mans start. And he was supposed to be unbeatable at that.

'So I led the race into the first corner and along part of the straight and then the pack started passing. The roadholding of the Sprite was very nice but it was not fast enough for the Abarths and I could not hold Stirling in his car, especially with my bad clutch. After an hour or so it was unusable so I started changing gear without it, but B.M.C. boxes are not all that good without a clutch and I became worried that I might wreck the gearbox. The owner was entered for the big race that night in the same car so, after an hour, I decided to pull in and let him know the position.

'He decided to take it on himself, probably to make sure he got a drive, because it would be pointless to start in the 12 Hour Race with the car in that condition and I do not think he had full facilities for repairs.'

In the 12 Hour Race, a sports Lola robbed the Sprites of class victory, the two Healey-entered cars finishing in second and third places. John Sprinzel recounts how he fared driving the car with Stirling Moss:

'We were leading our class fair and square when, after about three hours, the head gasket blew. This was a very common fault on the early "Sebrings". The regulations at Sebring say that you have to do all the work on the car yourself, using either tools from the pit or tools that are on board the car. I had to walk back to the pits which was some three miles away, collect all the tools and walk back again, accompanied by a marshal to make sure that I obeyed all the rules. I stripped off the head, removed the gasket and then found that there was a nasty burn on the cylinder head between the two cylinders, so there was nothing to do but push the damned thing all the way to the pit.

'That very nearly killed me and I don't think I would have made it but for this little short-legged marshal who ran beside me all the way, urging me on and keeping me going with bottles of orange squash. Of course, no one was allowed to help me with the pushing otherwise the car would have been disqualified.

'When I finally collapsed at the pits, the boys pinched a cylinder head from a car parked nearby, smuggled it into the pits and after about an hour got it fitted on to the race car. But it was all worth while because, despite spending some four of the 12 hours walking, we finally finished the event.'

For the 1963 Sebring 12 Hour Race the special-bodied 'works' coupé Sprite of John Colgate/Clive Baker performed brilliantly to lead the class and the index of performance until the 11th hour when a fractured oil pipe caused their retirement. Again, in 1964, at Sebring, the Colgate/Baker Sprite was eliminated with engine troubles within an hour of the finish when lying incredibly well placed.

Better fortunes came in 1965 when the Warwick-entered Sprites set out on a hat trick of Sebring class wins, Clive Baker and Rauno Aaltonen winning in 1965 and 1967, while Timo Makinen and Paul Hawkins took the honours in 1966.

The Sprite at Le Mans

For the 1960 Le Mans race, Donald Healey entered a single car, hardly recognizable externally as a Sprite, for the complex Le Mans regulations that year excluded cars of under 1,000 cc in the G T class. Thus the Sprite appeared with a very non-standard sports body to qualify for the sports-racing class. Nevertheless this strange little machine fulfilled its purpose and, driven by John Dalton and John Colgate, won its class by completing 2,055 miles in the 24 hours at an average speed of 85·6 mile/h. A pair of prettier fixed-head coupé Sprites contested the 24 Hour Race in the following year but one car was eliminated with mechanical troubles and the second crashed. In the 1963 race the John Whitmore/Bob Olthoff 'works' coupé Sprite performed splendidly to average fractionally over 100 mile/h for eight hours when an accident forced its retirement.

Clive Baker and Bill Bradley fared better in 1964, finishing 24th overall, while Paul Hawkins and John Rhodes won their class in the following year. Neither of the two works cars finished in 1966, but both Clive Baker/Andrew Hedges and Alec Poole/Roger Enever finished 15th overall in 1967 and 1968 respectively, both crews winning the *Motor* Trophy for the highest placed British crew and car.

Private owners

Of other racing successes, Geoff Williamson won his class in the Coupe du Salon at Montlhéry in 1959 and towards the close of that season, Team Sprite ('Mac' MacKenzie, Paddy Gaston and Chris Tooley) won the hotly contested Team Trophy and finished 1–2–3 in the class for the *Autosport* championship. John Sprinzel's 'Sebrings' had a highly successful racing season in 1961, drivers Ian Walker, Paul Hawkins and Cyril Simson scoring numerous national and club victories in addition to their international achievements. A team of six 'Sebrings' won the national Six-Hour Relay Race at Silverstone in 1961. Of other privateers, Paddy Gaston put up some determined drives with a supercharged Sprite against the higher capacity machinery with which he has raced.

Other successful Sprite privateers include Peter Jackson, Mike Reid, Mike White, John Harris, Mike Garton, John Moore and Jack Wheeler.

Although the Sprite has never achieved outstanding success in the field of international competition it is more widely known for its popularity in all branches of the sport at club level. The Sprite has proved to be an ideal club rally car, it has provided cheap and safe motor racing for many and it is unbeatable as a driving-test machine.

Since 1958 some 250,000 'Spridgets' have been built at Abingdon (125,000 Sprites and 125,000 Midgets); if not strictly a production record for one 'model', certainly a record for a basic sports car design which has served to bring to so many enthusiasts their first taste of sports car motoring.

CHAPTER 11

THE HEALEY-CLIMAX — THE FUTURE

The British Leyland merger and the end of production of the Austin-Healey '3000' in 1967 heralded the end of the 15-year association between the Donald Healey Motor Company and the British Motor Corporation.

Midway through the 1968 season it was announced that all future British Leyland Competition activities were to be centralized at the Competitions Department at Abingdon. Thus no further sponsorship would be possible for Donald Healey's racing programme as had been the case in the past. Inevitably this meant that the Warwick Company could not afford to continue racing Austin-Healeys – indeed it was not really now in their interests to do so.

Furthermore with the sales of the 'Sprite' comparing unfavourably with those of the MG Midget (particularly in the States) it was clear that British Leyland's plan of model rationalization would soon bring about the complete demise of the marque Austin-Healey.

Although the Warwick Company were at this time working on the production of a replacement for the '3000', using the Rolls-Royce 4 litre engine in a wider version of the 'big Healey' body, this design like the '3000' would have fallen foul of the American Safety and Air Polution Regulations. And so, as Donald Healey's contract with B.M.C. ran only until 1971, it was mutually agreed that there would be no new Austin-Healey models.

Although understandably sad at this state of affairs, Donald Healey met the challenge and, perhaps with an eye to future British Leyland Competition plans, produced for the 1968 Le Mans race the 2 litre Healey-Climax 'SR'.

In appearance the car resembled the classic profiles of the successful current sports racing prototypes, but its construction was entirely different, using a chassis-platform design (very similar to that of the Sprite) rather than the conventional space frame. This made the car immensely strong and, although the car had a 2 litre engine fitted, it was designed to take any power unit up to 4 litres. A further advantage of using a platform chassis was that it would be quite a simple job to put this sort of chassis into limited production which would not be the case with space frame construction.

The power unit used was the well-proven 2 litre V8 Coventry-Climax Grand Prix engine. Producing 240 b h p at 9,000 rev/min, the engine was fitted with Lucas fuel injection and the drive was through a Hewland five-speed gearbox. At 9,000 rev/min, speeds through the gears were impressive to say the least – 72 mile/h in 1st, 107 mile/h in 2nd, 135 mile/h in 3rd, 162 mile/h in 4th and 180 mile/h in top. The engine was centre-mounted in the chassis in conventional sports car racing fashion with twin radiators mounted at the side above the long fuel tanks.

The car was produced in a remarkably short time and with great secrecy behind locked doors at Warwick, the design being completely handled by Geoff Healey and Barrie Bilbie with the technical assistance of Wally Hassan from Coventry-Climax.

At Le Mans the car was driven by Clive Baker and Andrew Hedges and, although no one expected too much from a lone entry in its first outing, it was disappointing that the car was retired after less than two hours' running with gear selection troubles. However, the car's performance was certainly competitive for a 2 litre machine and this encouraged Healeys to enter a slightly lowered and lighter version of the original car for the 1969 Le Mans race, driven by John Harris and Clive Baker. The team suffered very bad luck to have a radiator punctured by a flying stone in the early stages of the race.

Looking to the future of the Healey Company is no easy task at the time of writing because an air of secrecy has always tended to surround the activities of the small but industrious Warwick firm. However, it is clear that Donald Healey has no regrets at the recent liberation from his B.M.C. committments. Now in his 72nd year and still retaining that eternal suntan and ageless appearance, Donald Healey is more than happy to develop some of his own quite revolutionary automobile engineering ideas. It is no secret that he is quite an expert on steam cars and he firmly believes (and is determined to prove) that steam power is a really practical solution to the current American Air Polution problems. Furthermore, I am sure that it will not be very long before we shall again be seeing the Healey Company producing a highly desirable, limited-production sports car under their own name.

Whatever the future holds in store, the name of Donald Healey will for all time be associated with a classic series of truly outstanding British sports cars.

INTRODUCTION TO THE APPENDICES

It has been the aim in the next part of this book to gather together all the available information on the various models of Healey and Austin-Healey cars into one compact volume.

In compiling these Appendices, I should like to express my thanks to John Gott and John Chatham for assistance with the 'big Healey' section, to Mike Garton for the 'Sprite' section, to Brian Dermott, Eric Hall, Robin Church and other members of the Healey Register of the Austin-Healey Club, for the section on Warwick cars. In addition, of course, a tremendous amount of assistance was freely given by Geoff Price, Geoff Healey and others at the Donald Healey Motor Company, by the British Leyland Motor Corporation and by many others.

The specifications are as accurate as it is possible to make them from contemporary material, but the authors must disclaim responsibility for the consequences of any inaccuracies. It is also important to bear in mind that most Healeys have by now seen a hard life, and care should be taken to ensure that all parts are in perfect condition before any attempt is made to improve the performance of the car.

The list of International results has only been taken to the end of 1968; since then the 'Sprite' has achieved further class awards at Sebring and elsewhere, but we had to stop somewhere!

LES NEEDHAM.

APPENDIX I

THE COMPETITION CAREER OF DONALD HEALEY

Year	Event	Car	Notes
1923	London–Lands End Trial	A.B.C.	First major event – wrecked valve gear on Porlock
1924	London–Lands End Trial	Riley	Car burnt out on way to start
		Substituted A.B.C.	Won first Gold Medal
	Lands End–John O'Groats Trial	Ariel 10	Gold Medal
1925	London–Lands End	Ariel 10	Gold Medal
	J.C.C. High Speed Trial, Brooklands	Ariel 10	First outing at Brooklands. Gold Medal
	Lands End–John O'Groats–Lands End (officially observed R.A.C. petrol consumption test)	Ariel 10	Petrol consumption 52 m p g at average speed of 20 mile/h
1926	London–Lands End	Fiat 7	Gold Medal
1927	London–Lands End	Rover 10	Gold Medal
1928	London–Lands End	Triumph 7	Silver Medal
	Bournemouth Rally	Triumph 7	Premier Award, starting from John O'Groats
1929	Monte Carlo Rally (Riga start)	Triumph 7	Unable to reach Riga, returned to Berlin and started there. 2 minutes outside time limit at Monte. Won class at Mont des Mules hill climb.
	London–Lands End	Triumph 7 supercharged	Gold Medal
	Brighton Rally	Triumph 7	Premier award, starting from John O'Groats
	Riga–Barcelona	Triumph 7	Class win, best British car
1930	Monte Carlo Rally (Tallinn start)	Triumph 7	Snow and ice all the way. Seventh overall, first British car.
	London–Lands End	Fiat 10	Gold Medal
	Austrian Alpine Trial	Invicta	Won Glacier Cup for penalty free run. Fastest climb of Arlberg Hill.

Year	Event	Car	Notes
1930	International Alford Alpine Trial	Invicta	Won Glacier Cup
1931	Monte Carlo Rally (Stavanger start)	Invicta	Made best time in final test. Won Rally outright.
	International 10,000 km Trial	Riley 2 litre	Longest trial ever organized traversing 37 countries in 14 days, finishing in Berlin. No marks lost, won First Award.
1931	Paris–Nice	Riley Nine	Class win
	La Turbie Hill Climb	Riley Nine	Class win
	International Alpine Trial	Invicta	Fastest climb of Galibier. Glacier Cup.
1932	Monte Carlo Rally (Umea start)	Invicta	Second overall, first British car
	International Alpine Rally	Invicta	Fastest climb of Stelvio. Won Glacier Cup.
	Klausen Hill Climb	Invicta	2nd in unlimited class
	Tourist Trophy Race	Invicta	Seized axle in practice
	Brighton Speed Trials	Invicta	Tied for fastest time in class with Kay Petre who borrowed and drove same car
	Paris–Nice Rally	Invicta	Won class
1933	Monte Carlo Rally (Tallinn start)	Invicta	Crashed in Poland
	International Alpine Rally	Brooklands Riley	2nd in class
1934	Monte Carlo Rally (Athens start)	Triumph 10	Second overall. First British car.
	International Alpine Rally	Triumph 10	Class fastest on Stelvio. Won Glacier Cup.
1935	Monte Carlo Rally (Umea start)	Triumph Dolomite	Hit train in Denmark – unhurt
1936	Monte Carlo Rally	Triumph Dolomite	Eighth overall, first British car
	International Alpine Rally	Triumph 14	Won Glacier Cup
1937	Monte Carlo Rally (Palermo start)	Triumph 12	Retired with engine trouble
1948	Mille Miglia	Healey 'Westland'	Ninth overall, first British car
	Rally des Alpes	Healey 'Westland'	Lost marks through stopping to aid injured driver.
1949	Mille Miglia	Healey 'Elliot'	Fourth in touring category (Son Geoff won touring category in Roadster)

Year	Event	Car	Notes
1949	Rally des Alpes	'Silverstone'	Lost one mark through hold up at Level Crossing
1950	Mille Miglia	Nash-Healey	Failed to qualify after going into ditch
1951	Mille Miglia	Nash-Healey	Finished 30th overall
1952	Mille Miglia	Nash-Healey Saloon	Crashed after busting tyre
1953	U.S.A. (Bonneville) Record Breaking	Austin-Healey '100'	International Records from 1,000 km to 5,000 km and 6 hours to 24 hours. American records from 1 km to 5,000 km and 24 hours. American flying mile 142·64 mile/h
1954	U.S.A. (Bonneville) Record Breaking	Austin-Healey '100-S'	International Records from 5 km to 5,000 km and 1 hour to 24 hours. American records 1 km to 5,000 km and 24 hours. American flying mile 192·62 mile/h
1956	U.S.A. (Bonneville) Record Breaking	Austin-Healey '100-Six'	Maximum speed reached 203·11 mile/h

APPENDIX II

TUNING THE RILEY-ENGINED, WARWICK-BUILT CARS

For this section we are indebted to Brian Dermott, Eric Hall and Robin Church who, in the course of a very informative evening, divulged the following information on the Riley-engined cars. There is naturally a bias towards the 'Silverstone', but a lot of the basic details also apply to the saloon and roadster models.

To quote Brian, 'Don't get the idea that the Healey is a fabulous car to go racing in – only just over 100 "Silverstones" were built, and then the Jaguar came along, which was a far better racing car. But if you want to have a lot of fun with a fairly ordinary car, the Healey takes a lot of beating.'

All the Healey chassis were basically the same; the front suspension was the unique Healey trailing link pattern, and the rear suspension remained basically the same for all models, although the saloons had lever-arm shock-absorbers whilst the 'Silverstone' had Woodhead-Munroe telescopic shockers. The 'F' and 'G' chassis were fitted with the later Riley back axles, with an open propellor shaft as distinct from the enclosed torque-tube pattern used on all the earlier cars. To get a better weight distribution on the 'Silverstone', the engine was 8 in. further back in the chassis, which had an extra cross member under the radiator.

It is important to realize that the Riley engine has a very long stroke (120 mm) and the normally accepted safe piston speed of 2,500 ft/sec. occurs at just under 70 mile/h with standard gearing. In addition, out of a total weight of 19 cwt, some 15 cwt is concentrated in: the engine and gearbox (7 cwt), back axle and torque tube (5–6 cwt), and the chassis ($1\frac{1}{2}$ cwt), so there is obviously not much scope for lightening. It might be possible to fit the later open prop-shaft to the car, but this would probably upset the balance of fore and aft weight distribution and would also rather get away from the spirit of preserving an historic car. The similar comments apply to the suggestion of fitting a Jaguar engine to the car – a modification which *can* be done if ample workshop facilities are available.

This chapter, therefore, is more concerned in the preparation of a standard car for racing, rather than with out-and-out tuning.

First of all, the car has got to be absolutely clean underneath the frame and on the running gear so that the scrutineer and others can see what is going on. All parts should be functioning properly, all the bearings should be tight, all the rubber grommets should be renewed and it should be in perfect road running condition.

Starting from the back of the car, from the racing point of view, one has got a situation where there is a 16-gallon petrol tank, sitting about 12 in.

above two batteries, and the division between the two is just a couple of sheets of tin! The bottom of the battery boxes should be reinforced with a piece of steel which should be cut to size and welded on. Two battery bolts should be either soldered or welded in position at the bottom of the boxes, so that the batteries can then be placed in position and clamped down (take care not to break the corners off by tightening up too hard). Then, to complete the job, a rubber cover should be fitted right across the top of the batteries, to stop any chance of petrol dropping on them. The two 6 volt batteries are connected by a cable which, under racing conditions, can chafe against the torque tube. A bracket and a P.K. screw can adequately fix this in a safe position.

The petrol tank itself is of very good construction and is firmly fitted into the chassis. The weak point is that the filler cap is fixed into the outside bodywork and if the car is knocked or crashed, the body flexing can move the hose between tank and filler. This should be replaced with convoluted hose, which has got more sideways give.

The spare wheel is removed (when regulations permit this). One of the works cars (Charles Mortimer's OPA2) had a panel in the resulting hole, but it is felt that it is best to leave the hole to assist cooling of the rear brakes and axle. It also enables the scrutineer to see the rear axle!

On the rear suspension three things require attention – shockabsorbers, clearance round the wheel arches and the panhard rod. The panhard rod must be correctly set up with the car jacked up by the back axle. Measure the distance from the brake drums to the chassis frame, and then adjust the rods accordingly. It is advisable to give an extra $\frac{1}{4}$ in. clearance on the offside to allow for the angle of the rod. The rubber bushes in the panhard rod are in fact exactly the same as the bushes in the Mini engine tie bar front end. They require replacing fairly frequently because they get chewed up quite a lot, due to the sideways thrust. On the saloons, there is a tendency for the bracket which attaches the panhard rod to the axle casing to break. This should be strengthened by welding extra steel bracing around it. It is also worth replacing the fixing bolts, which go through the bush and panhard rod, with high-tensile bolts as the original ones are fairly soft. Clearance under the 'Silverstone' wheel arches is pretty good, although every car seems to have its wings in a slightly different position. Take care that the wings are fitted with the bolt heads on the outside. If the shanks are outside, it is possible for the wheel to touch the inside of the wheel arch and to carve grooves in the tyres.

The original shockabsorbers are virtually unobtainable, as they were Woodhead-Munroe, with a very short travel. Koni do one that is suitable, and which can be fitted without too much trouble. The bottom mountings for the rear shockabsorbers can give trouble as they sometimes snap off due to fatigue. The back axle fixings should be checked and all bearings renewed. If it is desired to remove the pinion, a special tool is required (this consists of a piece of $\frac{1}{4}$ plate steel, machined to fit round the pinion and fitting into the two stops). There were several optional axle ratios, but for most racing purposes the normal 3·5:1 is probably the best compromise.

The bundy tubing to the brakes should be checked, in particular where it goes into the union for the rear axle (where rust can form) and where it comes out from the rear of the master cylinder (where it can chafe the bottom of the driver's floor). Replacement bundy tubing can be obtained quite easily from Edmunds Walker, who will bend it to pattern if required.

The handbrake presents no problems, other than usual maintenance. Whilst the 'D'-type 'Silverstone' has bucket type seats the 'E'-type has a bench seat which should be replaced for racing. The space available ($16\frac{1}{2}$ in.) is very narrow, so it virtually means getting a special shell made up and having it covered. The 'D'-type has a slightly smaller steering wheel.

The standard throttle cable is very prone to sticking. Two solutions are possible. Firstly, fit one of the SPQR Mini throttle pedal conversions to the bulkhead (after replacing the original steel cotter pin with a high-tensile one) and then use the throttle cable assembly from the saloon, which can be obtained from Jonathan Bowers (see note at end of this section). The Mini throttle cable could be used, but the Healey Saloon one is held positively in position. The alternative method of dealing with the throttle sticking problem is to retain the original outer cable, but to replace the inner with a piece of speedo cable, with the original cable ends brazed on. This gives a very smooth action. There must be an on-off ignition and pump switch on the dashboard, which must be clearly marked with its purpose and 'off' position.

The original exhaust pipe was aluminium, which went all the way round the inside of the rear wheel arch. It is probably better to shorten this so that the exhaust comes out of the side just in front of the rear wheel. The original silencers are still available – they are very long and thin to fit in the gap between the body and chassis. The usual mountings are quite adequate, but the flexible connection on the down pipe can give some trouble. It is possible to run with a completely welded-up, solid system, just relying on the movement in the rubber buffers on the silencer mounting but care should be exercised that engine movement doesn't cause breakages.

Make sure that the back of the gearbox is supported by the reinforced 'Silverstone' type gearbox mounting. The saloon mounting consisted of the usual two steel plates bonded together by rubber, but this, when fitted to the 'Silverstone', tended to vibrate badly, so an extra vertical piece of steel was added so that the rubber is supported on three sides. Also the check cable between the gearbox and the cruciform should be in good condition, otherwise the engine will continue through the radiator on braking!

This cable is adjustable, and when the engine is fitted, the cable should be tensioned until the rear engine mounting is upright.

The front suspension works very well, provided care is taken to keep all the bearings in perfect condition. (Replacement bearings are all readily available from Jonathan Bowers.) The weak point is the felt waterproofing seal on the trailing-link pivot-bearing housings. These should be greased very frequently to keep the bearings waterproofed although, when new, care should be taken not to burst the seal by pumping in too much grease. Moly-di-Sulphide grease is probably best for the job.

Check that the upright wheel brackets are not bent by putting a camber gauge on them. Hard knocks at the front end can bend these uprights, resulting in some very fancy readings with the gauge! Kingpins and stub axles are all obtainable from Jonathan Bowers, and should be replaced if there is any doubt about their condition. The correct fitting tolerances for these are quite critical. If the kingpin is loose in the wheel bracket, the only real solution is to have the bracket built up and then machined out. This, of course, is a common trouble encountered with beam axle front ends as well.

The central bearing of the steering swivel plate, which is located in the centre of the frame, requires replacing occasionally. Again the fit of the bearing and spindle is critical, it probably being best to get a slightly oversized bearing and have the pin turned to give a really positive fit. Once again Jonathan Bowers can give the necessary assistance. If the bearing is not absolutely tight on the pin, the swivel plate will wobble up and down slightly. It can be heard if you shake the steering wheel slightly in the garage with the engine switched off. The steering box itself is secured by means of a cast aluminium clamp (rather similar to a big end cap), which is not very strong. With continual tightening, the clamp can be distorted, which allows the box to move, thus tending to wear the aluminium away and aggravate the trouble. To cure this the cap should be removed, the shoulders filed slightly and the 'bearing' surface rescraped in the same way that old-style white metal bearings could be rescraped. Two drilled and tapped holes should be put in the cap, dimples put in the appropriate places in the steering box, and the whole lot reassembled with grub screws locating the box firmly in position. The steering box itself does not normally give any trouble.

The track 'toe in' should be set at $\frac{3}{16}$ in., or parallel if radial-ply tyres are being used.

Castor angle is very much a matter for personal preference, the car being very sensitive to change of castor. On the road, plenty of castor gives understeer, which is probably a good thing, but for racing this should be reduced quite a bit. The adjustment (an eccentric between the shockabsorber arm and suspension bracket) gives something like $\pm 2°$ of castor but, especially with radials, this is not always enough. By putting fibre rings ($\frac{1}{8}$ in. thick, $3\frac{1}{2}$ in. O D, $2\frac{5}{8}$ in. I D) under the springs it is possible to raise the front end, which also increases the amount of castor available. The front shockabsorbers, which of course form a very important part of the suspension, are very critical. The firm of P & R Hydraulics of Hersham, Surrey, have had a great deal of experience of reconditioning these components to suit the car and are well worth contacting.

Standard wheels are retained with something like 175 radial tyres. Anything larger fouls the wheel arch and does not really improve the performance of the car anyway.

The brake slave cylinders should be carefully checked, as the pistons tend to seize in the aluminium cylinders. Replacement Lockheed parts are still available for these wheel cylinders. If the brake drums are cracked or scored, Riley parts can be used at the rear, but the fronts were probably exclusively Healey. Brake materials – front, VG91; rear, MR41 (Ferodo).

The windscreen on the 'Silverstone' drops down into a slot for competition use, and this slot requires frequent cleaning, as dead leaves, twigs, etc., tend to accumulate in it. When the windscreen is lowered, it is advisable to remove the wiper blades, as if the wiper motor is accidentally started, the blades will hit the top of the screen and break off.

This more or less completes the body and chassis preparation but, before going on to the engine, a few points about the 'Elliot' Saloon raced by Eric Hall will show the differences in these heavier vehicles.

On the saloons, the battery boxes should still be carefully reinforced, but as they are situated under the seat they are not exposed to petrol spillage. The joining cable is also not so likely to chafe against the torque tube. The petrol tank is beneath the steel floor of the boot, with the filler cap inside the boot, so, other than ensuring that the cap is completely petrol proof, there is not much of a problem here. As mentioned earlier, the panhard-rod bracket on the rear axle is more liable to breakage on the saloon, so this should be suitably reinforced.

The rear shockabsorber set up is completely different, consisting of Girling PVA6 lever-type shockers. These, however, are no longer available. Eric Hall has solved this problem by fitting two Woodhead-Munroe telescopic shock-absorbers (not the 'Silverstone' type, but a longer travel pattern) so that they are angled forward to clear the seat pan. These, however, did not prove strong enough, so Eric also fitted two of the old-fashioned Hartford friction shock-absorbers transversely across under the seat pan and fixed by two plates round the axle. This improves the road holding tremendously and has the advantage of giving an adjustable setting. The seating in the saloon is not too bad, but full harness safety belts should be fitted, preferably to the transverse chassis member in front of the rear axle.

The silencing system on the saloon requires very careful attention, as the silencers themselves, which are tandem oval ones, lie in a narrow channel consisting of the side chassis member, the wooden floor above and a wooden body side member at the other side. It is probably safest to scrap the silencer completely and to run a 2 in. pipe right the way through, isolated from the bodywork by a stout bracket. For road use, the narrower 'Silverstone' silencer is probably the best replacement. A sheet of asbestos under the vulnerable points is well worth while.

With its extra weight, the saloon raises several problems regarding braking. Eric uses Ferodo AM4 linings at the front and AM3 at the rear, and he has fitted aluminium air scoops to the front of the front back plates, facing forward, and a similar one at the back of the back plates so that the air can get in and out. The back plates are drilled behind the scoops, and petrol gauze fitted over the orifice to prevent water getting in. Two small holes (about 4 × 2 in.) have been cut in the bodywork each side of the front number plate.

Some form of brake booster is probably advisable; Eric has used a Lockheed pressure intensifier, and he is also trying out a tandem braking system from an Austin taxi.

The early saloons had welded front suspension boxes which tended to split. The later Elektron ones are much better. Also the early cars did not have front anti-roll bars, but the 'Silverstone' or 'Tickford' bar can easily be fitted in position.

As far as wheels are concerned, wider wheels are definitely a help with the saloon. The wheels fitted to the Jaguar 3·4/3·8 have got 5 in. rims and the right stud centres. The centre bore of the wheel has to be relieved by $\frac{1}{16}$ in. all round, but there seems to be plenty of spare metal there.

When using the saloon competitively, care should be taken that the doors fit really securely as, with front opening doors, it would be very dangerous if they were to come open due to flexing, etc. Similarly the sunshine roof should be securely fixed, preferably with extra fixing straps.

The bonnets on all models should be firmly secured with leather straps right across from side to side.

Other than the general comments under the 'Silverstone', this completes the preparation of the saloon.

Engine preparation

The big problem encountered by everyone who races these Riley-engined cars is big-end failure, due to oil surge up the walls of the cylinders. The traditional (and effective) answer is to completely cover over the top of the sump with an aluminium plate, with just a single, central fore and aft slot for oil drainage and, of course, a hole for the oil pump. The size of the slot is obviously not critical; something like 1 in. wide and 8 in. long appears to be adequate. An additional vertical baffle finishing about 1 in. above the bottom of the sump helps to reduce the horizontal 'slop' as well. It is possible to fit the later RMB type oil pump, which picks up from the middle of the sump, but there would still be a tendency for the oil to go up the cylinder block and to get blown out of the breather.

Over a long period of time the crankshaft oilways tend to sludge up. There are sludge traps (large allen screws) in the end big-end journals and also in the inner crank webs (plain slotted-head screws) and it is very important that the oilways should be completely cleaned out. Obviously, as always when dealing with engine preparation, the crankshaft, connecting rods, pistons, flywheel, etc., should all be balanced, both individually and as an assembly. It is possible to lighten the flywheel by removing some of the excess metal, but care should be exercised that the flywheel is not unduly weakened. There appear to have been two types of flywheel used, one with a flat edge from the centre boss to the starter ring, the other with a $1\frac{1}{2}$ in. wide recess machined in the back. With the solid one it is possible to remove about 5 lb by machining a tapered face from the outside edge to the crankshaft flange and obviously most of this excess weight comes from the outside. In the case of the wheel with the recess already machined, this can be widened on the outside, and some 3 to 4 lb removed.

The early engines had white metalled big-ends, with a horizontal joint between the two halves of the rod. The later RMF Rileys (fitted with the RMB engine) had a diagonal joint and shell bearings. The top shell was lead indium, whilst the bottom shell was white metal. These are considered more robust than the original units and are easily fitted, although there is more end float between the big-ends and journals. It is possible to fit the lead top bearing in the bottom half of the cap if the locating tags are carefully removed. Big-end bolts are worth replacing, taking care that they are properly secured with *new* tab washers.

The early 'Silverstones' and 'A' and 'B' chassis cars had a 6·9:1 compression ratio. With the later RMB engine, which was probably fitted to some of the later chassis, this went down to 6·6:1. Pistons from the Riley 'Pathfinder' can be fitted and with the standard heads this will give about 7·25:1. Approximately 0·050 in. can be removed from the cylinder head to increase the compression ratio still further (more than this amount will cause the 'Pathfinder' pistons to hit the combustion chamber). This puts the compression ratio up to about 7·75:1. When machining the cylinder head, care should be taken over the water jacket holes which come out, on the head face, at a very oblique angle and thus get larger as the face is machined.

Not much can be done to the valves; the inlet valves are larger than the original Riley ones but the exhaust ones are the same. The normal modifications can be made to the valve gear, grinding off the non-contact areas of the rockers, and replacing the inter-rocker springs with copper or steel tube spacers and washers. When Harold Grace was racing 2½ litre Rileys, he used special valve springs, but these are no longer obtainable. They enabled the normal maximum rev/min of about 4,800 (5,200 in bursts) to be increased to about 6,000 at the expense of some phenomenal piston speeds. A point to note here is that at least some Healeys have an additional 'helper' spring between the cam follower and the bottom of the push rod. It is not certain whether they were on all Healey engines; they are certainly not on Riley engines, but they do help to raise the valve bounce rev/min.

It is possible to get proprietary camshafts ground to give between 40° and 45° overlap, but it is doubtful whether it is worth having this done. Similarly, although it is possible to fit two 1¾ in. SU carburetters, there does not appear to be much advantage in so doing. Both the inlet and exhaust manifolds differ from the original Riley units, and are now completely unobtainable, so great care should be taken over them. The usual lining up and polishing operations should be carried out on these components and on the cylinder head ports, and care taken that the square holes in the manifold gaskets line up accurately with the appropriate ports.

The original distributors on all these cars were designed for the very low octane 'pool' petrol which was all that was available just after the war, and had a manual advance and retard control. This can, of course, be converted to a more modern, high-lift-cam distributor with vacuum advance and retard. This entails turning the distributor through 180°, connecting the vacuum pipe under the first carburetter and retiming 180° up.

The 'Silverstone', in particular, runs very warm, especially if the original headlamps are left in place in front of the radiator, so an oil cooler is well worth fitting. This is quite simple, as all the oil pipes are external from the engine and it is just a matter of breaking into the system and putting the cooler in series. It is also very important to ensure that the baffles under the nose of the 'Silverstone' are in place to force the air through the radiator and to stop it going outside around the body. On the saloons, with their better cooling characteristics, it is possible to fit an electric cooling fan and save some b h p by dispensing with the ordinary fan blades.

The back axle tends to run hot under competition conditions and can pressurize itself, forcing an oil mist on to the rear brakes. This can be obviated by drilling a hole in the filler plug on the differential nose piece and brazing a piece of tube in place to act as a breather.

Spares

It is reported that glass fibre front and rear wings are now available for the 'Silverstone'. Metal ones are very expensive indeed.

Wherever Healey enthusiasts gather, eventually the name of Jonathan Bowers is mentioned. Briefly, some years ago the Donald Healey Motor Co. sold its entire stock of pre-B.M.C. spares to a garage. These were allowed to rot there and were eventually sold to a scrap dealer. Mr Bowers heard about this, and got to the garage at the same time as the scrap merchant and, after a lot of haggling, managed to purchase the entire stock. He then took nearly two years to clean, check, label and package all the bits and pieces. He now keeps them in immaculate condition and is extremely helpful to all Healey owners, even having small numbers of scarce parts specially manufactured and all this at very reasonable prices indeed. It is entirely due to his efforts that so many Healeys are still on the road and he can be contacted through the Healey Register of the Austin-Healey Club.

APPENDIX III

TUNING THE AUSTIN-HEALEY '100', '100-SIX' AND '3000'

The major difficulty encountered by anyone endeavouring to tune the various versions of the 'big Healey' is that most special parts are now virtually unobtainable. In this chapter it is intended to give brief details of the various modifications which have been suggested over the years by the Competitions Departments of B.M.C. and the Donald Healey Motor Co., and then to explain the methods adopted by two successful 'big Healey' owners, John Chatham and John Gott.

PREPARING THE AUSTIN-HEALEY '100' FOR RACING (1956)

Many cars have competed successfully in racing using the following modifications. For convenience, they are divided into sections as follows:

(a) Engine
(b) Rear axle and overdrive combinations
(c) Brakes
(d) Weight and wind resistance reduction
(e) Improved road holding
(f) Electrical.

(a) Engine

The 'Le Mans' Engine Kit consists of stronger inner and outer valve springs, new valve spring cups, two $1\frac{3}{4}$ in. SU carburetters, front and rear aluminium inlet manifolds, cold-air box and air tube, high-lift camshaft (1B2892), steel-faced cylinder-head gasket, special distributor (7H1727), valve-guide shroud and oil retainer, nuts, bolts and gaskets.

This kit, when correctly fitted, results in an increase in b h p from 90 at 4,000 rev/min to 110 at 4,500 rev/min.

It is possible to carry out the alterations without removing the engine from the chassis. The radiator and bonnet should first be removed, then cylinder head, carburetters and manifolds. Unbolt the front engine mountings so that the nose of the engine can be lifted. Extract the crankshaft pulley, take off the timing case cover, remove the camshaft gear and chain and withdraw the camshaft itself. Strip the cylinder head and carefully smooth off any roughness within the combustion chambers and ports. Match and fit the inlet and exhaust manifolds and carburetters, taking great care that no steps exist at the joints. It is important that the carburetters are carefully aligned so that the spindles are in line and the mechanism returns freely to its stops.

216

The valves should be lightly ground in until perfect seatings are obtained. Fit the special camshaft, chain and gear, ensuring that the valve timing markings are correctly lined up. Fit the new distributor with the timing set at 9° b t d c. Rebuild the engine, using jointing compound sparingly on the cylinder-head gasket. Set the valve clearances to 0·015 in. Check all head nuts after the engine has been warmed up (65/70 lb ft). In no circumstances should the cylinder head be machined to raise the compression ratio.

The thermostat should be removed for racing, to allow a greater flow of water. The recommended plug for racing is Champion NA10 (now N3) with a gap of 0·022 in.

(b) Rear axle and overdrive

The standard production rear axle is 4·125, with 3·667 available as an alternative. With the three available overdrive ratios, this gives the following possible overdrive top gear ratios:

4·125 axle with 0·778 overdrive.   Overdrive top gear ratio 3·21
4·125   0·756   3·12
4·125   0·820   3·38
3·667   0·778   2·86
3·667   0·756   2·77
3·667   0·820   3·01

(*Note* – later a 4·1 axle became available and the 0·756 overdrive ceased to be used.)

Relationship of road speed to engine rev/min

Based on Dunlop Road Speed tyres inflated to 29 lb/in², making allowance for tyre growth at high speeds.

mile/h	4·125 axle			3·667 axle		
	Direct Top	0·820 O D	0·778 O D	Direct Top	0·820 O D	0·778 O D
120	—	—	5,000	—	4,700	4,500
115	—	—	4,800	—	4,500	4,300
110	—	4,850	4,600	—	4,300	4,150
105	—	4,600	4,400	5,000	4,100	3,950
100	—	4,400	4,200	4,750	3,900	3,750
95	—	4,200	3,950	4,550	3,700	3,550
90	4,800	3,950	3,750	4,300	3,500	3,400
85	4,550	3,750	3,550	4,050	3,300	3,200
80	4,300	3,500	3,350	3,800	3,100	3,000

The choice of the best combination of ratios for different circuits is a
difficult matter, and can make a great deal of difference to lap times. Recommendations, based on the 'Le Mans' Engine Kit, and a single aero screen, are:

High-speed circuits with long straights	3·667 axle with 0·778 O D
Fast circuits	3·667 axle with 0·82 O D
Short circuits with many corners and short straights	4·125 axle with 0·82 O D
Sprints, etc.	4·125 axle with 0·82 O D

In general, the 3·667 axle with 0·82 O D is the most suitable compromise
for racing. The gearing should be such that 4,500 rev/min is reached on the
straights; 4,800 rev/min should not be exceeded. The 3·667 axle has the
advantage over the 4·125 in that it gives a higher speed in direct top. The
centrifugal governor switch for the overdrive should be shorted out for
racing. This is easily done by connecting a wire between the two terminals
of the switch. This switch is located on the extreme rear of the overdrive unit.

(c) Brakes

Brakes should be correctly adjusted in accordance with Girling's instructions. Alfin brake drums are available – these save weight and assist in heat
dissipation.

(d) Reducing weight and wind resistance

For racing it is suggested that the following items are removed: bumpers
and bumper irons, windscreen and side curtains, hood, tools (if not required
by the regulations), heater, windscreen wiper. A lightweight dynamo, bracket
and regulator are available.

(e) Improved road holding

The cornering power and stability can be improved by fitting: harder front
shockabsorbers, stiffer rear springs (both these items fitted as standard to cars
after chassis number 153855) and a stiffer anti-roll bar.

For most racing work Dunlop Road Speed tyres are suitable. They should
be inflated to 26 lb/in² (front) and 29 lb/in² (rear). For long distance racing
Dunlop R1 5·50×15 racing tyres should be used.

(f) Electrical

It is advisable that all wiring and connections should be checked before a
race. Particular attention should be paid to battery and starter leads, and leads
behind the panel. A second coil may be positioned near the original so as to
be available for a quick change.

AUSTIN-HEALEY '3000' TUNING (1959)

(a) Polish head and ports. (Use standard pistons and compression ratio of
9 to 1.)

(b) Fit camshaft, B.M.C. Pt No. AEC 865:

| I o 16° b t d c | E o 51° b b d c |
| I c 56° a b d c | E c 21° a t d c |

(c) Use standard inner valve springs, but use outer valve springs 1G 2887 (as for ZA Magnette).

(d) Fit 2 in. SU carburetters No. AUC938 (for pair). Open out the standard manifold to suit. Carburetters are complete with UVB needles and black and blue damper springs. Fit flare pipes to the end of each carburetter, 1 in. deep overall and to fit bore of the carburetter at the flange. The outer edge diameter to be $3\frac{1}{2}$ in. and the flare of the bell to be $1\frac{1}{2}$ in. radius.

(e) Static ignition setting, 6° b t d c. The standard distributor can be used satisfactorily, but a special distributor has been used sometimes (Lucas Experimental LT 17001).

(f) Use Champion N3 plugs.

(g) A special exhaust system can be made up consisting of an oval, glass-wool packed silencer, 27 in. long with two straight-through perforated internal pipes; also, welded to the rear, two $1\frac{3}{4}$ in. o d tail pipes, one 14 in. long and one 9 in. long, bent around to come out of the side of the car in front of the rear wheels. The silencer should have two short pipes approximately $2\frac{1}{4}$ in. long at the front to fit over the front exhaust pipes. The above system will need suitable mounting brackets.

(h) With the above tuning, 137 b h p has been recorded at the rear wheels. For improved handling for competition purposes, the higher rate front suspension springs 1H 4092 should be fitted (Mark III springs).

Alternative valve spring set up: Retain standard outer spring and fit 1H 1112 inner springs – 6,350 rev/min crash. Change both inner and outer springs – outer, AHH 7264; inner 1H 723 – 6,450 rev/min crash.

LIÈGE-ROME-LIÈGE REPLICA

In 1961, as a result of the success of the '3000' in the 1960 Liège Rally, a Liège-Rome-Liège Replica was offered for sale to a limited number of private owners. The specification was as follows:

Fit balanced crankshaft/flywheel/clutch assembly, carrying out normal balancing to connecting rods, etc. Fit polished, gas-flowed cylinder head, compression ratio 9·5:1 (works heads polished and prepared by Weslake). Fit special Servais free-flow six branch exhaust manifold. Fit special silencer assembly with outlet just in front of rear wheels. Fit three SU HD8 carburetters on special inlet manifold (some cars were fitted with two 2 in. HD8 carburetters and later 1962 cars were fitted with three 45 DCOE Webers). Fit stronger valve springs and different camshaft. Strengthen sump by welding additional sheet of metal around the front and bottom and fit recessed type sump drain plug. Move all wiring and pipework to less vulnerable position along the sides of the chassis members.

To fit three SU (or Weber) carburetters, it will be necessary to cut away the near side pedal box to give sufficient clearance, re-welding and strengthening as necessary (this modification is not possible on LH drive cars).

Fit cold-air scoop on to the scuttle, with suitable ducts to feed cold air to driver and passenger. Fit A35 van-type ventilator flap to hardtop roof. Fit 60-spoke wire wheels.

If a Mark I, fit Mark II front coil springs with packing pieces (H7939 obtainable from Donald Healey Motor Co., Warwick). The packing pieces increase the ground clearance and one should be fitted at the bottom and two at the top of the spring. Fit special adjustable shockabsorbers at the rear (Armstrong DAS 9) and competition setting shockabsorbers at the front. Fit a heavy-duty anti-roll bar. Fit 14-leaf rear springs. Fit disc brake assembly to the rear. Fit a two-speed wiper motor and high-output generator and coil and associated equipment. Fit special heavy-duty gearbox and 4·3:1 differential. Fit modified boot lid to allow two spare wheels to be carried. Fit large capacity fuel tank. Fit air-horns, trip recorder, special speedo, etc.

The total cost of this conversion, including labour, was some £850 on top of the price of the basic car, but the customer had a car which was virtually identical with the works cars of that time.

CAMSHAFTS

All the following have been used in various models of the 'big Healey':

	Inlet opens (b t d c)	Inlet closes (a b d c)	Exhaust opens (b b d c)	Exhaust closes (a t d c)
AEC 828 (touring)	5°	40°	40°	10°
AEC 865 (high lift)	16°	56°	51°	21°
690/1223 (high lift)	5°	45°	51°	21°

THE WORKS CARS

In 1959/60 the works rally cars were fitted with the standard cylinder head, two 2 in. SU carburetters, AEC 865 camshaft, and free-flow exhaust manifold, 11 in. disc brakes were fitted to the rear axles as well as the front, and the suspension was toughened up.

The 1961 cars were fitted with an aluminium cylinder head (to reduce weight at the front end – approximately 35 lb), three SU HD8 carburetters with UVB needles, and were bored out to give 2967·6 cc. The compression ratio remained at 9·03:1.

The camshaft was considerably hotter: I o 34° b t d c, I c 74° a b d c, E o 69° b b d c, E c 39° a b d c. Lift 11·12 mm. Later in 1961 three Weber 45 DCOE carburetters were used.

By 1964 the three Webers were standard fitting, usually with 38 mm choke, 170 main jet, 165 air correction, F.16 emulsion tube, 50F9 slow running, ·45 pump jet, 3·5 aux. venturi, and 7·5 mm float level. The compression ratio of the alloy head had gone up to 10:1, and an even higher lift cam was used: I o 50° b t d c, I c 70° a b d c, E o 75° b b d c, E c 45° a t d c. Lift 11·48 mm 60 lb inner and 140 lb outer valve springs were used, and the cylinder block was relieved to allow clearance for the valve heads. The flywheel was lightened to 20 lb. The thermostat was blanked off and a special exhaust manifold and system fitted. An extra strong gearbox was fitted, with the so-called 'Tulip' ratios – this had overdrive on 3rd and top. An alternative box, used for racing (known as the Sebring box) had close 1st and 2nd ratios, then a big gap and a close 3rd and top. This latter box was used without an overdrive, and with a very high rear axle ratio to cope with the long straights at Sebring. Removal of the overdrive in this case resulted in a worth-while saving in weight. The steering ratio of the works cars was altered to 12:1 from the standard 15:1. Naturally all the usual rally accessories were fitted.

In rally tune one of these works cars weighed about 24-25 cwt and they regularly produced some 170 b h p at the wheels at around 5,000 rev/min. The final works car was produced in 1967, when the 1964 Morley car was refurbished for the 1967 R.A.C. Rally. Most of its specification was the same as for the earlier cars, but a special experimental aluminium block was used for the engine. This did not give any increase in performance, but once again reduced the weight over the front axle considerably. Nevertheless, the extra weight of the sump and transmission guards still resulted in the car turning the scales at some 24 cwt. Unfortunately this car was never used in earnest, as the R.A.C. Rally was cancelled due to foot-and-mouth disease.

JOHN CHATHAM'S CARS

One of the most successful of the private owners is Bristol garage owner John Chatham. John started tuning an Austin-Healey '100' in 1960 and it was not long before his BN 1 (SAL75) was collecting awards. Naturally, a tremendous amount of trial and error went into the development of the car, but John's recommendations can be summarized as follows:

(a) Engine

Bore the block out 20 thou. and fit new pistons to give a 9·0:1 compression ratio. Lighten the flywheel by removing the heavy flange on the clutch side and relieving the back. Have the flywheel, crank, rods, etc., very carefully balanced. (Note that Healey rods are normally sold in sets of four or six, which are reasonably matched – an odd rod should never be fitted as it is likely to be as much as $\frac{1}{2}$ oz different from the others.) It is best to leave the head fairly standard – it is possible to increase the compression ratio to 10·0:1 by machining, but this tends to overstress the crankshaft without much increase in power. Clean up the ports, opening up the exhaust port in particular. Quite a lot can be removed from the exhaust valve guide where it projects into the exhaust port. The latest '3000' inlet and exhaust valves can be fitted, although the valve seats have to be opened up slightly to take them. The 'Le Mans' camshaft is no longer available, but it is always possible to get a cam reprofiled to the 'Sebring' or '100S' specification. The standard valve springs are quite adequate (provided that they are new) as 4,800 rev/min is the maximum worth-while rev. limit.

The '100M' inlet manifolds are no longer available, but a simple four-stud adaptor can be made up to take $1\frac{3}{4}$ in. SU carburetters, as fitted to the '100M'. Needles and damper springs should be as in the '100M' specification. For even greater performance, two 2 in. SUs can be fitted – the suggested needles in this case being UH. Naturally care should be taken in lining up the new carburetters with the manifold and inlet ports. On the exhaust side, a Derrington extractor manifold is well worth fitting to improve the gas flow. The '100M' distributor was Lucas part No. 40520A – it is believed to be unobtainable now, but a similar pattern might be available.

This completes the engine modifications, but John stresses that accurate balancing and careful assembly are by far the most important items if maximum performance is required.

(b) Transmission

With the extra power the standard clutch is inclined to give trouble. Chatham first solved this by fitting an old Austin taxi clutch, but the best solution is to fit the Mark III '3000' diaphragm clutch. This bolts straight on, but the bell housing has to be relieved to allow sufficient clearance for it to operate. It is possible to fit the '3000' gearbox to the '100', but only six of the nine bolt holes line up; however this seems to be sufficient to hold the unit. The first motion shaft has to be shortened about 1 in., and the small cross member in front of the cruciform has to be cut back or taken out. The '3000' rear gearbox mountings can be used, drilling the chassis accordingly. The overdrive solenoid is liable to knock against the chassis as a result of engine movement – the chassis should be relieved to give sufficient clearance. It is not necessary to alter the prop-shaft length for this modification, but if a '3000' rear axle is fitted the prop-shaft has to be shortened. On the early cars it is a big advantage to fit a '3000' rear axle, because the BN 1 had a fairly weak spiral bevel rear drive (the BN 2 had a much stronger hypoid drive) and also the brake shoes are wider on the '3000' than the early '100'. The latest Mark III '3000' radius arms improve the handling of the car, the original panhard tie rod being removed. Fitting these does, however, involve some quite tricky chassis welding. Adjustable Armstrong shockabsorbers are fitted, and these are normally set about three clicks back from maximum. At the front end a standard '3000' disc brake set up can be fitted to BN 2s and later cars. Mark I coil springs are probably the best, as the later springs are a bit too hard for the four-cylinder car. The normal pattern shockabsorbers are generally suitable although, if a stiffer set up is required, the Mark III '3000' shockers can be used. The '3000' front anti-roll bar should be fitted. On the braking side, the '3000' brakes are a great improvement on the original units, but a servo is almost essential – this again can be taken from a '3000'.

Some care should be taken to ensure good balance between front and rear brakes with the disc/drum set up – Chatham has found it necessary to reduce the size of the rear brake cylinder from 1 in. to $\frac{3}{4}$ in. on spiral bevel drive cars. On later hypoid drive cars, use '3000' wheel cylinders. Chatham reckons that on this car $5\frac{1}{2}$J wheels with 165 × 15 tyres are the most suitable, although the 60-spoke wire wheels from the Mark III '3000' are an improvement on the standard '100' wheels. It is worth noting that the MGC wire wheels are 5J

and will fit without too much difficulty. (Mark III '3000' – 4½J.) Care should
be taken when fitting wide wheels that they do not catch the inside of the
wheel arches when on full bump and full lock conditions.

'100-Six'

The early '100-Six' had a four-port, siamesed head, which was rather
inefficient. This was later replaced by the six-port head which was much
better. The two heads are interchangeable.

The larger capacity '3000' engine will fit into the '100-Six' without much
difficulty.

'3000'

It is important to realize that virtually none of the parts used to modify
the '3000' to full works specification are now available. Thus a major conversion on this car is a difficult and expensive operation. The earlier Mark I
and Mark II cars can very easily be brought up to Mark III specification (at
least as far as the engine is concerned) and this is a very worthwhile operation
for road use.

For more serious tuning most of the comments about the '100' apply.
Again the flywheel should be lightened, and the crankshaft, flywheel and
con rods carefully balanced. The cylinder head can be planed to give about
10·0:1 compression ratio. The combustion chamber should be opened up
around the inlet valve head to improve gas flow, and the block itself should
be relieved to allow clearance for the valves if a high-lift cam is fitted. The
Mark III valve springs are satisfactory up to about 7,000 rev/min. With a
high-lift camshaft it is advisable to fit solid steel rocker pedestals. The block
can be bored to 30 thou. oversize – pistons this size still being available. This
gives a capacity of about 2,967 cc. When the car is fitted with twin or triple
SU carburetters, Chatham has found that the best camshaft is the standard
Mark III. With triple 45 DCOE Webers, however, he has found that a high-
lift race cam gives a big increase in performance. With the race cam it is
essential to have a different distributor, and Chatham has found that a
DMA 40662A is best. The Competitions Department manifolds for triple
Webers are no longer available, but Derringtons make a suitable manifold.
They also do an exhaust manifold that is suitable for all models of '3000'.
The original competition exhaust manifold is still available from Servais
Silencers, but this can only be used on a triple carburetter set-up. With these
extractor exhaust systems, it is best either to fit the Mark III exhaust pipe
system for road use or to fabricate a new system to finish about the middle
of the near-side door for competition use. On earlier cars, the rear silencers
of the Mark III system must be omitted, because of the reduction in ground
clearance. John uses Lodge RL49 plugs, which he finds last him a complete
racing season.

To fit an oil cooler it is easiest to alter the filter so that it fits on to the chassis
side member, and then to take the oil cooler outlet pipes from an adaptor on
the block. It is possible that the new MGC oil filter could be used, which
would simplify this job. Chatham does not normally use a fan, but if one *is*

used, a pulley with a deeper V should be fitted to avoid throwing belts. The thermostat is taken out and replaced with a competition MGB bypass blanking plate.

The works-type straight-cut gearboxes are no longer available. Competition clutches can be obtained from Borg & Beck and competition overdrive units from Laycocks. It is more convenient to move the overdrive switch on to the gear-lever. To lower the front end for racing, it helps to fit Mark I coil springs as the later springs are too hard. In addition, spacers can be fitted between the wishbone and the spring seat. It is also advisable to soften the rear springs slightly; this can be done by removing one or two leaves. Adjustable Armstrong shockabsorbers are fitted to the rear; this necessitates drilling fresh holes as the original ones do not line up. At the front, standard Mark III units are used, and competition valves can be obtained if required. The heavy-duty anti-roll bars are no longer available – John uses a Mark II 'Sprite' one, quite successfully, with his very wide wheels. (NB. The stiffer the roll bar, the more the understeer.) John uses Ferodo DS11 disc brake pads and Mintex M20 rear linings.

More recently it has been apparent that the greatest improvement in lap times can be achieved by fitting bigger and still bigger tyres. In Britain the maximum size rim that is permitted on 3 litre 'Production Sports' cars is 10 in., and Chatham has used a 10·30 × 13 Firestone tubeless tyre with a B.10 mix on such a rim. John is firmly convinced that it is cheaper and easier to fit wide wheels to bolt-on fittings rather than to the splined (knock-on) type fittings. At the front, $\frac{1}{2}$ in. spacers are required to ensure that the disc calipers do not foul. The studs fitted to the rear drum brakes are longer than the standard front studs, so these can be used to go through the spacers.

At the rear, with a drum braked axle (disc wheels) no spacers or longer studs are required as these are already built in. If you are fortunate enough to have an ex-works car with disc brakes at the rear it is necessary to use a 1 in. spacer. Disc brake conversions for the rear are no longer available, although it might be possible to fit (say) Jaguar units if sufficient workshop equipment is available.

As with the '100', it is advisable to fit the later Mark III pattern radius arms, but using Triumph Herald differential-mounting Metalastik bushes, as they are stiffer than the '3000' bushes.

Generally, a large amount of weight can be saved on the bodywork, most panels now being available in glass fibre from various proprietary sources. Chatham favours a 14 in. leather-covered steering wheel for racing use, because the high ratio steering boxes are no longer available.

JOHN GOTT'S CAR

John Gott joined the B.M.C. works rally team in 1955 and drove the '100-Six' in earnest for the first time in 1958. From then, until he left the works team in 1962, he was almost solely a Healey man, and when he finally departed from Abingdon he took his old faithful works Healey '3000', SMO 746, with him. Since those days John has regularly competed in club race meetings with the car, which has seen just about every stage of development that is possible with a '3000'.

SMO 746 was one of the first three works rally cars and originally ran in the 1959 Alpine Rally. In those days the cars were running with a standard disc/drum brake set-up, 4 in. wire wheels and twin $1\frac{3}{4}$ in. SU carburetters. Later the brakes were altered to discs all round, and the two SUs were replaced with triple $1\frac{1}{2}$ in. SUs. At the same time the rear end was stiffened by the fitting of 14-leaf rear springs, which helped to counteract the effect of the 25 gallon fuel tank and twin spare wheels which weighed down the tail. Later still, a spur-type gearbox was fitted which was much stronger than the standard box. About this time John entered a couple of races at Silverstone in SMO and returned a best lap time of 1 min. 19 secs, and it is noteworthy that eight years later the same car with the same driver is lapping the same circuit some 11 secs faster.

After triple SUs (2 in. by now) the works cars went on to triple Weber, 45 DCOEs, and about the same time they were fitted with aluminium cylinder heads. These heads did not materially increase the power output, but they did reduce the weight over the front wheels (by about 35 lb) and thus reduced the tendency to understeer. This, then, was basically the state of John's car when he handed it over to Jock Thin to look after, and it was decided to start a methodical development programme. The first thing they tackled was the tyre equipment – the car at that time was running on $4\frac{1}{2}$ Js and the first move was to fit $5\frac{1}{2}$ Js from an Aston-Martin which improved the Silverstone lap times by something like a second a lap. John, incidentally, has knock-on type wheels, but more of this later. He then went on to Minilite knock-ons with $6\frac{1}{2}$ J at the front and 7J at the rear.

Even this was not sufficient and so finally J. A. Pearce 10J magnesium wheels were fitted. By this time John had a good assortment of various size knock-on type wheels and so it was decided to retain this type of fitting with the 10Js, but both John and Jock feel now that this was a mistake. Firstly, it is much easier to fit wide wheels on to the stud-type fittings. The fittings themselves save something like 5 lb per wheel unsprung weight. They are cheaper and, finally, especially with the very wide wheels, there seems to be a tendency for the spinner on the knock-on type wheels to work loose under the stress of hard braking. In fact John lost a wheel at Silverstone for this very reason, and he has now swopped his splined hubs over so that the left hub is on the right of the car and vice versa. This could cause trouble through rapid acceleration and, as a precaution, the ears of the hubs are wired with soft iron wire. At the moment it appears that this problem is not fully understood, the different coefficients of heat of the various metals in the spline, hub and spinner all contributing to the trouble, so there seems no doubt that the simplest and safest answer is to use a stud-fixing wheel.

When fitting any wide wheel the main problem is to ensure adequate clearance on the inside. There is a cast-iron bracket bolted on the inside of the rear arch that has to be removed and, in addition, spacers have to be fitted to clear the spring hanger bracket. The insides of the front wheel arches require relieving a bit, slightly more on the near side than the off-side. Both front and rear wheel arches have to be flared on the outside to comply with the regulations. John runs with 2 lb more pressure in the front tyres than the rears, but obviously this is a purely personal preference. His tyres are low profile Dunlop 475/1130 tubeless.

As far as suspension and transmission are concerned the front end was lowered by removing the packing pieces from the top of the coil spring and fitting a 1 in. spacer below the spring (subsequently changed to a $\frac{3}{4}$ in. spacer as a result of bottoming on Hawthorn Bend at Brands Hatch). The works 14-leaf springs were replaced firstly by a standard 7-leaf one, and then by 9-leaf springs re-cambered the other way to reduce the ground clearance a bit more. This latter proved quite successful, the car holding the road very well indeed. Adjustable Armstrong shockabsorbers are used at the back, set fairly firmly. At tight circuits like Brands, John still found that he was having trouble with rubbing under the wings. This was finally cured by cutting out the inside of the wheel arches and building up boxes to give the required strength. At the same time, the opportunity was taken to take out all the double skinning, to fit a small, light-weight fuel tank and to replace, with aluminium or glass fibre, as many interior panels as possible. The position of the battery was moved from behind the seats to the off-side of the boot to help with the weight distribution for the majority of British circuits which are right-handed. Don't forget, of course, that this car started as a rally machine, and so was very much heavier than a standard car. Altogether something like 2 cwt was removed as a result of these operations.

John is convinced that it will never be possible to race a 'big Healey' successfully on the original drum/disc brake set up. The discs from a Jaguar can be fitted, but it is necessary to have a new forged back plate made up, which is rather difficult unless you can get hold of a copy to work from.

SMO has been converted to a dual-braking system, which requires twin servo-units and a special master cylinder. Cars such as the MGC, which were built for the American market, were fitted with these dual master cylinders as standard, but great care must be taken to get the balance right between front and rear brakes.

The works had a wide range of axle ratios, of which the best was probably the special 4·3:1, although this is useless with low profile tyres when a 3·9:1 is most suitable. If a 4·3:1 is unobtainable and ordinary profile tyres are used, then the best compromise is probably the 4·1:1. Changing the axle ratios for different circuits is probably not worth while unless the absolute ultimate in performance is required. John uses a limited slip differential (an American No-Spin) but has doubts about whether it is very beneficial.

John normally uses the so called 'Tulip' ratio gearbox, with overdrive on third and top. The lightweight racing cars had the 'Sebring' gearboxes, which were four speed boxes without an overdrive, but with a close third and top. This was used at Sebring with a 3·5:1 rear axle, but it is not very practical for the normal British circuits. To save about $\frac{1}{2}$ cwt in weight, no overdrive was fitted. Some competitors have tried using the 'Sebring' box with an overdrive, but this results in the odd situation where the car goes faster in overdrive third than top. Both these boxes are now very rare.

Regarding the engine, both John and Jock feel certain that there is not much that can be done to increase the power output other than careful balancing and assembly. SMO has a compression ratio of about 11:1 – higher than this causes piston and gasket trouble. The engine is bored 40 thou. over-size, which gives a capacity of 2,982 cc, but pistons to this size are virtually unobtainable now. If pistons with a fourth ring below the gudgeon are used, the bottom ring should be removed. Three 45 DCOE 13 Weber carburetters on the works inlet manifold provides the correct mixture, although John feels that nearly as good results could be obtained with three well-tuned 2 in. SUs. At least one competitor has tried six Amal carburetters, but here the problem is that the flexing encountered on the circuit tends to send them out of balance with each other. Needle valves on the Webers should be of the spring-loaded type to stop flooding and should be changed fairly often. John does not feel that Nimonic inlet and exhaust valves are essential for club racing, although possibly worth while for long distance events. The valve gear need not be lightened but rough edges should be cleaned up on rockers, etc., and MGB valve springs used. Special rockers without a top oil hole are used to reduce the amount of oil pumped out of the head through the breathers. The springs between the rockers are replaced by bushes to reduce friction slightly. John normally doesn't use more than 5,800–6,000 rev/min, although the engine will rev. higher. He prefers to use a chronometric rev. counter, with a tell-tale indicating maximum revs used.

John uses one of the ex-works camshafts, but he reckons that the Mark III cam is a very good next best. If a high-lift cam is used, it is essential to relieve the cylinder block by about $\frac{1}{8}$ in. to clear the valve heads. It is an advantage to have a nitrided crankshaft but a tip regarding this is that the front engine pulley should be fixed in position with Loctite. With a nitrided crank, when the pulley is removed, it tends to pull the threads, which then become powdery when the pulley is replaced. It thus becomes difficult to ensure that the pulley is done up to the correct tightness. The competition diaphragm clutch tends to go out of balance very easily if the engine is over-revved – the reverse thrust as the engine slows down again seems to push it a little bit out of balance and cause a serious vibration.

On twisty circuits in particular, there is quite a problem with surge of both fuel and oil. The float chamber level should be high enough to counteract this, bearing in mind the danger of fire due to flooding. The petrol tank should be well baffled, as should the sump. It is also advisable to put a splash plate above the oil pump to prevent oil being splashed and pumped up the cylinder walls. This plate should be made of duralumin, as a steel one will tend to vibrate and break. The generator pulley should be replaced with a larger one to stop the generator being driven too fast and thus burning itself out. John races with the fan removed, but it is replaced for tuning purposes as the engine tends to boil when stationary. John finds that Champion N6OY plugs are most suitable for a well-tuned Healey, whilst N9Ys are best for a mildly tuned model.

GEARBOX RATIOS

At various times the following alternative gearbox ratios were homologated for the Austin-Healey '3000':

					('Tulip' box)
First	.	.	2·413:1	2·207:1	2·64:1
Second	.	.	1·722:1	1·575:1	1·88:1
Third	.	.	1·195:1	1·093:1	1·43:1
Fourth	.	.	Direct	Direct	Direct
Reverse	.	.	3·1:1	2·83:1	3·39:1

APPENDIX IV

TUNING THE SPRITE AND MIDGET

The Sprite has far more potential for tuning than the 'big Healey' and is in the fortunate position that most parts are still readily available, especially for the later models. Part numbers, when quoted below, are the British Leyland (ex-B.M.C.) numbers and many of these parts are available from the Special Tuning Department at Abingdon. It is worth noting that the Sprite and Midget are mechanically identical, the only differences being of trim and such things as dashboard layout. There was no MG equivalent of the original 'bug-eyed' Sprite, so the Mark I Midget corresponds with the Mark II Sprite, the Mark II Midget with the Mark III Sprite, and the Mark III Midget with the Mark IV Sprite.

The original Sprite had a 948 cc engine, with the serial number prefix 9C, and this was followed in 1961 by the 9CG engine which had the same capacity (948 cc) but a higher compression ratio, different cylinder head, larger valves, double valve springs and larger carburetters.

When tuning the early model, it is possible to gain an improvement by interchanging parts from the 9C and 9CG engines.

The first stage in any simple tuning is to polish the ports, remove all casting marks, etc., from the combustion chambers, and gradually radius the centre projection without removing it altogether. Inlet and exhaust manifolds should be carefully lined up with the ports, carefully grinding away any step at the joint. A further improvement at this stage can be obtained by enlarging the inlet manifold, so that the template shown in Fig. 1 can just be inserted through the neck. Take care not to exceed this shape as the wall is very thin at this point.

The compression ratio of the 9C engine can be raised by fitting flat topped 9CG pistons (to about 9·3:1). The same effect can be obtained by removing about 0·065 in. from the face of the cylinder head, but take great care as the bottom of the rocker feed oilway is very close to the surface. It is worth while putting a piece of stiff steel wire down the rocker feed hole to check the depth of this oilway before starting machining operations. Reset ignition to 3° b t d c. This will then give approximately 47 b h p.

Of great importance in any head-tuning operation is to ensure that all the combustion chambers are the same capacity. The volume of each chamber should be carefully measured. Grinding will then enable you to get the chambers to identical volume.

To take advantage of the raised compression ratio, the 997 cc Mini Cooper camshaft 88G 229 should be fitted (table on page 232 shows alternative part numbers). This has a higher lift than the standard cam, as well as a greater valve overlap, but the standard valve springs can be retained, being good for up to 6,400 rev/min, which is more than recommended for the standard bottom end of the 9C unit. With all this improvement it is obviously pointless to retain the 9C carburation, and so a 9CG inlet manifold with H2 carburetters should be fitted, after carefully matching up the manifold and ports. At the same time a good three-branch exhaust manifold should be obtained.

The standard distributor is not suitable for this set-up, but should be replaced by the special competitions one (C–27H–7766), set at between one and two degrees b t d c . Carburetter needles should be V3, with blue damper springs. This should have increased the power of the 9C unit to some 55 b h p at 5,800 rev/min, which is about the most that the unit can stand without substantial work to the bottom end.

An essential operation to the crankshaft, con rod, flywheel assembly is to have it carefully balanced both individually and as an assembly. Two stronger crankshafts which have been available in the past were the so-called 'red crank' (C–AEA 406) and the nitrided Formula Junior crank (C–AEA–461), but these are now unobtainable. A new Tuftrided crank (C–AEA 792) is, however, available and this should be safe to some 7,500 rev/min. It is advisable when contemplating these high revs to 'strap' the centre main cap. This entails machining the cap flat and fitting a $\frac{1}{2}$ in. steel billet on top, holding this with longer high-tensile studs and self-locking nuts.

The table on page 232 shows details of the various factory camshafts produced for 'A' series in-line and transverse engines.

By the time modifications have reached this stage, it is advisable to be using the 9CG block, with shell bearings for all the camshaft journals. This block can be bored oversize and pistons with fully floating gudgeon pins used. The standard con rods should be discarded if maximum power is to be obtained, replacements being the standard 9FA Cooper type 12G123/126, which fitted with 12A 674 pistons in a 2·543 in. bore (0·065 in. oversize) gives 998 cc. Alternatively the Formula Junior pistons C–AEA 639 with special rods C–AEA 620/621 (gudgeon pin is larger) and bore size 2·538 (0·060 oversize) gives 995 cc.

By now thought should be given to changing the head to either the 9CG type or, better still, to the MG 1100/Mini Cooper 998 cc head, 28G 222. This gives a larger inlet valve head (1·219 in.). These heads should, of course, be carefully polished as before, making sure that there are no sharp edges in the combustion chamber, taking particular care over the ports, spark plug orifice, etc. The 9CG head with 12A 674 pistons gives approximately 9·8:1 compression ratio, whilst the Mini Cooper head with the same pistons gives 9·1:1. With the C–AEA 639 piston, however, this goes up to 10:1 as the pistons rise above the top of the block slightly. With the 12A 674 pistons, a similar compression ratio can be obtained by taking about 0·045 in. off the head. The maximum compression ratio permissible with reasonable tractability is 11:1, which entails machining 0·095 in. off the head for the 12A 674 pistons, or 0·050 in. off for the C–AEA 639 pistons.

A third alternative is to use the current Mark IV Sprite head, 38G 399, with 12A 674 pistons. This would give 11:1 again. With the C–AEA 639 pistons and AEG 226 gasket fitted with this head, the resulting compression ratio would be about 12·3:1. This head has the added advantage of even larger inlet and exhaust valves and has a very good standard of finish.

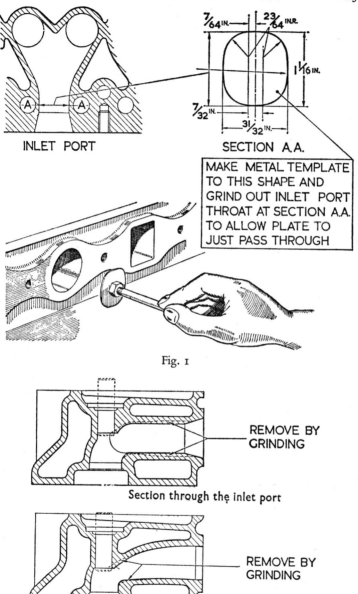

INLET PORT

SECTION A.A.

MAKE METAL TEMPLATE
TO THIS SHAPE AND
GRIND OUT INLET PORT
THROAT AT SECTION A.A.
TO ALLOW PLATE TO
JUST PASS THROUGH

Fig. 1

REMOVE BY
GRINDING

Section through the inlet port

REMOVE BY
GRINDING

Section through the exhaust port

Fig. 2

THE VARIOUS FACTORY CAMSHAFTS PRODUCED FOR 'A' SERIES IN-LINE AND TRANSVERSE ENGINES

								Not available with pin drive	
Part Nos. (with pin type oil pump drive)	8G 712 2A 297 2A 571	12G 165 AEA 630	AEG 148	88G 229 2A 948 12A 122	AEG 510	C-AEA 731	C-AEA 648		
Marking	—	2 rings	—	1 ring	1 ring	3 ring	AEA 649		
Cam lobe width	⅜ in.	⅜ in.	½ in.	⅜ in.	½ in.	⅜ in.	½ in.		
Standard use	Mini	1100 and Midget	Cooper 'S' Midget II	Cooper 997 cc	Cooper 'S' 1966 Later		Race	Sprint	Super Sprint
Inlet opens b t d c	5°	5°	5°	16°	10°	24°	50°	60°	60°
closes a b d c	45°	45°	45°	56°	50°	64°	70°	80°	80°
Exhaust opens b b d c	40°	51°	51°	51°	51°	59°	75°	75°	85°
closes a t d c	10°	21°	21°	21°	21°	29°	45°	45°	55°
Inlet period	230°	230°	230°	252°	240°	268°	300°	320°	320°
Exhaust period	230°	252°	252°	252°	252°	268°	300°	300°	320°
Cam lift	·221 in.	·250 in.	·250 in.	·250 in.	·250 in.	·252 in.	·315 in.	·315 in.	·315 in.
Valve lift	·285 in.	·318 in.	·318 in.	·318 in.	·318 in.	·320 in.	·394 in.	·394 in.	·394 in.
Running clearance	·012 in. (·30 mm)	·012 in. (·30 mm)	·012 in. (·30 mm)	·015 in. (·38 mm)	·015 in. (·38 mm)	·015 in. (·38 mm)	·015 in. (·38 mm)	·015 in. (·38 mm)	·015 in. (·38 mm)
Part Nos. (With flange pump drive 12G 729)	12A 1065 Auto Mini	12G 726 Auto 1100	AEG 522 AEG 538	C-AEG 567	C-AEG 542	—	C-AEG 529	C-AEG 597	C-AEG 595
Cam lobe width	⅜ in.	⅜ in.	½ in.	½ in.	½ in.		½ in.	½ in.	½ in.
Markings	—	—	—	AEG 567	AEG 543		AEG 530	AEG 598	AEG 596
"	—	2 rings	—		1 ring				

For identification see markings and cam lobe width (⅜ in.=9·5 mm, ½ in.=12·7 mm):
For checking the valve timing on camshaft 8G 712, 12G 165 and 88G 229 set the rocker clearance to 0·019 in. (0·48 mm).
For checking the valve timing on camshafts AEG 148, AEG 510, C-AEA 731, C-AEA 648, C-AEG 595, C-AEG 597, C-AEG 529 and AEG 522 set the rocker clearance to 0·021 in. (0·53 mm).
Camshaft AEG 522 was fitted to 1275 cc Sprite and Midget engine prefix 12CC and to 1300 transverse range with 12H prefix.

The standard valve springs fitted to all these heads should be capable of preventing valve bounce up to some 7,000 rev/min. As can be seen from the table there is a large number of camshafts available, the most popular being the 88G 229, already mentioned, the C–AEA 731 ($\frac{3}{4}$-race cam) and the C–AEA 648 (full-race cam). With this last cam in particular, but also to a certain extent with the others, care should be taken if larger valves are used as a result of fitting different heads, to relieve the cylinder block to give a clearance of at least 0·060 in. With the increased cam lift, the standard timing chain becomes unsuitable at high rev/min, so this should be converted to Duplex by fitting Mini Cooper 'S' components. British Leyland Special Tuning Department market a special kit for this purpose (C–AJJ-3325). A lightened steel camshaft sprocket to suit this kit is also available (C–AEG 578).

The original pressed-steel rocker gear should be discarded and replaced by the Mini Cooper 'S' forged type (12G 1221) which can be further lightened by radiusing the bosses and valve contact area shoulders. The rocker shaft itself should be changed to the stronger AEG 399, and the rocker locating springs changed to spacers and washers (C–AEG 392 and AEG 168) which should be adjusted to ensure that the rocker arms are central over the valve stems. This rocker shaft requires a tapped pedestal, 12G 1927, and three pedestals, 12G 1926, complete with locking plate and locating screw.

With all these head modifications, it is pretty obvious that the carburation will have to be attended to, the alternatives being a pair of $1\frac{1}{2}$ in. SUs with AM or CP4 needles, ·090 jets, and blue damper springs mounted on a Mark IV Sprite manifold, suitably opened up, or a 45 DCOE9 Weber.

If the latter is used with manifold kit C–AJJ 3360 the following jets will provide a starting point for tuning, bearing in mind that these will vary, depending upon the exact state of tune:

Choke	36
Main jet	1·50/1·55
Correction air jet	1·75
Idling jet	·50/·60
Pump jet	·60
Emulsion	F2
Auxiliary	3·5 mm
Float	7·0 mm

With all these modifications either the competition distributor (C–27H–7766) already mentioned, or the Mini Cooper 'S' distributor (12G 445), is still suitable, with the static setting about t d c. Power by now should be some 75 b h p at 6,500 rev/min.

To ensure adequate cooling, the thermostat should be removed and replaced with a blanking sleeve (11G 176), which ensures adequate circulation around the head and valve seats. Make sure that the radiator matrix is getting a full flow of air and that there are no gaps between the cowling and the radiator. The oil cooler should be placed alongside the radiator and not in front of it, with its own air intake. Incidentally, whilst building the engine, it is as well to fit the 12G 793 oil pump, which is more efficient than the standard one.

Coming now to the transmission, it is possible to carefully lighten the flywheel, as shown in Fig. 3. Do not exceed the limits shown, as a fractured flywheel is not only expensive but also dangerous! Don't forget to have the machined flywheel re-balanced.

A stronger competition clutch is essential, and this can be obtained from Automotive Product (Borg & Beck) stockists. They normally recommend a nine-spring $6\frac{1}{4}$ in. unit with the part numbers: cover ass. 50333 driven plate 45585/41, release bearing 50345, spacer washers (6 off) 50332.

The gearbox fitted to the 9C engine could be improved slightly by changing to the 9CG ratios as shown below.

9C							9CG
3·628	.	.	.	First	.	.	.	3·2
2·374	.	.	.	Second	.	.	.	1·916
1·412	.	.	.	Third .	.	.	.	1·357
Direct	.	.	.	Fourth	.	.	.	Direct
4·664	.	.	.	Reverse	.	.	.	4·114

The parts required for this conversion are, however, no longer available from B.M.C.

No alterations are possible to the 9CG gearbox as the later gearboxes have larger diameter mainshafts. It is possible, however, to fit the later 1098/1275 gearboxes complete, and this has the double advantage of permitting the use of the close ratio, spur gear set C–AJJ 3319 (ratios: first, 2·573:1; second, 1·722:1; third, 1·255:1) and also the 1098's $7\frac{1}{4}$ in. competition clutch C–BHA 4448, with the driven plate C–BHA 4449 and flywheel 12G 180, all of which fit into the larger bell housing.

Whichever gearbox is fitted, the later, stronger layshaft (22G 673) should always be used.

A wide variety of axle ratios have been used in various vehicles using the 'A' series rear axle, and although some of these are no longer available now, they can sometimes be found in breakers' yards with the crownwheel and pinion in a serviceable condition. The table below lists the various ratios available.

Ratio	Originally used	Diff. Assembly Part No.
3·727	Early Riley 1·5	ATA 7239
3·9	Competition	ATA 7353
4·22	Standard Sprite to H–AN7–24731	ATA 7326
4·55	Minor '1000' Van	ATA 7093
4·375	A35 Van	2A 7230
5·3	GPO Minor '1000' Van	ATA 7073

These can be readily fitted to early Sprites, but if the crown wheel and pinion are changed by themselves, care must be taken as the inside diameter of the pinion bearing can be either 1 in. or 1·1875 in. The latest half shaft from the Mark IV Sprite (BTA 607) should always be used as the earlier shafts were prone to shearing under the extra power being applied. Special racing shafts are also available (C–BTA 940).

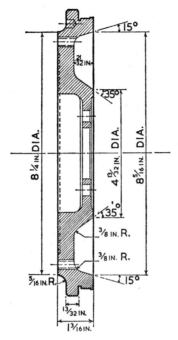

Fig. 3

Limited slip differentials are available and are a considerable advantage when racing, particularly on rough tracks (C–BTA 1226).

From the suspension point of view, not much can be done to the early Sprites. If it is intended to use the car mainly for racing, it is possible to lower the front by using spacers above the spring pan. This reduces the pre-load of the springs by extending the fitted length. Roll bars are available in a variety of diameters from $\frac{9}{16}$ in. to $\frac{5}{8}$ in.; the thicker the bar the more the car will understeer (as it will from lowering the front end). This can be useful to counteract any oversteer resulting from fitting lighter bonnets, etc.

Bottom wishbone links, already drilled for fitting roll bars, can be obtained (AHA 7029/7030), or the existing links can be drilled. Competition shock-absorbers are also available.

At the rear a number of possibilities are available. A stiffer, heavy-duty, quarter-elliptic spring (AHA 5468) can be fitted or, alternatively, it is possible to reduce the number of leaves in the standard spring, especially if lightened bodywork is being used. The ride height can be varied at the rear by inserting special wedges (AHA 6456) between the mounting and spring. From model No. H–AN5–4333 the shockabsorber mounting brackets were changed and adjustable shockabsorbers (C–AHA 6453/6454) could be fitted, but unfortunately these are no longer available.

The standard wheels have only a $3\frac{1}{2}$ in. rim (4J on the Mark IV wire wheels). A 5 in. wire wheel is also available from British Leyland Special Tuning, but, as far as disc wheels are concerned, the only real alternative is alloy or magnesium wheels. Care should be taken over the use of spacers when fitting wider wheels, as these considerably increase the load on studs and bearings. A 1 in. spacer can result in an increase in stress of some 25%.

For road use, a maximum wheel width of 5 in. is adequate, although for racing, low-profile tyres on 7 in. and 8 in. rims are frequently used. The tyre manufacturers' recommendations should be sought in these cases.

The rear hub-bearing locking nut must be absolutely tight, as any play will let the bearings turn on the casing and ultimately lead to the half-shaft flange fracturing under side thrust. The front stub axles should be replaced with the later stronger type (BTA 744/745).

The normal brakes are quite adequate for road use, but fade badly under severe competition conditions. Ferodo VG95 linings can help to reduce this, but the only real answer is to go over to disc brakes. The original Sebring Sprites had 8 in. Girling disc brakes at the front and 8 in. Girling drum brakes at the rear, but this was a special application for this particular model.

The production disc brakes fitted to the Mark II Sprite can be fitted with care to the earlier models. Note that the master cylinder must be changed as well, the new part being BHA 4365. Take great care that the brake hoses do not foul when the wheels are turned from lock to lock, allowing for suspension movement as well. Harder disc pads are available (C–AHT16), but the normal rear drum linings should be retained to ensure correct fore and aft balance. The original Mark I Sprite was so popular that a variety of proprietary head modifications were offered by firms such as Speedwell, Sprinzel, Alexander Engineering and so on. Some of these were quite interesting technically, with special seven-port alloy-heads (centre exhaust port still siamesed), cross-flow heads and so on. Most of these tended to be somewhat unreliable, mainly due to warping or porosity.

Shorrocks produced a supercharger kit which was very effective, but of course this is not really suitable for competition use as it affects the classification of the car.

A number of different engine capacities were also introduced, including some development B.M.C. units which were identified by the prefix XSP before the engine number. Special capacities available for competition purposes were:

960 cc = (948 cc bored + 0·020 in.) 2·498 in. × 3 in.
995 cc = (948 cc bored + 0·060 in.) 2·538 in. × 3 in.
999 cc = 2·82 in. × 2·438 in.
1,098 cc = 2·667 in. × 3 in. (short stroke) (1·75 in. mains)
1,138 cc = 2·59 in. × 3·3 in. (1·75 in. mains or 2 in. mains)
1,293 cc = 2·8 in. × 3·2 in. (2 in. mains)

The Mark II Sprite

The early Mark II Sprites continued in production with a 948 cc unit, prefix 9CG. This had a slightly better profile camshaft, larger inlet valves in an improved head and $1\frac{1}{4}$ in. carburetters as standard. Most of the comments in the previous section apply also to this engine.

In October 1962 the engine size was increased to 1,098 cc (engine prefix 10CG, car HAN-7). This retained the $1\frac{3}{4}$ in. main bearing of the smaller unit, and in addition had a poor internal head design, which resulted in severe local overheating. Other than mild polishing and balancing no tuning is recommended for this model.

With the change in engine, disc brakes became standard fitting at the front end and at the same time wire wheels became a factory option. Previously these had only been available as a special conversion on the Sebring model.

Mark III Sprite

With the HAN-8 model, introduced in March 1964, the rear suspension was altered to half-elliptic springs, and the engine, whilst still remaining at 1,098 cc (prefix 10CC) became much more amenable to tuning. The cylinder head was redesigned with larger inlet valves, the main bearings went up to 2 in. diameter and the whole unit was far more robust.

Starting with the head again the usual polishing operations can be carried out, taking care not to radius the combustion chamber/head face angle. The throat width in the inlet ports can be taken out to an absolute maximum of $1\frac{1}{32}$ in. on this head. Larger inlet valves (C–AEA 628) can be fitted if the seats are suitably ground out.

Approximately 0·060 in. can be ground off the face of the head, and this would give a compression ratio of about 10:1. The ordinary pistons have to be retained because of their short compression height. With the 88G 229 camshaft, the competition distributor C–27H–7766 and ignition set at t d c, power will be something over 65 b h p at 6,000 rev/min. Further slight gains can be achieved by removing the air cleaners (this necessitates changing to AH2 carburetter needles and red damper springs), fitting a three-branch exhaust manifold and modifying the rocker gear (see page 233).

Competition valve springs C–AEA 494 and C–AEA 524 raise the valve bounce point to 7,350 rev/min, whilst lighter cam followers C–AEG 579 help to reduce stresses.

To give even more power, the Mark IV head should be used which gives a compression ratio of 11:1 and larger inlet and exhaust valves. With this head, either the C–AEA 731 or C–AEA 648 camshafts should be used, but care should be taken that the valves do not touch the cylinder block. At least 0·060 in. clearance should be allowed. Similarly, check that there is 0·060 in. clearance between the central coils of the valve spring in the compressed state – this ensures that the springs do not bind and the valve clears the block even under bounce conditions. It is essential before fitting these cams, however, to ensure that the bottom end of the engine has been balanced individually and as an assembly.

If it is intended to rebore the block, 0·060 in. takes the capacity up to 1,144 cc. More than this takes the car out of the popular 1,150 cc capacity class.

With this amount of tune, it is advisable to fit either two $1\frac{1}{2}$ in. SUs or a 45 DCOE twin-choke Weber carburetter. The $1\frac{1}{2}$ in. SUs will fit on the standard inlet manifolds, which should be carefully polished to the correct size. Twin flare or ram pipes should replace the air cleaners. With the 648 cam, use No. 7 needles otherwise No. 6 are suitable; set the competition distributor previously mentioned to give a static timing of 2° to 3° b t d c. All this will give about 80 b h p at 6,000 rev/min.

The Weber will, of course, require a special manifold and fitting kit (C–AJJ 3360). As always, the jets used will depend upon the exact state of tune, but a good starting point would be:

Choke	38 mm
Main jet	1·85/1·90 mm
Air correction	2·10 mm
Slow running	50 F2
Pump jet	·60 mm
Auxiliary	3·5 mm
Float	5 mm

To make full use of this a racing extractor-type exhaust manifold should be used when some 85 b h p at 7,000 rev/min should be obtained. The Mark IV pipe and silencer can be connected to this for road use.

The front suspension is dealt with as on the earlier models, although slightly stronger springs were fitted to later Mark III and all Mark IV models. Special lowered half-elliptic rear springs can also be fitted (C–AHA 8272). Adjustable shockabsorbers are also available (C–AHA 7906/7907). The normal braking system, with DS11 pads at the front, is quite adequate for most competition use.

With the extra power either the $7\frac{1}{4}$ in. competition clutch C–BHA 4448/4449 can be fitted or advice should be obtained from Automotive Products Competition Department at Leamington Spa.

As mentioned earlier, there is a variety of different rear axle ratios that can be used, but from HAN–7–24732 the differential assembly was redesigned. The new one can be identified by the oil filler being on the case and not on the carrier assembly.

Whilst the complete differential assemblies are interchangeable between the early and late axles, the crown wheels and pinions are not interchangeable.

Three alternative ratios are available for the later axle:

Ratio	Originally used	Diff. Assembly Part No.
3·727	Later Riley 1·5	BTA 551
3·9	Sprite from H–AN9–66226	BTA 1222
4·22	Sprite to H–AN9–66225	BTA 550
4·55	Special Competition ratio (No longer available)	C–BTA 916 (crown wheel and pinion only)

The limited slip differential will fit all these ratios.

Sprite Mark IV

With the Mark IV model, the Sprite achieved the same capacity as the 1,275 cc Mini Cooper 'S' model, but it is still detuned compared to its older cousin, giving about 65 b h p at 6,000 rev/min. Inlet and exhaust valves, although larger than the Mark III Sprite, are still smaller than the Mini Cooper, whilst the pistons have a large 'dish' in the crown to keep the compression ratio down to 8·8:1.

The original pre-production cars had a standard-material crankshaft, which was changed to a nitrided crank for the first batch of production models. This crank is marked AEG 517. Later production cars have a slightly different nitrided version (marked AEG 565) which was subsequently changed to a tuftrided version with the same markings. For all practical purposes these two later shafts can be considered equally good. The connecting rods, although heavier, are, if anything, an improvement on the Mini Cooper 'S' rods so, as far as the bottom end is concerned, all that is required is the usual careful balancing. If required, a lightened flywheel (C–AHT 70) and competition diaphragm clutch can be fitted (C–AEG 546/547).

The head should be cleaned up as usual, taking care not to alter the shape of the combustion chamber and ports. The manifold should be opened up to take 1½ in. SU with No. 6 needles and blue damper springs. Flare pipes and exhaust manifolds should be fitted as with the Mark III. The static ignition setting should be about 8° b t d c with either of the standard distributors. This will give approximately 10 b h p more than standard at 6,000 rev/min.

Further power can, of course, be gained by changing the camshaft. The shafts used on the earlier models will not fit the Mark IV, as the oil-pump drive has been changed from a pin type to a spider type to give a stronger coupling. The equivalent of the old 88G 229 cam is the C–AEG 567, and this should be used with the competition distributor and a t d c ignition setting. Naturally with these modifications the compression ratio should be increased, which can be done in several ways. Mini Cooper 'S' pistons come in two types – dished top (8G 2434) giving a compression ratio of 9·75:1, or the alternative flat-top pattern giving a compression ratio of 12:1 which is rather on the high side. If the cylinders are rebored +0·020 in. the capacity goes up to 1,293 cc, which is nicely at the top of the 1,300 cc class; 0·060 in. can be taken off the cylinder head to push the compression ratio up still further to 11·5:1. Lightened cam sprocket (C–AEG 578) and followers (C–AEG 579) should be used, and the power by now will be up to about 83–85 b h p, usable to 6,500 rev/min. Fitting the Mini Cooper 'S' head, similarly polished and machined, would raise this figure still further to 90 b h p at 6,500 rev/min.

For out and out racing the C–AEG 529 camshaft (equivalent of the old 648 cam) can be fitted. This provides no power below 3,000 rev/min but pulls well from 4,500 to 7,500 rev/min, with a peak of about 95 b h p at 6,500. As the valves are open for longer periods, the springs are not stressed as much as with peakier cams, so they can go to a higher figure without bouncing. Stronger springs (C–AEA 652/524) can be fitted if desired, however.

With extremely careful preparation, the power output can be pushed up to 104 b h p at 7,000 rev/min; this necessitates using a 529 cam, 8G 2434 pistons, grinding 0·060 in. off the head face, opening the inlet up to take the C–AEG 544 valve (1·406 in. diameter), the competition distributor set to t d c and fitting a 45 DCOE Weber carburetter with the following settings:

Choke	38
Main jet	1·95
Air correction	1·75
Idling	50 F2
Pump jet	60
Emulsion	F2
Auxiliary	3·5
Float	7 mm

Suspension and transmission should be treated as described earlier.

It is now possible to obtain light-weight body panels, bonnets, boots, etc., for all models of Sprite. Before fitting any of these, make certain that they are suitable for the proposed use of the car. Some of the extremely light-weight bonnets and rear ends, for example, whilst perfectly adequate for racing use, would not last a week on a car used for daily journeys on the road. If your aim is to lighten the car for racing, take care that you do not affect the inherent strength of the basic structure, as this can have disastrous results. Never forget that some Sprites are getting quite old now, so before commencing any modifications ensure that the basic parts are in a sound condition.

The works Le Mans and Sebring Sprites

There have been some 30 of these one-off racing models produced by the Donald Healey Motor Co. at Warwick, and naturally their specifications varied from year to year and from event to event. It is interesting to note that for the 1967/68 events a special five-speed gearbox was fitted, giving the following ratios: first, 2·45:1; second, 1·620:1; third, 1·268:1; fourth, direct; fifth, 0·85:1; and reverse, 3·201:1. Normally a 3·727:1 rear axle was used with this arrangement, and with Lucas fuel injection the 1,293 cc engine gave some 120 b h p at 7,000 rev/min. The car which ran at Le Mans in 1968 averaged something like 95 mile/h for the full 24 hours, including all pit stops – ample proof of the development since the original 1958 'bug-eyed' model.

'Fly-off' handbrake

On most cars the handbrake lever incorporates a ratchet, so that the brake can be applied by a simple pull, and will then be automatically held in the 'on' position until deliberately released by pressing a catch.

A few years ago the sports car was always distinguished from more routine transportation by the fact that it had a 'fly-off' handbrake. This means that the ratchet works in the opposite sense to usual: on pulling up the lever the usual clicking sound is absent and the lever is quite free to move in either direction. Pressing the catch puts the ratchet into engagement when required to hold the brake on. To release the brake, one pulls the lever up to take the tension off the pawl, whereupon the catch pops out and the lever is quite free again and, if released, will 'fly-off'.

The idea was to facilitate holding the car on the starting line of a race or hill climb, so that when the flag fell the driver simply let go of the lever without having to hold the catch at all. Nowadays, it is a great advantage in the violent manoeuvres called for in gymkhanas and driving tests; the 'handbrake turn' is a standard trick and a quick handful of rear brakes is made much easier if the ratchet is disengaged. Even on the road, a clean restart on a gradient is easier to manage with a fly-off than with the standard handbrake.

The only reason that Sprites are fitted with standard handbrakes is that so many new owners (particularly overseas) find the fly-off type unfamiliar and are unwilling to teach themselves a new technique. Car-park and garage attendants, too, go blue in the face trying to release a fly-off by pressing the button, which in fact clamps it on harder!

A simple conversion for Sprite handbrakes to fly-off operation is:

Remove the left-hand seat cushion and backrest to give room to work. Remove the clevis pin from the handbrake cable where it joins the compensator on the rear axle.

Remove the two cross-head screws holding the handbrake lever assembly to the propeller shaft tunnel and pull the lever away from the tunnel sufficiently for removal of the nut securing the short lever to the handbrake fulcrum. This will allow the assembly to be removed from the car. Take care that the short lever does not fall back into the tunnel; secure it with wire.

It will be seen that the standard operation of the spring-loaded release is to keep the pawl in contact with the ratchet. We must reverse this action so that the spring holds it off.

Make up a plate from $\frac{1}{16}$ in. sheet steel as shown, and rivet one end to the pawl. Heat the handbrake release rod at the bend and reshape to the opposite angle so that when the pawl is reassembled the rod will connect with the spare hole in the new plate.

Pressing the release button will now bring the pawl into engagement with the ratchet and the tension in the brake cable will hold it in engagement. A twitch of the lever will take the load off the pawl and the spring will pull it clear of the ratchet. Reassembly is in the reverse order of dismantling.

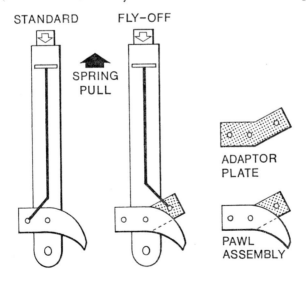

STANDARD   FLY-OFF

SPRING
PULL

ADAPTOR
PLATE

PAWL
ASSEMBLY

APPENDIX V

TECHNICAL SPECIFICATIONS

The specifications on the following pages are based on information found in the official workshop manuals and other official sources. For details of tolerances, etc., these publications should be consulted. All dimensions are quoted in inches unless otherwise noted.

Abbreviations

Bearing surfaces:	WM	White metal, cast direct
	WMB	White metal lined on bronze shells
	TW WM	Thin wall, white metal lined
	SWM	Steel and white metal
	TW RB	Thin wall, rolled bush
	D	Front bearing – steel-backed white metal; middle and rear – direct in crankcase
	TM	Detachable, steel-backed tri-metal
	LIS	Steel-backed, lead indium
	CLS	Steel-backed, copper-lead lined
	WMSLI	White metalled steel shell, lead-indium plated
	CLI	Steel-backed, copper, lead, indium plated
Clutches:	SDP	Single dry plate
	DSP	Diaphragm spring pattern
Fuel pumps:	SU El	SU Electric pattern
	AC Me	AC Mechanical pattern
General:	N/A	Not applicable

WARWICK BUILT HEALEYS

	Westland, Elliot, Duncan, Sportsmobile	Silverstone	Tickford, Abbott	Nash	Sports-Convertible (Alvis)
Approx. Production dates	1946–50	1949–50	1950–54	1950–54	1951–53
Serial numbers	—	D1 to D51 E52 to E104	C 1842 on BT 1999 on F 3001 on	—	G501 to G528
Make of engine/Number of cylinders	Riley 4	Riley 4	Riley 4	Nash 6	Alvis 6
Bore/Stroke (mm)	80·5 × 120	80·5 × 120	80·5 × 120	85·72 × 111·12 (after 1952 88·9 × 111·12)	84 × 90
Capacity (cc)	2,443	2,443	2,443	3,848 (after 1952 4,138)	2,993
Compression ratio	6·5: 1 (later 6·9: 1)	6·9: 1	6·9: 1	8·1: 1 (after 1952 8·25: 1)	7·0: 1
Firing order	1, 2, 4, 3	1, 2, 4, 3	1, 2, 4, 3	1, 5, 3, 6, 2, 4	1, 5, 3, 6, 2, 4
Torque (lb ft@rev/min)	132@3,000	132@3,000	132@3,000	210@1,600	140@2,000
B m e p (lb/in²)	125	125	125	—	—
B h p (@rev/min)	104@4,500	104@4,500	104@4,500	125@4,000 (after 1952 135@4,000)	106@4,200
Valves:					
Lift	0·390	0·390	0·390	—	—
Head diam.: inlet	1·856	1·856	1·856	—	—
exhaust	1·604	1·604	1·604	—	—
Stem diam.	0·3125	0·3125	0·3125	—	—
Rocker clearance (engine hot): inlet	0·003	0·003	0·003	0·012	0·012
exhaust	0·004	0·004	0·004	0·016	0·015
Valve timing:					
Rocker gap	0·005	0·005	0·005	—	0·020
Inlet opens (b t d c)	17°	17°	17°	—	13°
Inlet closes (a b d c)	43°	43°	43°	—	—
Exhaust opens (b b d c)	45°	45°	45°	—	—
Exhaust closes (a t d c)	20°	20°	20°	—	—
Pistons: Clearance at skirt	0·0022	0·0022	0·0022	—	—
Piston rings:					
Number	4	4	4	4	—
Width, compression	0·0932	0·0932	0·0932	0·0937	—
oil	0·1570	0·1570	0·1570	0·1562	—
Ring gap	0·010	0·010	0·010	—	—
Gudgeon pin: Type	Floating	Floating	Floating	Floating	—
Fit	Hand push @70°C	Hand push @70°C	Hand push @70°C	—	—
Diam.	0·866	0·866	0·866	0·8745	—
Connecting rods:					
length, centres	8·625	8·625	8·625	—	—
side clearance	0·005	0·005	0·005	—	—
Big-ends:					
Type	WM	WM	WM	—	—
Diametrical clearance	0·0015	0·0015	0·0015	—	—
Crankshaft:					
Journal diam.	2·559	2·559	2·559	2·479	—
Crankpin diam.	2·362	2·362	2·362	2·000	—
Max. crankpin undersize	−0·040	−0·040	−0·040	—	—
Main bearings:					
No. and type	3 WMB	3 WMB	3 WMB	7	7
Length, front and centre	1·938	1·938	1·938	—	—
rear	2·7559	2·7559	2·7559	—	—
Running clearance	0·002	0·002	0·002	—	—

WARWICK BUILT HEALEYS—*continued*

	Westland, Elliot, Duncan, Sportsmobile	Silverstone	Tickford, Abbott	Nash	Sports-Convertible (Alvis)
Lubrication:					
Pump type	Straight gear	Straight gear	Straight gear	Gear	—
Pressure running (lb in²)	25 to 40	25 to 40	25 to 40	30	40
idling (lb/in²)	12	12	12	—	—
Sump capacity (pints)	12	12	12	12	12
Ignition:					
Contact breaker gap	0·012 to 0·015	0·012 to 0·015	0·012 to 0·015	0·018 to 0·024	0·012 to 0·015
Static setting	4° b t d c	4° b t d c	4° b t d c	t d c	2° b t d c
Spark plug type	Champion L7	Champion L7	Champion L7	Autolite AL5	—
gap	0·025	0·025	0·025	0·030	0·025
Fuel system:					
Pump type	2 SU El	2 SU El	2 SU El	AC Me	AC Me
Carburetter	2SU HV4	2SU H4	2SU H4	2SU H6 (later 2 Carter)	2SU H4
Needles, standard	AM	AM	EE	SO	ES
rich	S6	S6	CY	—	L
weak	AJ	AJ	EM	—	—
Air cleaner	cold air box	cold air box	air filter	dry	—
Damper spring colour	—	—	—	—	Red
Tank capacity (gals)	16	17	16	20	16
Cooling system:					
Capacity (pints)	24	24	24	34	28
Clutch: Size/Type	9 or 10 in. SDP	10 in. SDP	10 in. SDP	10 in. SDP	10 in. SDP
Gearbox ratios: First	3·646: 1	3·646: 1	3·646: 1	2·57: 1	2·57: 1
Second	2·155: 1	2·155: 1	2·155: 1	1·55: 1	1·922: 1
Third	1·418: 1	1·418: 1	1·418: 1	Direct	1·315: 1
Fourth	Direct	Direct	Direct	N/A	Direct
Overdrive	N/A	N/A	N/A	0·7: 1	N/A
Reverse	3·646: 1	3·646: 1	3·646: 1	—	—
Oil capacity (pints)	2¼	2¼	2¼	2¼ + 1¼ (O/D)	—
Rear axle:					
Type	¾ floating prop shaft in torque tube	¾ floating prop shaft in torque tube	(F chassis- Salisbury open prop shaft)	Nash with with torque tube	Salisbury open prop shaft
Final drive	Helical bevel	Helical bevel	(F chassis- hypoid)	Hypoid	Hypoid
Ratio	3·5: 1	3·5: 1	3·77: 1	4·1: 1	3·77: 1
Alternatives		3·0; 3·1; 3·28; 3·25; 3·64; 3·78; 3·88			
Oil capacity (pints)	3¼	3¼	—	4	—
Suspension:					
Castor angle	0°	1°	1°	1°	1°
Camber angle	0° to 1°	0° to 1°	0° to 1°	−½° to +1½°	0° to 1°
Swivel pin inclination	9°	9°	9°	9°	9°
Rear shockabsorbers type	Lever	Telescopic	(F chassis- telescopic)	Telescopic	Telescopic
Brakes: Type/diam. front	Drum 11 in.	Drum 11 in.	Drum 11 in.	Drum 10 in.	Drum 11 in.
rear	Drum 10 in.	Drum 10 in.	F chassis Drum 11 in.	Drum 10 in.	Drum 11 in.
Make	Lockheed	Lockheed	(F chassis Girling)	Bendix	Girling
Total friction area (in²)	150	150	(F chassis 170)	176	170
Steering: Track toe in	⅛ to ¼	⅛ to ¼	⅛ to ¼	3/16	⅛ to ¼
Wheels:					
Tyre size standard	5·75 × 15	5·50 × 15	5·75 × 15	6·40 × 15	6·40 × 15
Pressure, front (lb/in²)	20	20	22	24	22
rear	20	20	24	24	24
Electrical:					
Voltage	12	12	12	6 (later 12)	12
Battery capacity (amp hrs)	63	63	63	105	63
Dimensions:					
Wheelbase	8 ft 6 in.	8 ft 6 in.	8 ft 6 in.	8 ft 6 in. (Farina – 9 ft)	8 ft 6 in.

WARWICK BUILT HEALEYS—*continued*

	Westland, Elliot, Duncan, Sportsmobile	Silverstone	Tickford, Abbott	Nash	Sports-Convertible (Alvis)
Overall length	14 ft (Sportsmobile – 15 ft)	14 ft (without front bumpers – 13 ft 6 in)	14 ft 9 in.	14 ft 4 in.	14 ft 6 in
Overall height	Elliot & Duncan 4 ft 10 in. Westland 4 ft 7 in. Sportsmobile 4 ft 6 in.	3 ft 7 in.	4 ft 7 in.	4 ft 4¾ in.	4 ft 8 in
Overall width	5 ft 5½ in.	5 ft 3 in.	5 ft 7 in.	5 ft 6 in.	5 ft 5 in.
Ground clearance	7 in.	7 in.	7 in.	6 in.	7 in.
Track front	4 ft 6 in.	4 ft 6 in.	4 ft 6 in.	4 ft 5 in.	4 ft 5 in.
rear	4 ft 5 in.	4 ft 5 in.	(F chassis 4 ft 7 in)	4 ft 7 in.	4 ft 7 in.
Approx. weight (cwt)	Elliot 22½ Westland 23 Duncan 26	18½	26½	24	24¾

Performance:

	Elliot	Westland	Silverstone	Tickford, Abbott	Nash	Sports-Convertible (Alvis)
0–30 mile/h (sec.)	3·7	4·3	—	5·0	—	4·4
0–50	8·4	10·2	6·6	10·5	—	9·7
0–60	12·3	14·7	11·0	14·6	9·5	13·5
0–70	17·8	19·2	15·0	19·6	—	18·8
0–80	23·5	28·3	—	28·3	—	—
Standing ¼ mile	—	—	—	19·3	—	19·9
Max. speed (mile/h.)	102	104	—	104	110	100

H.A.H.—17

AUSTIN-HEALE"

	Hundred BN 1	Hundred BN 2	100 S	100 M	100-Six BN 4	100-Six BN 4/BN 6
Basic Identification	3-speed gearbox	4-speed gearbox	Racing model	Modified engine	4 inlet port head	6 inlet port head BN 4—2 sea BN 6—2/4 se
Approximate production dates	1953–55	1955–56	Feb.-July 1955	1955–56	from Aug. 1956	1959 to March
Chassis serial numbers	138031 to 228046	228047 to 233455	3501–10 3601–10 3701–10 3801–10 3901–10	—	50759 onwards	to BN 4 7770 and BN 6 50 to 4650
Engine prefix	—	—	1B	—	—	26D
Engine serial numbers	—	—	222701 to 222750	—	—	60449 to 26D 77766
Number of cylinders	4	As BN I	As BN I	As BN I	6	As BN 4
Bore/stroke (mm)	87·3×111·1	„	„	„	79·365×88·9	„
Capacity (cc)	2,660	„	„	„	2,639	„
Compression ratio	7·5:1	„	8·3:1	8·1:1	8·25:1	8·7:1
Firing order	1,3,4,2	„	1,3,4,2	1,3,4,2	1,5,3,6,2,4	1,5,3,6,2,
Torque (lb ft@rev/min)	150@2000	„	168@2500	144@2000	142@2400	150@3000
B m e p (lb/in^2)	139	„	157	—	139	—
B h p (@rev/min.)	90@4000	„	132@4700	110@4500	102@4600	117@4750
Valves: Lift	0·390	„	0·435	0·435	0·3145	0·3145
Diam. head, inlet	1·725	„	1·813	As BN I	1·690	1·750
exhaust	1·415	„	1·625	„	1·420	1·560
stem, inlet	0·3420	„	—	„	0·3420	0·3420
exhaust	0·3420	„	—	„	0·3420	0·3420
Rocker clearance	0·012	„	0·015	0·015	0·012	0·012
Valve guides: length, inlet	2·1406	„	—	As BN I	2·266	—
exhaust	2·8281	„	—	„	2·578	—
Valve spring, freelength: inner	1·9531	„	—	„	1·969	—
outer	2·1718	„	—	„	2·047	—
fitted length, inner (@lb)	1·5@22·5	„	—	„	1·517@25·3	1·504@26
outer	1·703@65	„	—	„	1·607@54·2	1·594@55·7
Tappets: Diameter	0·999	„	—	„	0·937	As BN 4
Length	3·03	„	—	„	2·548	„
Rocker bushes type	TW WM	„	—	„	SWM	„
inside diam. (reamed)	0·812	„	—	„	0·812	„
Clearance	0·012	„	—	„	0·012	„
Camshaft: Journal diam, front	1·789	,,	As BN I	,,	1·789	,,
middle front	1·749	„	„	„	1·769	„
middle rear	N/A	„	„	„	1·749	„
rear	1·623	„	„	„	1·729	„
End-float	0·005	„	„	„	0·005	„
Bearings, No. and type	3 TW WM	„	„	„	4 TW RB	„
Reamed inside diam.: Front	1·7905	„	„	„	1·7905	„
Middle front	1·7505	„	„	„	1·7705	„
Middle rear	N/A	„	„	„	1·7505	„
Rear	1·6245	„	„	„	1·7305	„
Valve timing: Chain pitch	0·375	„	„	„	0·375	„
No. of pitches	62	„	„	„	62	„
Rocker clearance for timing	0·021	„	„	„	0·0234	„
Inlet valve opens (b t d c)	5°	„	10°	10°	5°	5°
closes (a b d c)	45°	„	50°	50°	45°	45°
Exhaust valve opens (b b d c)	40°	„	45°	45°	40°	40°
closes (a t d c)	10°	„	15°	15°	10°	10°
Pistons: Skirt clearance, top	0·0015	„	—	As BN I	0·002	As BN 4
bottom	—	„	—	—		

1ODELS

3000 3N 7/BT 7	3000 Mk II BN 7/BT 7	3000 Mk II BJ 7	3000 Mk III BJ 8	Sprite AN 5	Sprite Mk II AN 6	Sprite Mk II AN 7	Sprite Mk III AN 8	Sprite Mk IV AN 9
BN 7 BT 7	triple carbs 2 seat 2/4 seat	twin carbs 2/4 seat	2/4 seat		948 cc engine	1998 cc engine		
1959–61	1961–62	1962–64	1964–67	1958–61	1961–62	1962–64	1964–66	1966 on
101 to 13750	13751 to 19853	17551 to 25314	25315 to 43026	501 to 50116	101 to 24731	24732 to 38828	38829 to 64734	64734 on
29D 101 to 26212 6	29E 101 to 5799 As Mk I	29F 101 to 6188 As Mk I	29K 101 onwards As Mk I	9C 101 to 49201 4	9CG 101 to 36711 As AN 5	10CG 101 to 21048 4	10CC 101 onwards As AN 7	12CC 101 onwards 4
3·34×88·9	„	„	„	62·94×76·2	„	64·58×83·72	„	70·61×81·28
2,912				948		1,098		1,275
9·0:1				8·3:1	9·1:1	8·9:1		8·8:1
, 5, 3, 6, 2, 4	„	„	„	1, 3, 4, 2	1, 3, 4, 2	1, 3, 4, 2		1, 3, 4, 2
162@2700	—	165@3000	165@3000	52@3300	52·8@3000	62@3200	65@3500	72@3000
142	—	—	—	136				139
124@4600	132@4750	131@4750	148@5200	43@5200	46@5500	56@5500	59@5750	65@6000
0·3145	0·368	As Mk II BN 7	As BJ 7	0·28	0·312	0·312	0·312	0·318
1·750	As Mk I	„	„	1·0937	1·153	1·215	1·215	1·310
1·560	„	„	„	1·00	1·00	1·00	1·00	1·154
0·3420	„	„	„	0·2795	0·2795	0·2795	0·2795	0·2795
0·3420	„	„	„	0·2790	0·2790	0·2790	0·2790	0·2790
0·012	„	„	„	0·012	0·012	0·012	0·012	0·012
2·266	„	„	„	1·687	1·687	As AN 6	As AN 7	1·6875
2·578	„	„	„	1·687	1·687	„	„	1·6875
1·969	„	„	„	single spring only	1·672	„	„	1·703
2·047	2·031	„	„	1·750	1·750	„	„	1·828
1·504@26	As Mk I	„	„	N/A	1·179@18·5	„	„	1·27@25
·594@55·7	1·594@67·5	„	„	1·297@57·5	1·291@52	„	„	1·383@51
As BN 4	As BN 7	„	„	0·812	As AN 5	„	„	As AN 8
„	„	„	„	1·505	„	„	„	„
„	„	„	„	0·563	0·563	0·563	0·563	0·563
„	„	„	„	—	—	—	—	—
‚‚	‚‚	‚‚	‚‚	1·666	As AN 5	As AN 6	As AN 6	As AN 6
„	„	„	„	1·623	„	„	„	„
„	„	„	„	N/A	„	„	„	„
„	„	„	„	1·373	„	„	„	„
„	„	„	„	0·005	„	„	„	„
„	„	„	„	3 D	3 SWM	„	„	„
„	„	„	„	—	1·667	„	„	„
„	„	„	„		1·6245	„	„	„
„	„	„	„	N/A	N/A	„	„	„
„	„	„	„		1·375	„	„	„
0·375 62	„	„	„	0·375 52	As AN 5 „	„	„	„
0·030 5° 45° 40° 10°	0·030 5° 45° 51° 21°	0·030 5° 45° 51° 21°	0·030 16° 56° 51° 21°	0·019 5° 45° 40° 10°	0·029 5° 45° 51° 21°	„	„	„
	From I.O. I.C. E.O. E.C.	29F 2286 10° 50° 45° 15°						
0·0037 0·0012	As BN 7 „	As BN 7 „	As BN 7 „	0·001 —	0·004 0·002	0·003 0·0007	As AN 7 „	0·0033 0·0018

AUSTIN HEALE*

	Hundred BN 1	Hundred BN 2	100 S	100 M	100-Six BN 4	100-Six BN 4/BN 6
Width of ring groove, compression	0·0962	As BN 1	—	As BN 1	0·0957	As BN 4
oil	0·1585	,,	—	,,	0·1895	,,
Max. piston oversize	0·040	,,	—	,,	0·040	,,
Piston rings: Number	3+1	,,	2+1	,,	3+1	,,
Width, compression	0·0935	,,	—	,,	0·0935	,,
oil	0·1557	,,	—	,,	0·187	,,
Ring gap, compression	0·013	,,	—	,,	0·011	,,
oil	0·013	,,	—	,,	0·011	,,
Gudgeon pin: Type	Floating	,,	Fully floating	,,	Clamped (Floating after 40500)	Fully floating
Fit	Push @ 70°	,,	—	,,	Selective fit	Selective fit
Diameter	0·8749	,,	—	,,	0·8749	0·8749
Connecting rods:						
Length, centres	8·185	,,	—	,,	6·603	6·603
Side clearance	0·010	,,	—	,,	0·0055	0·0055
Big-end type	TW WM	,,	TM	,,	TW WM	LIS
Diametrical clearance	0·0012	,,	—	,,	0·0012	0·0012
Crankshaft:						
Journal diam.	2·479	,,	—	,,	2·3745	As BN 4
Crankpin diam.	2·000	,,	—	,,	2·000	As BN 4
Max. undersizes	0·040	,,	—	,,	0·040	,,
End-float	0·0025	,,	—	,,	0·004	,,
Main bearings:						
No. & type	3 SWM	,,	3 TM	,,	4 SWM	,,
Length	Front 1·75 Middle & rear 1·995	,,	—	,,	1·50	,,
Running clearance	0·0017	,,	—	,,	0·002	,,
Lubrication pump: Type	Straight gear	,,	High pressure	,,	Rotor	,,
Oil pressure, running (lb/in²)	50–55	,,	—	,,	55–60	,,
idling (lb/in²)	—	,,	—	,,	25–30	,,
Sump capacity (pints)	11¾	,,	11¾	,,	12	,,
Ignition: Distributor type	Lucas DM2P4	,,	—	—	Lucas DM6A	,,
Contact breaker gap	0·015	,,	0·015	0·015	0·015	,,
Static setting (b t d c)	6°	,,	—	9°	6°	,,
Stroboscope setting	—	,,	—	—	—	—
Spark plug—type	N 5	,,	N 3	N 3	UN12Y	,,
gap	0·025	,,	—	0·022	0·025	,,
Fuel pumps: Type	SU El	,,	2SU El	SU El	SU El	SU El
Carburetters:						
Type	2 SU H4	,,	2 SU H6	2 SU H6	2 SU H4	2 SU HD6
Needles, standard	QW	,,	KW1	OA7	AJ	CV
rich	QA	,,	KW	OA6	4	RD
weak	AT	,,	SA	OA8	M1	SQ
Jet size	0·090	,,	0·100	0·100	0·090	0·100
Damper spring colour	Yellow	,,	Red	Red	Red	Yellow
Petrol tank capacity (galls)	12	,,	20	12	12	12
Radiator capacity (pints)	20	,,	20	As BN 1	20	As BN 4
Thermostat setting °C	73	,,	73	,,	70	,,
Clutch: Type and size	9 in. SDP	,,	10 in. SDP	,,	9 in. SDP	,,
Total axial press. (lb)	1260	,,	—	,,	1260	,,

MODELS—*continued*

3000 BN 7/BT 7	3000 Mk II BN 7/BT 7	3000 Mk II BJ 7	3000 Mk III BJ 8	Sprite AN 5	Sprite Mk II AN 6	Sprite Mk II AN 7	Sprite Mk III AN 8	Sprite Mk IV AN 9
0·145	As BN 7	As BN 7	As BN 7	—	—	—	—	0·049
0·160	„	„	„	—	—	—	—	0·1583
0·040	„	„	„	0·040	0·040	0·040	0·040	0·020
3+1	„	„	„	3+1	As AN 5	3+1	As AN 7	3+1
0·130	„	„	„	0·070	„	0·062	„	—
0·130	„	„	„	0·125	„	0·125	„	—
0·015	„	„	„	0·009	„	0·009	„	Top 0·013 2nd & 3rd 0·911
0·015 ully floating	„	„	„	0·009 Clamped	Semi-floating	0·009 Fully floating	„	0·020 Pressed in
Selective fit 0·8749	„	„	„	0·0002 0·6245	0·0002 0·6245	Push fit —	„	Push fit 0·8124
6·603	„	„	„	5·75	5·75	As AN 6	„	5·75
0·007	„	„	„	0·010	0·010	„	„	0·008
LIS	„	„	„	CLS	LIS	„	„	LIS
0·0025	„	„	„	0·0017	0·0017	„	„	0·0017
2·3745	„	„	„	1·7507	As AN 5	„	2·0007	2·0007
2·000	„	„	„	1·6257	„	„	1·6257	1·6257
0·020	„	„	„	0·020	„	„	0·020	0·010
0·004	„	„	„	—	—	—	—	0·0025
4 WMSLI	„	„	„	3 LIS	„	3 LIS	As AN 7	3 CLI
1·50	„	„	„	1·1875	„	1·0625	„	0·980
0·002	„	„	„	0·0012	„	0·0012	„	0·0018
Gear	„	„	„	Eccentric rotor	„	As AN 6	„	Gear
50	„	„	„	30–60	„	„	„	40–70
20	„	„	„	10–25	„	„	„	20
12¾	„	„	„	6½	„	„	„	6½
DM6A	„	(from 29F3562–Lucas25D6)	Lucas 25D6	Lucas DM2 PH4	Lucas DM2 P4	Lucas 25D4	„	Lucas 23D4 or 25D4
0·015	„	0·015	0·015	0·015	0·015	0·015	„	0·015
5°	„	5° (from 29F3562–10°)	10°	5°	4°	5°	„	7°
15°@600	„	—	15°@600	—	6°@600	8°@600	„	22°@1000
UN12Y	„	As BN 7	As BJ 7	N	N 5	N 5	N 5	UN12Y or N9Y
0·025				0·025	0·025	0·025	0·025	0·025
SU El	SU El	SU El	SU El	AC Me	AC Me	AC Me	SU El	SU El
2 SU HD6	3 SU HS4	2 SU HS6	2SU HD8	2 SU H1	2 SU HS2	2 SU HS2	2 SU HS2	2 SU HS2
CV	DJ	BC	UH	GG	V3	GY	AN	AN
RD	DK	RD	UN	EB	V2	M	H6	H6
SQ	DH	TZ	UL	MOW	GX	GG	GG	GG
0·100	0·090	0·100	0·125	0·090	0·090	0·090	0·090	0·090
Green	Red	Green	Red and green	—	Light blue	Blue	Blue	Light blue
12	12	12	12	6	6	6	6	6
18	As BN 7	18	18	10	10	10	As AN 7	10
70	„	70 or 83	83	73	65–70	82	„	82
10 in. SDP	„	10 in. SDP (from 29F 4898— 9 in. DSP)	9 in. DSP	6¼ in. SDP	As AN 5	7¼ in. SDP	„	6½ in. DSP
1680	„	—	—	570	„	—	—	—

	Hundred BN 1	Hundred BN 2	100 S	100 M	100-Six BN 4	100-Six BN 4/BN
Gearbox ratios: First	2·25 : 1	3·073 : 1	3·075 : 1	As BN 1 or BN 2	3·076 : 1	As BN 4
Second	1·42 : 1	1·915 : 1	1·907 : 1	„	1·913 : 1	„
O/D Second	1·074 : 1 (from O/D No. 1292/1 1·129 : 1	N/A	N/A	„	N/A	„
Third	Direct	1·332 : 1	1·328 : 1	„	1·333 : 1	„
O/D Third	0·756 : 1 or 0·795 : 1	1·034 : 1	N/A	„	1·037 : 1	„
Fourth	N/A	Direct	Direct	„	Direct	„
O/D Fourth	N/A	0·776	N/A	„	0·778	„
Reverse	4·98 : 1	4·18 : 1	4·17 : 1	„	4·16 : 1	„
Oil capacity (standard) (pints)	N/A	N/A	3	N/A	5	„
(withoverdrive)	5½	5¼	N/A	As BN 1 or BN 2	6¼	„
Rear axle:						
Ratio, standard	N/A	N/A	2·92 : 1	„	3·91 : 1	„
with overdrive box	4·125 : 1	4·1 : 1	N/A	„	4·1 : 1	„
alternatives	—	—	2·69 : 1 3·66 : 1, 4·125 : 1	3·667 : 1	—	—
Final drive, type	Spiral bevel	Hypoid	Spiral bevel	As BN 1 or BN 2	Hypoid	„
capacity (pints)	2¼	3	2½	„	3	„
Suspension:						
Castor angle	1¾°	As BN 1	—	„	2°	„
Camber angle	1°	„	—	„	1°	„
Swivel pin inclination	6½°	„	—	„	6½°	„
Front spring: type	Coil	„	Coil	„	Coil	„
Rear spring: Type	Semi-elliptic	„	Semi-elliptic	„	Semi-elliptic	„
Number of leaves	7 (from chassis 152233–8)	8	—	8	7	„
Shock absorbers	Lever	Lever	Double acting	„	Lever	„
Brakes: Type and diam. front	11 in. Drum	As BN 1	11½ in. Disc	„	11 in. Drum	„
rear	11 in. Drum	„	11½ in. Disc	„	11 in. Drum	„
Steering: Type	Cam and peg	„	Cam and peg	„	Cam and peg	„
ratio	12·6 : 1	„	—	„	14·1 : 1	„
Track toe in	1/16 to ⅛	„	⅛	„	1/16 to ⅛	„
Wheel size: Standard	5·90 × 15	As BN 1	5·50 × 15	„	5·90 × 15	„
Pressures front (lb in²)	20	„	23	26	20	„
rear	23	„	26	29	23	„
Type of wheel	Wire	„	Wire	Wire	Disc or wire	„
Electrical: Voltage	12	„	12	As BN 2	12	„
Battery capacity (20 hr rate)	57	„	38	„	58	„
Generator: Cut in speed	1100–1250	„	—	„	1100–1250	„
Max. output amps	22	„	—	„	22	„
Dimensions: Wheelbase	7 ft 6 in.	„	7 ft 6 in.	„	7 ft 8 in.	„
Overall length	12 ft 7 in.	„	12 ft 4 in.	„	13 ft 1½ in.	„
Overall height	4 ft 1½ in.	„	3 ft 6 in.	„	4 ft 1 in.	„
Ground clearance	5½ in.	„	5½ in.	„	5½ in.	„
Track, front	4 ft 1 in.	„	4 ft 1⅝ in.	„	4 ft 0¾ in.	„
rear	4 ft 2¾ in.	„	4 ft 2¾ in.	„	4 ft 2 in.	„
Turning circle	35 ft	„	35 ft	„	35 ft	„
Approx. weight (lb)	2176	„	1924	„	2436	„
Performance figures:						
0–30 mile/h (sec.)	3·3	„	3·4	—	4·3	3·6
0–50	7·6	„	7·2	—	9·3	8·2
0–60	10·3	„	9·8	—	12·9	11·2
0–70	13·4	„	12·5	—	17·5	14·8
0–80	18·0	„	15·4	—	22·6	20·1
0–90	25·6	„	19·0	—	32·3	25·8
0–100	—	—	24·4	—	—	37·7
Standing ¼ mile	17·5	—	16·8	—	18·8	18·1
Maximum speed (mile/h)	111	„	125	—	103	111

MODELS—*continued*

3000 BN 7/BT 7	3000 Mk II BN 7/BT 7	3000 Mk II BJ 7	3000 Mk III BJ 8	Sprite AN 5	Sprite Mk II AN 6	Sprite Mk II AN 7	Sprite Mk III AN 8	Sprite Mk IV AN 9
2·93:1*	2·83:1	As Mk II	2·637:1	3·627:1	3·200:1	As AN 6	As AN 7	As AN 8
2·053:1*	2·06:1	„	2·071:1	2·374:1	1·916:1	„	„	„
N/A	N/A	„	N/A	N/A	N/A	„	„	„
1·309:1*	1·31:1	„	1·306:1	1·412:1	1·357:1	„	„	„
1·075:1*	1·076:1	„	1·071:1	N/A	N/A	„	„	„
Direct	Direct	„	Direct	Direct	Direct	„	„	„
0·822	0·822	„	0·820	N/A	N/A	„	„	„
3·78:1* (* later cars as Mk II)	3·72:1	„	3·391:1	4·664:1	4·114:1	4·120:1	„	„
5	As BN 7	„	As BJ 7	2¼	As AN 5	As AN 6	„	„
6¼	„	„	„	N/A	„	„	„	„
3·545:1	„	„	„	4·22:1	„	„	„	4·22:1 (from 77573 3·9:1)
3·909:1	„	„	„	N/A	„	„	„	N/A
4·1:1	„	„	4·1:1, 4·3:1, 4·875:1	—	—	—	—	—
Hypoid	„	„	As BJ 7	Hypoid	„	„	„	As AN 8
3	„	„	„	1¾	„	„	„	„
2°	„	„	„	3°	„	„	„	„
1°	„	„	„	1°	„	„	„	„
6½°	„	„	„	6½°	„	„	„	„
Coil	„	„	„	Coil	„	„	„	„
Semi-elliptic	„	„	„	¼ Elliptic	„	„	Semi-elliptic	Semi-elliptic
7	„	„	7 (from BJ 8 26705–6)	15	„	„	5	5
Lever	„	„	Lever	Lever	„	„	Lever	As AN 8
11 in. Disc	„	„	As BJ 7	7 in. Drum	„	8¼ in. Disc	As AN 7	„
11 in. Drum	„	„	„	7 in. Drum	„	7 in. Drum	„	„
Cam and peg	„	„	„	Rack and pinion	„	As AN 6	„	„
15·1:1	„	„	„	2¼ turns	„	„	„	„
1/16 to 1/8	„	„	„	0 to 1/8	„	„	„	„
5·90×15	„	„	„	5·20×13	„	„	„	„
20	„	„	„	18	„	„	„	„
25	„	„	„	20	„	„	„	„
Disc or wire	„	„	„	Disc	Disc or wire	„	„	„
12	„	„	„	12	As AN 5	„	„	„ (later cars neg. earth)
58	„	„	„	43	„	„	„	„
1100–1250	„	„	1250	1050–1200	„	„	„	„
25	„	„	30	19	„	22	„	„
7 ft 7¾ in.	„	„	As BJ 7	6 ft 8 in.	„	As AN 6	„	„
13 ft 1½ in.	„	„	„	11 ft 5⅝ in.	„	„	„	„
4 ft 2¾ in.	„	„	„	4 ft 1¾ in.	„	„	„	„
4⅝ in.	„	„	„	5 in.	„	„	„	„
4 ft 0¾ in.	„	„	„	3 ft 9¾ in.	„	3 ft 10⅜ in.	„	„
4 ft 2 in.	„	„	„	3 ft 8¾ in.	„	3 ft 8¾ in.	„	„
35 ft 7 in.	„	„	„	32 ft	„	32 ft	„	„
2460	„	„	„	1400	1460	1466	1490	1510
3·5	3·8	3·3	3·5	5·1	5·7	4·7	4·2	4·2
8·0	8·3	7·5	6·9	13·7	13·3	11·6	9·8	9·2
11·4	10·9	10·3	9·8	20·7	19·2	16·9	14·7	13·0
14·3	14·3	13·4	12·5	33·6	30·8	26·2	20·4	19·1
18·9	19·2	17·6	15·6	—	58·4	37·4	33·4	27·8
24·8	25·9	23·0	19·5	—	—	—	—	—
32·8	36·4	29·8	24·7	—	—	—	—	—
17·9	18·3	17·4	17·0	21·7	21·7	21·0	19·7	19·1
114	113	116	122	81·5	86·5	88·4	91·4	95·1

PRODUCTION FIGURES

Warwick built cars

Chassis type	Total	Elliot	Westland	Duncan	Sportsmobile	Silverstone	Tickford	Abbott	Nash	Sports Convertible	Others	Date introduced
'A'	97	15	15	8							59	Oct. 1946
'B'	231	85	41	31	23						51	Mid 1947
'C'	170	1	8				124	27			10	1950
'D'	51					51						Sept. 1949
'E'	54					54						Mar. 1950
'BT'	50						36	14				Mid 1951
'F'	100						64	36				Nov. 1951
'N'	253								253			Mid 1950
'N' Farina	151								151			Feb. 1952
'G'	28									25	3	Oct. 1951
Totals	1,185	101	64	39	23	105	224	77	404	25	123	

Austin-Healey '100S' 50

Longbridge built cars

Austin-Healey '100', BN 1 10,688
                 BN 2 3,924
Austin-Healey '100-Six', BN 4 . . . 6,045

Abingdon built cars

Austin-Healey '100-Six', BN 4 . . . 4,241
                 BN 6 . . . 4,150
Austin-Healey '3000' Mark I BT 7 . . 10,825
                 BN 7 . . 2,825
         Mark II BT 7 . . 5,095
                 BN 7 . . 355
                 BJ 7 . . 6,113
         Mark III BJ 8 . . 17,703

Austin-Healey Sprite Mark I . . . 48,999
                     Mark II (948 cc) . . 19,285
                     Mark II (1,098 cc) . 11,215
                     Mark III . . . 25,905
                     Mark IV   over 20,000 (still in production)

APPENDIX VII

INTERNATIONAL COMPETITION RESULTS

THE ELLIOT SALOON AND WESTLAND ROADSTER

Date	Event	Drivers	Model	Details of car	Results
December 1946	Timed Run, Milan–Como Autostrada, Italy	Motor road test staff	Saloon		104·65 mile/h flying $\frac{1}{2}$-mile; 17·8 secs standing $\frac{1}{4}$-mile
July 1947	Alpine Rally, France	T. Wisdom Mrs B. Wisdom	Roadster		1st 2–3 litre class
July 1947	Timed Run, Jabbeke-Aeltre Highway, Belgium	D. Healey	Saloon	FWD 695	110·8 mile/h measured mile
April 1948	Targa Florio, Sicily	J. Lurani Serafini	Saloon	CUE 722 (76)	13th overall; 1st unlimited touring cars; 2nd overall touring cars
May 1948	Mille Miglia, Italy	D. Healey G. Healey	Roadster	GWD 43 (44)	9th overall; 2nd unlimited sports class

Date	Event	Drivers		Reg. (No.)	Result
		J. Lurani C. Sandri	Saloon	CUE 722 (76)	13th overall; 1st touring car class
July 1948	Spa 24 Hour Race, Belgium	N. Haines R. Haller	Saloon		Retired
		N. Haines T. Wisdom	Saloon	GWD 42 (80)	2nd 2–3 litre class
July 1948	Alpine Rally, France	D. Healey N. Haines	Roadster	GWD 43 (34)	1st 2–3 litre class
September 1948	Paris 12 Hour Race, Montlhéry	L. Johnson N. Haines	Saloon	(11)	Retired
		T. Wisdom N. Black	Roadster		Retired
October 1948	Timed Run, Montlhéry	T. Wisdom	Saloon		103·76 miles in one hour (flying start) 101·7 miles in one hour (standing start)
April 1949	Mille Miglia, Italy	T. Wisdom G. Healey	Roadster	GWD 43	1st touring class
		D. Healey G. Price	Saloon	192 AC (356)	4th touring class
May 1952	Silverstone Production Touring Car Race	K. Wharton	Saloon	FGD 288 (23)	2nd overall; 1st 2–3 litre class

THE HEALEY 'SILVERSTONE'

Date	Event	Drivers	Car	Results
July 1949	Alpine Rally, France	D. Healey/I. Appleyard	JAC 100 (104)	2nd overall; 1st British; 1st class
August 1949	Silverstone Production Car Race	A. Rolt		4th overall; 2nd class + Team
		L. Chiron	GCY 145	6th overall; 4th class + Team
		T. Wisdom	JAC 100	17th overall; 5th class + Team
January 1950	Palm Beach Races, Florida	B. Cunningham		2nd overall
		P. Walters		5th overall; 1st 3 litre class
		J. Rutherford		2nd class
April 1950	Targa Florio, Sicily	T. Wisdom/A. Hume		1st British; 4th class; overall 16th
April 1950	Mille Miglia, Italy	P. Monkhouse/P. Wood		Crashed

Date	Event	Driver		Result
July 1950	Alpine Rally, France	R. Richards/R. Lord		Crashed
		Mosters/Castelbarco		38th overall; 8th class
		G. Wilkins/Mrs. Wilkins		Crashed
		G. Walker/G. Parkes		Crashed
		E. Wadsworth		Crashed
		L. O. Bartlett		Crashed
August 1950	Silverstone Production Car Race	D. Hamilton		1st class
		C. Mortimer	OPA 2	5th class
		G. Gale		6th class
September 1950	Tourist Trophy, Dundrod	E. Wilkinson		4th class; 9th overall
		R. Richards		5th class; 11th overall
		C. Masters		6th class; 12th overall
		C. Mortimer		7th class; 14th overall
		R. Oliver		8th class; 15th overall
		W. Freed		Crashed

257

Date	Event	Drivers	Car	Results
September 1950	Watkins Glen Sports Car G.P.	B. Cunningham		2nd overall
	Watkins Glen (Seneca Cup Race)	P. Walters		1st overall
June 1951	Manx Cup Races, I.O.M.	P. Simpson		5th overall
July 1951	Alpine Rally, France	E. Wadsworth/C. Corbishley		Coupe des Alpes; 1st class
		A. Tasker/J. Blackwell	(73)	Crashed
August 1951	Liège–Rome–Liège	P. Riley/W. Lamb	DVG 807 (29)	1st class; 8th overall
September 1951	Tourist Trophy, Dundrod	J. Buncombe	(26)	14th overall; 5th class
August 1952	Goodwood 9 Hour Race	D. Boston/R. Shattock		8th overall; 4th class

THE NASH-HEALEY

Date	Event	Drivers	Car	Results
April 1950	Mille Miglia, Italy	D. Healey/G. Healey	'Silverstone' Prototype	9th class; 177th overall
June 1950	Le Mans 24 Hour Race, France	D. Hamilton/A. Rolt	'Silverstone' Prototype (14)	3rd class; 4th overall
April 1951	Mille Miglia, Italy	D. Healey/G. Healey	Standard body (406)	4th class; 30th overall
May 1951	B.R.D.C. Production Car Race, Silverstone	A. Rolt	Standard body	6th overall
June 1951	British Empire Trophy, I.O.M.	R. Parnell	Standard body (26)	Retired
June 1951	Le Mans 24 Hour Race, France	D. Hamilton/A. Rolt	Coupé Prototype (19)	4th class; 6th overall
May 1952	Mille Miglia, Italy	D. Healey/G. Healey	Coupé Prototype (550)	Crashed
		L. Johnson/W. McKenzie		4th class; 7th overall

Date	Event	Drivers	Car	Results
June 1952	Le Mans 24 Hour Race, France	L. Johnson/T. Wisdom	Coupé Prototype modified as open (10)	1st class; 3rd overall; 1st British; 2nd index
		G. Cabantous/P. Veyron	'Silverstone' Prototype	Retired
July 1952	Alpine Rally, France	E. Wadsworth		Crashed
May 1953	Mille Miglia, Italy	J. Fitch/— Willday	Special body (540)	Retired
June 1953	Le Mans 24 Hour Race, France	L. Johnson/H. Hadley		11th overall; 4th index
		G. Cabantous/P. Veyron		Retired

Date	Event	Drivers	Results
March 1953	Lyons–Charbonnières Rally	G. Grant/P. Reece	50th overall; 11th class
April 1953	Mille Miglia	A. Hadley/Mercer J. Lockett/J. Reid	Retired Retired
June 1953	24 Hour Race, Le Mans	M. Gatsonides/J. Lockett M. Becquart/G. Wilkins	12th overall; 2nd class 14th overall; 3rd class
August 1953	9 Hour Race, Goodwood	J. Lockett/K. Rudd	10th overall; 8th class
January 1954	Auckland G.P., New Zealand	R. Jenson	6th overall
March 1954	Paris – St Raphael Rally	Miss B. Haig/Miss E. Riddell	7th overall; 1st class
March 1954	Sebring 12 Hour Race	W. Wellenberger/W. Wonder J. Guibardo/Smyth Grundage/Orr	Retired Retired Retired
March 1954	R.A.C. Rally	F. Davis/Mrs V. Davis G. Rollings/W. McCormick R. Lane/D. Plant A. Coakley/J. Noble	18th overall; 1st class 25th overall; 2nd class 47th overall; 6th class 87th overall; 12th class

Date	Event	Drivers	Results
March 1954	R.A.C. Rally	J. Richmond/W. Shepherd	131st overall; 16th class
		G. Sharp/A. Rollason	145th overall; 18th class
		F. Baker/ —	150th overall; 20th class
		F. Still/W. Kindred	159th overall; 22nd class
		D. Perring/G. Griffiths	Retired
		P. Thomson/M. Mander	Retired
		J. Somervall/ —	Retired
April 1954	Rallye Soleil	P. Lalisee/R. Devries	15th overall; 1st class
April 1954	Tulip Rally	L. Hengst/W. Metternich	25th overall; 4th class
		N. Blockley/J. Kat	128th overall; 8th class
		K. Fraser/C. MacIntyre	Crashed
May 1954	G.P. de Spa Sports Car Race	C. Goethais	4th class
		R. Overstraten	8th class
May 1954	Hedermorslopp Sports Car Race, Sweden	C. Lincoln	5th overall
		G. Olsson	6th overall
		R. Finnila	7th overall
June 1954	Scottish Rally	F. Marsh/ —	3rd class
		J. Furrhinan/ —	Retired
		J. Richmond/W. Shepherd	Retired

Date	Event	Driver(s)	Result
June 1954	Midnight Sun Rally	G. Olsson/ —	3rd class
July 1954	Leinster Trophy	A. Coleman	7th overall
July 1954	Alpine Rally	R. Flower/E. McMillen	25th overall; 3rd class
		A. Stross/H. Mason	26th overall; 4th class
		Marion/Marion	Retired
		Vegler/ —	Retired
		Mrs N. Mitchell/Miss S. Hindmarsh	Crashed
July 1954	British G.P. Sports Car Race, Silverstone	J. Deeley	20th overall; 4th class
		D. Shale	Crashed
August 1954	Sports Car Race, Snetterton	D. Shale	2nd class
		R. Weaver	3rd class
		B. Tucker	4th class
August 1954	Wakefield Trophy, Curragh, Ireland	A. Coleman	7th overall
		C. Carter	20th overall
September 1954	Skarnacksloppet Sports Car Race, Sweden	E. Carlsson	4th overall
		A. Lindberg	5th overall
		H. Sjoqvist	6th overall
		H. Holck-Clausen	7th overall
		G. Olsson	8th overall
		S. Burlin	9th overall
		I. Hellestrom	10th overall
		I. Morrison	11th overall

Date	Event	Drivers	Results
September 1954	Austrian Alpine Rally	J. Teese/ —	9th overall; 3rd class
October 1954	Kanonloppet Sports Car Race, Sweden	E. Carlsson R. Sjoqvist I. Hellestrom G. Oisson S. Burlin	2nd overall 3rd overall 4th overall 5th overall 6th overall
October 1954	B.A.R.C. Sports Car Race, Aintree	J. Deeley D. Shale	3rd overall 4th overall
October 1954	Rheinlandfahrt Rally	R. Shaffer	1st (tied) overall; 1st class
November 1954	Great American Mountain Rally	E. Buick/W. Buick W. Kolackowski/D. Stanfill	2nd overall; 1st class 9th overall; 2nd class
March 1955	Sebring 12 Hour Race	Sir S. Oakes/Lady Oakes J. Guibardo/Wolfe W. Wondar/W. Wellenberger	Crashed 18th overall 26th overall
March 1955	R.A.C. Rally	L. Griffiths/R. Wingfield F. Marsh/ — I. Walker/I. Nix A. Coakley/J. Noble G. White/V. Domleo	26th overall; 9th class 58th overall; 19th class 86th overall; 21st class 91st overall; 22nd class 126th overall; 31st class

Date	Event	Driver	Result
March 1955	Paris – St Raphael Rally	Mlle M. Olivet/ —	19th overall; 12th class
March 1955	Lyons–Charbonnières Rally	de Gruyter/Ducourthial	36th overall; 3rd class
April 1955	Tulip Rally	H. Herweiger/J. Boekhout	54th overall; 2nd class
		C. Bussler/B. Bergkist	70th overall; 3rd class
		L. Griffiths/P. Legget	119th overall; 4th class
		K. Fraser/Mrs M. Fraser	126th overall; 5th class
		N. Blockley/J. Kat	Retired
		E. Ross/C. Matthews	Retired
		J. van der Pije/P. van Ewijk	Retired
April 1955	Rallye de Nantes	P. Houdusse/ —	9th overall; 4th class
April 1955	Mille Miglia	G. Verilla/B. Ferrari	88th overall; 4th class
May 1955	Ulster Trophy	A. Coleman	6th overall
May 1955	Elaintarhanajo Sports Car Race, Helsinki	N. Kozarovitsky	9th overall; 4th class
		A. Paananen	11th overall; 7th class
May 1955	Hockenheim Sports Car Race	G. Smith	1st overall
		Geisinger	3rd overall
June 1955	Scottish Rally	B. Potts/ —	4th class
		K. Best/ —	Retired
		Sir S. Oakes/ —	Retired
June 1955	Mobilgas Economy Rally	H. Kendrick	1st class

Date	Event	Drivers	Results
August 1955	Liège–Rome–Liège Rally	J. Maquet/R. Gutenkauf Franssen/Moineau	Retired Retired
September 1955	Skarpacksloppet Sports Car Race, Sweden	A. Lindberg N. Kozarovitsky	3rd overall; 1st class 8th overall; 2nd class
November 1955	Great American Mountain Rally	E. Buick/W. Buick B. Kinne/R. Dewees	3rd overall; 2nd class 9th overall; 3rd class
November 1955	Tour of Belgium	Franssen/Moineau	3rd overall; 2nd class
December 1955	Governor's Trophy Race, Nassau	R. Fergus P. Pohanka	14th overall 37th overall
	Nassau Trophy Race	F. Pohanka P. Stiles R. Jackson-Moore J. Orr	31st overall 34th overall 49th overall Retired
March 1956	R.A.C. Rally	L. Griffiths/T. Underhill	15th overall; 2nd class
April 1956	B.A.R.C. Sports Car Race, Goodwood	R. Green	2nd class
May 1956	Tulip Rally	H. Herweiger/J. Boekhout J. Dathan/Miss D. Dathan	83rd overall; 9th class Retired
March 1958	R.A.C. Rally	D. Mackay/D. Needham	5th class

AUSTIN-HEALEY '100S'

Date	Event	Drivers	Results
March 1954	12 Hour Race, Sebring	L. Macklin/G. Huntoon	3rd overall; 1st in class
May 1954	Mille Miglia	L. Macklin L. Chiron T. Wisdom/M. Morris-Goodall	23rd overall; 5th class; 1st British Retired Retired
November 1954	Pan-American Road Race	L. Macklin/D. Healey C. Shelby/R. Jackson-Moore	Retired Retired
March 1955	12 Hour Race, Sebring	S. Moss/L. Macklin W. Brewster/C. Rutan W. Cook/G. Rand J. Cooper/R. Jackson-Moore R. Fergus/H. Watts F. Allen/G. Erhman J. Ferguson/R. Keith	6th overall; 1st class 14th overall; 2nd class 17th overall; 3rd class 40th overall Retired Retired 32nd overall
April 1955	British Empire Trophy, Oulton Park	L. Macklin R. Flockhart J. Dalton D. Shale	14th overall Failed to qualify for the final

267

Date	Event	Drivers	Results
April 1955	Mille Miglia	G. Abecassis L. Macklin R. Flockhart D. Healey/J. Cashmore	11th overall; 1st class; 1st British 36th overall; 2nd class Crashed Retired
May 1955	B.R.D.C. Sports Car Race, Silverstone	L. Macklin	17th overall; 6th class
June 1955	24 Hour Race, Le Mans	L. Macklin/ L. Leston	Crashed
August 1955	'Daily Herald' Trophy, Oulton Park	L. Macklin	12th overall
August 1955	Liège-Rome-Liège Rally	P. Reece/D. Scott	Crashed
September 1955	Tourist Trophy, Dundrod	L. Macklin/J. Dalton E. McMillen/M. Llewellyn	Crashed 14th overall; 10th class
December 1955	Nassau Trophy, Bahamas	S. Moss F. Allen	Retired Retired
March 1956	R.A.C. Rally	J. Winby/R. James	112th overall; 7th class

March 1956	12 Hour Race, Sebring	P. Stiles/G. Huntoon	11th overall; 3rd class
		L. Macklin/A. Scott-Brown	Retired
		R. Jackson-Moore/F. Robinson	Retired
April 1956	B.A.R.C. Sports Car Race, Goodwood	J. Dalton	3rd overall; 1st class
April 1956	Mille Miglia	T. Wisdom/W. Monaco	77th overall; 2nd class
		L. Brooks/S. Asbury	Crashed
June 1956	12 Hour Race, Rheims	R. Flower/C. Davis	8th overall

AUSTIN-HEALEY 'Ioo-SIX'

Date	Event	Drivers	Results
March 1957	Sestrière Rally	T. Wisdom/A. Wisdom	10th class; 83rd overall
March 1957	12 Hour Race, Sebring	G. Geitner/R. Cuomo J. Bentley/P. Stiles R. Jackson-Moore/F. Robinson	2nd class; 26th overall Retired Retired
April 1957	Acropolis Rally	J. Hocquard/R. Barthelemy	Retired
May 1957	Mille Miglia	T. Wisdom/C. Winby	1st price class; 37th overall
June 1957	Midnight Sun Rally	J. Hocquard/R. Barthelemy	9th class; 160th overall
January 1958	Monte Carlo Rally	T. Wisdom/C. Smith	Retired
March 1958	R.A.C. Rally	J. Sears/P. Garnier D. Shale/ —	5th class; 52nd overall Retired
March 1958	12 Hour Race, Sebring	G. Geitner/H. Kunz/R. Cuomo P. Stiles/G. Ehrman B. Kinchelve/F. Moore	14th, 17th and 23rd overall; Manufacturers' Team Prize
April 1958	Tulip Rally	J. Sears/P. Garnier	Retired

Date	Event	Crew	Result
May 1958	German Rally	J. Hocquard/W. Bosco	3rd class; 38th overall
July 1958	Alpine Rally	W. Shepherd/J. Williamson	2nd class; 7th overall; Coupe des Alpes
		P. Moss/A. Wisdom	4th class; 10th overall; Coupe des Dames
		J. Sears/S. Moore	5th class; 11th overall
		N. Mitchell/G. Wilton-Clark	6th class; 12th overall
		J. Gott/C. Tooley	Retired
August 1958	Liège–Rome–Liège Rally	P. Moss/A. Wisdom	1st class; 4th overall; Coupe des Dames
		G. Burgess/S. Croft-Pearson	4th class; 10th overall
		N. Mitchell/A. Hall	6th class; 15th overall
		J. Johns/S. Moore	Crashed
			Manufacturers' Team Prize; Club Team Prize with 'MGA' (Gott/Brookes)
April 1959	Tulip Rally	J. Sears/P. Garnier	1st class; 8th overall
		P. Moss/A. Wisdom	Crashed
		E. Judge/C. Seward	Crashed
May 1959	B.R.D.C. G.T. Race, Silverstone	J. Sears	3rd class; 4th overall

Date	Event	Drivers	Results
May 1959	Acropolis Rally	P. Moss/A. Wisdom	Crashed
November 1959	R.A.C. Rally	P. Smith/E. Lodge	Retired
May 1960	Tulip Rally	K. Karolus/G. Plörer	7th class; 111th overall
May 1961	Tulip Rally	E. Judge/C. Seward	9th class; 93rd overall

AUSTIN-HEALEY '3000'

Date	Event	Drivers	Results
June 1959	Alpine Rally	J. Gott/C. Tooley W. Shepherd/J. Williamson J. Sears/S. Moore	5th in G.T. category; 2nd in class Retired Retired
September 1959	Liège-Rome-Liège Rally	P. Riley/R. Jones J. Gott/K. James J. Sears/P. Garnier G. Burgess/S. Croft-Pearson	7th in G.T. category; 1st class Retired Retired Crashed
September 1959	Gold Cup Meeting Sports car race, Oulton Park	J. Sears	1st class
October 1959	German Rally	P. Moss/A. Wisdom	2nd overall; 1st class; Coupe des Dames
November 1959	R.A.C. Rally	D. Morley/E. Morley J. Sears/W. Cave J. Williamson/J. Milne	4th overall; 1st class 17th overall; 2nd class Retired
December 1959	Portuguese Rally	P. Moss/A. Wisdom	53rd overall; 4th class; Coupe des Dames

Date	Event	Drivers	Results
March 1960	12 Hour Race, Sebring	G. Geitre/J. Louis-Spencer J. Sears/P. Riley F. Spross/ —	15th overall; 2nd class 3rd class Crashed
March 1960	Circuit of Ireland	G. Parkes/G. Howarth P. Moss/A. Wisdom	1st class Retired
March 1960	Lyons–Charbonnières Rally	P. Moss/A. Wisdom	Crashed
April 1960	Geneva Rally	P. Moss/A. Wisdom	7th overall; 1st class; Coupe des Dames
May 1960	Tulip Rally	P. Moss/A. Wisdom D. Morley/E. Morley	8th overall; 1st class Coupe des Dames 21st overall; 3rd class
May 1960	Acropolis Rally	P. Moss/A. Wisdom P. Riley/A. Ambrose	Retired Crashed
June 1960	24 Hour Race, Le Mans	J. Sears/P. Riley	Retired
June 1960	Alpine Rally	P. Moss/A. Wisdom	2nd overall; 1st class; Coupe des Dames

Date	Event	Drivers	Results
August 1960	Tourist Trophy, Goodwood	J. Gott/W. Shepherd D. Morley/E. Morley R. Adams/J. Williamson	8th overall; 2nd class 14th overall; 3rd class Retired (All Team Prizes)
August 1960	Liège–Rome–Liège Rally	P. Riley J. Bekaert	19th overall 25th overall
		P. Moss/A. Wisdom	1st overall; 1st class; Coupe des Dames
		D. Seigle-Morris/V. Elford J. Gott/R. Jones P. Riley/A. Ambrose	5th overall; 2nd class 10th overall; 3rd class Retired (All Team Prizes)
October 1960	German Rally	D. Seigle-Morris/S. Turner D. Morley/B. Hercock P. Moss/A. Wisdom	8th overall; 1st class 12th overall; 2nd class 16th overall; 3rd class
November 1960	R.A.C. Rally	D. Morley/E. Morley P. Riley/A. Ambrose R. Adams/J. Williamson P. Smith/G. Bryant D. Dixon/C. Bond-Smith L. Griffiths/G. Brown A. Griffiths/H. Liddon J. Casewell/H. Davenport	3rd overall; 1st class 10th overall; 2nd class 39th overall; 4th class 41st overall; 5th class 57th overall; 7th class 63rd overall; 8th class 94th overall; 10th class Retired (Team Prize)

275

Date	Event	Drivers	Results
May 1961	Tulip Rally	P. Moss/A. Wisdom	11th overall; 1st class; Coupe des Dames
		D. Morley/E. Morley	14th overall; 2nd class
		D. Grimshaw/ B. Melia	52nd overall; 5th class
		P. Smith/C. Bond-Smith	74th overall; 6th class
		M. Day/R. Douglas	76th overall; 7th class
		A. Vicat-Cole/H. Mainz	81st overall; 8th class
		D. Allen/J. Hill	95th overall; 10th class
		F. Powell/J. Tait	102nd overall; 11th class
May 1961	1,000 km Race, Nürburgring	G. Gonzalo/G. van Opheim	35th overall
May 1961	Acropolis Rally	P. Riley/A. Ambrose	3rd overall; 1st class
		G. Parkes/J. Sprinzel	Crashed
June 1961	Midnight Sun Rally	P. Riley/A. Ambrose	12th overall; 2nd class
June 1961	24 Hour Race, Le Mans	J. Bekaert/D. Stoop	Retired
June 1961	Alpine Rally	D. Morley/E. Morley	1st overall; 1st class
		J. Gott/W. Shepherd	15th overall; 3rd class
		P. Moss/A. Wisdom	Crashed
		P. Riley/A. Ambrose	Crashed
		D. Seigle-Morris/V. Elford	Crashed

Date	Event	Crew	Result
August 1961	Polish Rally	D. Astle/S. Turner	2nd class
August 1961	Liège-Rome-Liège Rally	D. Seigle-Morris/A. Ambrose J. Gott/W. Shepherd P. Moss/A. Wisdom D. Grimshaw/R. Jones	6th overall; 1st class Retired Retired Crashed
November 1961	R.A.C. Rally	P. Moss/A. Wisdom D. Seigle-Morris/A. Ambrose D. Grimshaw/B. Melia D. Morley/E. Morley	2nd overall; 1st class; Coupe des Dames 12th overall; 3rd class 64th overall; 4th class Retired
November 1961	Tour of Corsica	P. Moss/A. Wisdom	17th overall; 1st class; Coupe des Dames
January 1962	Monte Carlo Rally	D. Seigle-Morris/A. Ambrose W. Marriott/R. Marriott D. Grimshaw/G. Humble	18th overall; 1st class Retired Retired
April 1962	Circuit of Ireland	G. Parkes/G. Howarth	3rd overall; 1st class
May 1962	Tulip Rally	D. Morley/E. Morley P. Riley/D. Astle A. Verschoor/A. van Jaarsveld	14th overall; 1st class 18th overall; 2nd class 6th class
May 1962	Acropolis Rally	P. Moss/P. Mayman	8th overall; 1st class; Coupe des Dames

277

Date	Event	Drivers	Results
May 1962	Police Rally	J. Gott/D. Nicholson	1st class
June 1962	Alpine Rally	D. Morley/E. Morley	1st overall; 1st class
		P. Moss/P. Mayman	3rd overall; 3rd class; Coupe des Dames
		D. Seigle-Morris/A. Ambrose	8th overall; 5th class
		P. Riley/D. Astle	Retired (Team Prize)
June 1962	24 Hour Race, Le Mans	R. Olthoff/J. Whitmore	Retired
August 1962	Polish Rally	P. Moss/P. Mayman	2nd overall; 1st class; Coupe des Dames
August 1962	Liège–Rome–Liège Rally	L. Morrison/R. Jones	5th overall; 2nd class
		D. Seigle-Morris/B. Hercock	8th overall; 3rd class
		P. Hopkirk/J. Scott	Retired
		R. Aaltonen/A. Ambrose	Retired
November 1962	R.A.C. Rally	P. Hopkirk/J. Scott	2nd overall; 1st class
		P. Moss/P. Mayman	3rd overall; 2nd class; Coupe des Dames
		D. Morley/E. Morley	Crashed
		P. Riley/H. Nash	Crashed
		D. Grimshaw/ G. Allen	Retired
		M. Day/M. Mobsby	Retired

278

January 1963	Monte Carlo Rally	T. Makinen/C. Carlisle W. Marriott/R. Marriott — Amy/— Casey	13th overall; 1st class Retired Retired
March 1963	12 Hour Race, Sebring	R. Olthoff/R. Bucknum P. Hopkirk/D. Morley	12th overall; 4th class 26th overall; 6th class
April 1963	Tulip Rally	D. Morley/E. Morley L. Morrison/R. Finlay D. Astle/D. Grimshaw	2nd G.T. category; 1st class Retired Crashed
April 1963	Circuit of Ireland	L. Morrison/R. Finlay	Crashed
May 1963	Police Rally	J. Gott/D. Nicholson	6th class
May 1963	G.T. Race, B.R.D.C. Silverstone	R. Olthoff	6th overall
June 1963	Alpine Rally	D. Morley/E. Morley T. Makinen/M. Wood P. Hopkirk/J. Scott L. Morrison/R. Finlay	Retired Retired Crashed Crashed
June 1963	Scottish Rally	G. Parkes/B. Whitmarsh	3rd class
June 1963	Midnight Sun Rally	T. Makinen/A. Ambrose	Disqualified
July 1963	Grovewood Trophy Race, B.R.S.C.C. Mallory Park	C. Baker	7th overall

Date	Event	Drivers	Results
September 1963	Liège–Rome–Liège Rally	P. Hopkirk/H. Liddon T. Makinen/G. Mabbs L. Morrison/M. Wood P. Moon/A. Cowan R. Aaltonen/A. Ambrose B. Russell/P. Scott	6th overall; 1st class Crashed Retired Retired Crashed Retired
October 1963	Geneva Rally	P. Moon/J. Davenport	11th overall; 1st class
November 1963	R.A.C. Rally	T. Makinen/M. Wood D. Morley/E. Morley P. Moon/R. Mackie B. Petch/H. Miller R. Aaltonen/A. Ambrose	5th overall; 1st class 9th overall; 2nd class Retired Retired Crashed
December 1963	Governor's Trophy Race, Nassau	C. Baker	14th overall; 1st class
March 1964	12 Hour Race, Sebring	P. Hopkirk/G. Clark	Crashed
April 1964	Italian Flowers and Perfumes Rally	P. Moon/J. Davenport	1st class
April 1964	Tulip Rally	D. Morley/E. Morley P. Moon/Miss D. McCluggage E. Grabowski/H. de Graaf	1st G.T. category 3rd class Retired

Date	Event	Drivers	Result
May 1964	Austrian Alpine Rally	P. Hopkirk/H. Liddon	1st overall
June 1964	Alpine Rally	D. Morley/E. Morley P. Moon/M. Wood	2nd overall; 1st class 10th overall
August 1964	Spa-Sofia–Liège Rally	R. Aaltonen/A. Ambrose P. Hopkirk/H. Liddon T. Makinen/D. Barrow	1st overall Retired Retired
November 1964	R.A.C. Rally	T. Makinen/D. Barrow D. Morley/E. Morley	2nd overall; 1st class Retired
March 1965	12 Hour Race, Sebring	P. Hawkins/W. Banks	17th overall; 1st class
April 1965	Tulip Rally	D. Morley/E. Morley	5th category; 1st class
May 1965	Targa Florio Race	T. Makinen/P. Hawkins	20th overall; 2nd class
June 1965	Geneva Rally	D. Morley/E. Morley	7th overall; 1st class
June 1965	Scottish Rally	T. Makinen/P. Easter	Retired
July 1965	Alpine Rally	D. Morley/E. Morley	2nd in category
November 1965	R.A.C. Rally	T. Makinen/P. Easter D. Morley/E. Morley	2nd overall; 1st class Retired

Date	Event	Drivers	Results
April 1966	B.A.R.C. G.T. Race, Goodwood	T. Worswick	2nd class
May 1966	International Police Rally	J. Gott/Holdsworth	5th overall; 2nd class
May 1966	International Journalists' Rally	Count Czernin	2nd overall; 1st class
May 1966	Targa Florio Race	T. Worswick/A. Minshaw	Retired
May 1966	Tulip Rally	A. Raylor/G. Franklin	3rd class
		G. Smit/L. Smit	4th class
		E. Grabowski/H. de Graaf	Retired
November 1966	R.A.C. Rally	T. Harrison/E. Worswick	58th overall
		N. Jenkins/I. Woodruffe	Retired
April 1967	Tulip Rally	B. Petch/H. Miller	6th category; 3rd class
May 1967	Targa Florio Race	T. Worswick/R. Bond	9th overall; 2nd class
August 1967	B.O.A.C. 500 Race	T. Worswick/P. Clark	Not classified
May 1968	Targa Florio Race	T. Worswick/R. Bond	29th overall

AUSTIN-HEALEY SPRITE

Date	Event	Drivers	Results
July 1958	Alpine Rally	J. Sprinzel/W. Cave T. Wisdom/J. Hay R. Brookes/R. Wells-West	1st class; 15th overall 2nd class; 19th overall 3rd class; 25th overall
September 1958	Liège-Rome-Liège Rally	J. Sprinzel/R. Bensted-Smith	Retired
January 1959	Monte Carlo Rally	J. Sprinzel/W. Cave T. Wisdom/D. Johns R. Baxter/J. Reece D. Wilson–Spratt/J. Bayliss	3rd class; 14th overall 5th class; 63rd overall Retired Retired
February 1959	Sestrière Rally	T. Wisdom/J. Lucas	5th class; 39th overall
March 1959	Sebring 12 Hours	H. Sutherland/P. Stiles E. Leavens/H. Kunz/J. Colgate F. Hayes/J. Christy	1st class; 31st overall 2nd class; 36th overall 3rd class; 38th overall
March 1959	Circuit of Ireland	S. Moore/A. Spence R. McKinney/F. Erskine	1st class; 13th overall 2nd class; 15th overall
April 1959	Tulip Rally	Lord and Lady Strathcarron	Retired
May 1959	Targa Florio	T. Wisdom/B. Cahier	6th class; 17th overall

Date	Event	Drivers	Results
May 1959	Scottish Rally	S. Moore/ — D. Thompson/ —	1st class; 2nd overall 2nd class
June 1959	Alpine Rally	T. Wisdom/J. Hay Artalo/Bourdillon	2nd class; 2nd G.T. category Retired
September 1959	Liège–Rome–Liège Rally	J. Sprinzel/S. Turner F. Powell/Jones	1st class; 12th overall Crashed
November 1959	R.A.C. Rally	T. Gold/M. Hughes Miss R. Seers/Miss I. Robinson D. Wilson–Spratt/J. Bayliss R. Wall/A. Jakes H. Appleby/R. McGhie C. Molyneux/K. Allen D. Guttridge/J. Patterson R. Smith/M. Tyson	1st class; 2nd overall Retired Retired Retired Retired Retired Retired Retired
October 1959	Coupe du Salon, Montlhéry	G. Williamson	1st class
December 1959	Portuguese Rally	B. Vilarinho/ — F. Oliveira/ — S. Pinto/ —	1st class; 8th overall 2nd class; 19th overall 3rd class; 45th overall

Date	Event	Drivers	Results
January 1960	Monte Carlo Rally	D. Wilson-Spratt/J. Bayliss	5th class; 148th overall
March 1960	Sebring 4 Hours	S. Moss S. Moore/Lilley	1st class; 2nd overall Retired
April 1960	Sebring 12 Hours	J. Sprinzel/J. Lumkin J. Colgate/Spross	1st class; 41st overall Crashed
April 1960	Circuit of Ireland	A. Boyd/M. Johnston C. Vard/J. Scott G. Whaley/ — S. Moore/ — R. Woodside/ — Mrs M. Cordner/ —	1st class; 1st overall 2nd class; 3rd overall 3rd class; 18th overall 4th class; 20th overall 5th class; 25th overall 6th class; 30th overall
April 1960	B.A.R.C. Goodwood Closed car race	L. Adams J. Sprinzel	1st class 2nd class
April 1960	B.A.R.C. Aintree Closed car race	P. Hawkins E. Foden	1st class 3rd class
May 1960	Tulip Rally	T. Gold/M. Hughes R. Wall/D. Allen R. Domey/L. Needham H. Appleby/R. McGhie P. Barnsly/M. Baker	3rd class; 92nd overall 4th class; 96th overall Crashed Retired Retired

Date	Event	Drivers	Results
May 1960	Acropolis Rally	J. Sprinzel/R. Domey	Crashed
May 1960	Nürburgring 1,000 km	P. Hawkins/C. Simson	6th class
June 1960	Le Mans 24 Hours	J. Dalton/J. Colgate	1st class; 20th overall
June 1960	Alpine Rally	J. Sprinzel/W. Cave T. Wisdom/J. Hay D. Margulies/J. Campbell-Jones	Retired Retired Retired
August 1960	B.R.S.C.C. Brands Hatch, G.T. Race	D. Harris H. Elwes	2nd class 3rd class
August 1960	Tourist Trophy, Goodwood	C. Simson/P. Hawkins	7th class; 20th overall
August 1960	B.R.S.C.C. Brands Hatch, G.T. Race	J. Gaston L. Adams	1st class 2nd class
September 1960	Nürburgring 500 km	C. Simson/P. Hawkins	1st class
September 1960	Liège-Rome-Liège Rally	J. Sprinzel/J. Patten D. Margulies/S. Turner N. Blockley/Broomfield	1st class; 3rd overall Retired Retired

Date	Event	Driver(s)	Result
September 1960	German Rally	J. Sprinzel/Miss N. Sprinzel	2nd class; 24th overall
November 1960	R.A.C. Rally	J. Sprinzel/R. Bensted-Smith	1st class; 2nd overall
		P. Moss/A. Wisdom	2nd class; 20th overall
		J. Kirkham/P. Baldham	3rd class; 24th overall
		J. Patten/P. Hawkins	4th class; 37th overall
		C. Williams/B. Culcheth	7th class
		P. Barsby/M. Baker	10th class
		D. Wilson-Spratt/J. Bayliss	13th class
		Mrs. M. Cordner/Mrs D. Bleakley	14th class
		R. Wall/A. Martin	15th class
		T. Gold/M. Hughes	Retired
		B. Shawzin/G. Fields	Retired
		S. Guttridge/J. Tetley	Retired
November 1960	Tour of Corsica	P. Moss/A. Wisdom	Retired
December 1960	Nassau T.T. Race	P. Jackson	1st class
January 1961	Monte Carlo Rally	D. Wilson-Spratt/J. Bayliss	Retired
		I. Miller/Mrs Miller	Retired
		T. Wisdom/J. Hay	Retired
March 1961	Sebring 4 Hour Race	W. Hansgen	2nd overall
		B. McLaren	4th overall
		S. Moss	5th overall

Date	Event	Drivers	Results
March 1961		E. Leavens	6th overall
		P. Moss/R. Hawkins	7th overall
		B. Cunningham	8th overall
	Sebring 12 Hour Race	J. Buzetta/G. Carlson	2nd class; 15th overall
		E. Leavens/J. Colgate	3rd class; 25th overall
		J. Sprinzel/C. Simson/P. Hawkins	37th overall
March 1961	Circuit of Ireland	R. Woodside/T. Harriman	1st class; 2nd overall
		I. Woodside/E. Crawford	2nd class; 7th overall
March 1961	Lyon–Charbonnières Rally	B. Shawzin/B. Culcheth	5th class
May 1961	Tulip Rally	T. Gold/M. Hughes	1st class; 8th overall
		J. Sprinzel/W. Cave	2nd class; 17th overall
		B. Shawzin/J. Makin	4th class; 77th overall
		L. von Almkerk/S. Hanser	5th class; 111th overall
May 1961	Nürburgring 1,000 km Race	W. McCowen/A. Hedges	4th class; 32nd overall
		P. Hawkins/C. Simson	Retired
May 1961	Mille Miglia	B. Shawzin/J. Makin	2nd class; 33rd overall

Date	Event	Drivers	Result
June 1961	B.R.S.C.C. G.T. Race, Brands Hatch	I. Walker J. Gaston P. Hawkins	1st class 2nd class 3rd class
June 1961	La Chatre G.T. Race	P. Jackson	1st overall
June 1961	Le Mans 24 Hour Race	J. Colgate/P. Hawkins N. Sanderson/J. McKay	Retired Crashed
July 1961	Alpine Rally	J. Sprinzel/W. Cave T. Gold/M. Hughes D. Wilson-Spratt/A. Piggott B. Shawzin/Preiskal	2nd class; 17th overall Retired Retired Retired
July 1961	Claremont 6 Hour G.T. Race	P. Jackson	3rd class
July 1961	G.P. Aintree, G.T. Race	V. Preston J. Gaston	2nd class 3rd class
August 1961	Tourist Trophy, Goodwood	J. Gaston	6th class; 18th overall
September 1961	Liège-Rome-Liège Rally	J. Sprinzel/S. Actman N. Blockley/Broomfield	Retired Retired
September 1961	Nüburgring 500 km Race	R. Melville/P. Jackson A. Hedges/P. Kuderil I. Walker/P. Hawkins	3rd overall 4th overall 7th overall

Date	Event	Drivers	Results
November 1961	Tour of Corsica	D. Margulies/P. Jackson	Retired
November 1961	R.A.C. Rally	D. Wilson-Spratt/D. Thompson	4th class; 35th overall
		H. Appleby/R. McGhie	6th class; 48th overall
		I. Miller/Mrs Miller	9th class; 78th overall
		P. Hawkins/V. Elford	Retired
		A. Boyd/M. Johnston	Retired
		H. Folts/M. Bishop	Retired
		B. Shawzin/W. Barlow	Retired
		R. Wall/R. Moody	Retired
		R. Dewar/ —	Retired
		T. Baker/W. Ross-Dallas	Retired
January 1962	Monte Carlo Rally	J. Sprinzel/C. Carlisle	4th class; 94th overall
		D. Wilson-Spratt/J. Bayliss	7th class; 136th overall
		D. Burgess/ —	10th class; 223rd overall
		I. Miller/Mrs Miller	Retired
March 1962	Sebring 4 Hour Race	S. Moss	5th overall
		P. Rodriguez	6th overall
		I. Ireland	7th overall
		S. McQueen	9th overall
	Sebring 12 Hour Race	S. McQueen/J. Colgate	Retired

Date	Event	Drivers	Result
April 1962	Circuit of Ireland	F. Johnston/I. Turkington A. Boyd/M. Johnston	1st class 2nd class
May 1962	Tulip Rally	T. Gold/M. Hughes R. Wall/R. Moody	3rd class; 38th overall 6th class; 80th overall
May 1962	B.R.D.C. Silverstone G.T. Race	M. Reid J. Sparrowe P. Clarke	4th class; 18th overall 5th class; 19th overall 6th class; 20th overall
May 1962	Nürburgring 1,000 km Race	M. Reid/J. Sparrowe	2nd class
June 1962	Alpine Rally	J. Williamson/D. Hiam B. Shawzin/S. Smith	2nd class; 20th overall Retired
June 1962	Scottish Rally	A. Mickel/G. Mickel J. Hall/ — D. Hall/ —	1st class 2nd class 3rd class
June 1962	Midnight Sun Rally	H. Appleby/R. McGhie	5th class
August 1962	Tourist Trophy, Goodwood	J. Gaston/B. Wood	11th class; 18th overall
August 1962	Liège–Sofia–Liège Rally	B. Shawzin/Denny	Retired
September 1962	Nürburgring 500 km Race	M. Reid J. Milne/J. Williamson P. Jackson/C. Baker	4th class 5th class Crashed

Date	Event	Drivers	Results
October 1962	Geneva Rally	B. Shawzin/Denny	4th class; 24th overall
November 1962	R.A.C. Rally	D. Wilson-Spratt/A. Piggott T. Gold/ —	Retired Retired
January 1963	Monte Carlo Rally	D. Wilson-Spratt/B. Harper C. Twigdon/L. Chilvers	Retired Retired
March 1963	Sebring 3 Hour Race	C. Stockhard B. Cleland P. Rodriguez R. Noseda	4th overall 5th overall Retired Retired
	Sebring 12 Hour Race	J. Colgate/C. Baker	Retired
April 1963	Circuit of Ireland	I. Woodside/E. Crawford	1st class; 1st overall
April 1963	Tulip Rally	B. Culcheth/J. Davenport B. Harper/T. Baker	4th class; 9th G.T. category 5th class; 13th G.T. category
May 1963	Nürburgring 1,000 km Race	C. Carlisle/C. Baker	2nd class; 17th overall
May 1963	Police Rally	P. Bird/R. Sullivan R. Cross/N. Bangs P. Perks/R. Maslin	1st class; 1st overall 14th class; 42nd overall 18th class; 28th overall

June 1963	Scottish Rally	I. Woodside/A. Boyd	1st class; 5th overall
		J. Hall/ —	2nd class
		Mrs A. Mickel/Mrs. M. Currie	3rd class
June 1963	Le Mans 24 Hour Race	J. Whitmore/J. Olthoff	Crashed
July 1963	B.R.D.C. Silverstone G.T. Race	R. Bunting	2nd class
		C. Carlisle	Crashed
August 1963	B.R.S.C.C. Brands Hatch G.T. Race	M. Garton	3rd class
September 1963	Nürburgring 500 km Race	J. Williamson	4th class
		M. Garton	Retired
November 1963	R.A.C. Rally	I. Woodside/ —	Retired
January 1964	Welsh Rally	A. Poole/J. Bilton	12th overall
March 1964	Sebring 12 Hour Race	J. Colgate/C. Baker	Retired
March 1964	B.A.R.C. G.T. Race, Goodwood	M. White	4th class
March 1964	Circuit of Ireland	J. Eakin/M. Hart	1st class; 11th overall
April 1964	Targa Floria	P. Hopkirk/T. Wisdom	Retired

Date	Event	Drivers	Results
January 1964	Welsh Rally	A. Poole/J. Bilton B. Harper/R. Crellin	12th overall Retired
March 1964	Sebring 12 Hours Race	C. Baker/J. Colgate A. Pease/Miss D. Mimms	25th overall; 1st class (not running at finish) Retired
March 1964	B.A.R.C. G.T. Race Goodwood	M. White	4th class
March 1964	Circuit of Ireland	J. Eakin/M. Hart R. White A. Poole	11th overall; 1st class Retired Retired
April 1964	Targa Florio Race	P. Hopkirk/T. Wisdom	Retired
May 1964	B.R.D.C. G.T. Race, Silverstone	M. Garton	4th class
May 1964	1,000 km Race, Nürburgring	C. Baker/B. Bradley	29th overall; 3rd class
June 1964	Le Mans 24 Hour Race	C. Baker/B. Bradley	24th overall
August 1964	B.A.R.C. G.T. Race, Goodwood	J. Harris	13th overall
August 1964	G.T. Race, Nürburgring	M. Garton	2nd class

Date	Race	Driver(s)	Result
September 1964	500 km Race, Nürburgring	M. Garton	Retired
December 1964	Nassau Races	C. Baker	15th overall; 1st class
March 1965	Sebring 12 Hour Race	C. Baker/R. Aaltonen P. Hopkirk/T. Makinen	15th overall; 1st class 18th overall
May 1965	Targa Florio Race	R. Aaltonen/C. Baker	15th overall; 2nd class
May 1965	1,000 km Race, Nürburgring	C. Baker/J. Moore	28th overall; 1st class
June 1965	Le Mans 24 Hour Race	P. Hawkins/J. Rhodes R. Aaltonen/C. Baker	12th overall; 1st class Retired
June 1965	Crystal Palace	M. Garton	5th class
August 1965	Nürburgring	M. Garton	4th class
September 1965	500 km Race, Nürburgring	C. Baker/K. Greene M. Garton P. Jackson J. Moore/J. Harris	6th overall; 1st class 10th overall; 2nd class 15th overall; 3rd class 18th overall
December 1965	Nassau	C. Baker	1st class
February 1966	Daytona 24 Hour Race	R. Cuomo/Richards	21st overall; 1st class
March 1966	Sebring 12 Hour Race	T. Makinen/P. Hawkins R. Aaltonen/C. Baker	18th overall; 1st class 29th overall

Date	Event	Drivers	Results
May 1966	1,000 km Race	J. Harris/A. Poole M. Garton/J. Moore	11th overall; 3rd class 13th overall
May 1966	Targa Florio Race	C. Baker/R. Aaltonen H. Martin/J. Wheeler	16th overall; 3rd class Crashed
June 1966	1,000 km Race, Nürburgring	C. Baker/J. Moore A. Poole/M. Garton White/Grant	23rd overall; 2nd class 27th overall; 3rd class 2nd class
June 1966	Le Mans 24 Hour Race	P. Hopkirk/A. Hedges C. Baker/J. Rhodes	Retired Retired
July 1966	Circuit of Mugello	C. Baker/J. Moore	2nd class
August 1966	500 km Race, Hockenheim	De Klerk	10th overall
September 1966	500 km Race, Nürburgring	J. Moore A. Poole	4th overall; 2nd class Retired
October 1966	1,000 km Race, Montlhéry	J. Moore/S. Neale	Retired
April 1967	Sebring 12 Hour Race	R. Aaltonen/C. Baker R. Enever/A. Poole/C. Baird B. Burner/Y. Fretina	13th overall; 1st class 18th overall; 2nd class 27th overall; 1st class

Date	Race	Drivers	Result
May 1967	Targa Florio Race	R. Aaltonen/C. Baker J. Wheeler/M. Davidson	Retired after accident 6th class
May 1967	1,000 km Race, Nürburgring	M. Pigneguy/Cave	3rd class
June 1967	Le Mans 24 Hour Race	C. Baker/A. Hedges	15th overall
July 1967	Circuit of Mugello	C. Baker A. Hedges	4th class Retired
November 1967	Tour de Corse	C. Baker/M. Wood	Retired
March 1968	Sebring 12 Hour Race	C. Baker/M. Garton	34th overall; 1st class
May 1968	1,000 km Race, Nürburgring	C. Baker/J. Handley	1st class
May 1968	1,000 km Race Spa/Francorchamps	M. Pigneguy/W. Tuckett	22nd overall
May 1968	Targa Florio Race	R. Aaltonen/C. Baker	Retired
July 1968	Circuit of Mugello	C. Baker/A. Hedges M. Pigneguy/W. Tuckett D. Lucas/A. Appleby J. Wheeler/M. Franey	15th overall; 1st class 3rd class 6th class Retired
July 1968	Watkins Glen 6 Hour Race	C. Baker	2nd class

Date	Event	Drivers	Results
September 1968	Le Mans 24 Hour Race	A. Poole/R. Enever	15th overall
September 1968	500 km Nürburgring	W. Tuckett/M. Pigneguy M. Franey	18th overall 25th overall

APPENDIX VIII

INTERNATIONAL RECORDS HELD BY AUSTIN-HEALEYS

1953. Austin-Healey '100' at Bonneville Salt Flats.
International Class 'D' (2,000–3,000 cc) Records:

1,000 km	. . . . .	127·00 mile/h
1,000 miles	. . . . .	122·66 mile/h
2,000 km	. . . . .	123·13 mile/h
2,000 miles	. . . . .	123·03 mile/h
5,000 km	. . . . .	103·93 mile/h
6 hours	. . . . .	123·75 mile/h
12 hours	. . . . .	122·91 mile/h
24 hours	. . . . .	104·30 mile/h

1954. Austin-Healey '100S' at Bonneville Salt Flats.
International Class 'D' Records:

5 km (flying start)	. . .	182·3 mile/h
5 miles (,,)	. . .	182·7 mile/h
10 km (,,)	. . .	183·8 mile/h★
10 miles (,,)	. . .	181·1 mile/h★
50 km (standing start)	. . .	151·32 mile/h★
50 miles (,,)	. . .	153·88 mile/h★
100 km (,,)	. . .	154·62 mile/h★
100 miles (,,)	. . .	155·95 mile/h★
200 km (,,)	. . .	156·22 mile/h★
1,000 km (,,)	. . .	132·81 mile/h
1,000 miles (,,)	. . .	132·59 mile/h★
2,000 km (,,)	. . .	132·72 mile/h★
2,000 miles (,,)	. . .	132·38 mile/h★
3,000 km (,,)	. . .	132·18 mile/h
3,000 miles (,,)	. . .	132·16 mile/h
4,000 km (,,)	. . .	132·02 mile/h
5,000 km (,,)	. . .	132·27 mile/h★
1 hour (,,)	. . .	156·97 mile/h★
6 hours (,,)	. . .	133·06 mile/h
12 hours (,,)	. . .	132·47 mile/h
24 hours (,,)	. . .	132·29 mile/h

★ Records still current.

1956. Austin-Healey '100-Six' at Bonneville Salt Flats.
    International Class 'D' Records:

200 miles (standing start) . . .	152·58 mile/h
500 km (,,) . . .	152·95 mile/h
500 miles (,,) . . .	153·14 mile/h
1,000 km (,,) . . .	150·98 mile·h
3 hours (,,) . . .	153·06 mile/h★
6 hours (,,) . . .	145·96 mile/h★

1959. Austin-Healey Sprite EX 219.
    International Class 'G' (750–1,100 cc) Records:

50 km	145·56 mile/h★
50 miles	145·48 mile/h★
100 km	145·08 mile/h★
100 miles	146·17 mile/h★
200 km	146·64 mile/h★
200 miles	138·15 mile/h★
500 km	138·85 mile/h★
500 miles	137·72 mile/h★
1,000 km	138·39 mile/h★
1,000 miles	138·55 mile/h★
2,000 km	138·86 mile/h★
1 hour	146·95 mile/h★
3 hours	139·38 mile/h★
6 hours	139·09 mile/h★
12 hours	138·75 mile/h★

★ Records still current.

APPENDIX IX

THE WORKS RALLY CARS

Reg. No.	Date	Chassis No. / Engine No.	Event	History
PMO 201	1958	BN6-1136 / 26D/R/63599H (100/6)	1958 Alpine Liège	Pat Moss – Coupe des Dames Pat Moss – Coupe des Dames, 4th overall Sold to J. Mahles
PMO 202	1958	BN6-1137 / 26D/R/63818H (100/6)	1958 Alpine Liège	Bill Shepherd – Coupe des Alpes, 7th overall Gerry Burgess – 9th overall Sold to Bill Shepherd
PMO 203	1958	BN6-1138 / 26D/R/62823H (100/6) converted to 3000 spec 1959	1958 Alpine Liège 1959 Tulip Liège	Jack Sears – 11th overall Joan Johns – Retired Jack Sears – 8th overall Gerry Burgess – Crashed Sold to Small and Parkes
SMO 744	1959	HBN7-1343 / XSP/1813I/8HC	1959 Alpine Liège 1960 Sestrière Circuit of Ireland Acropolis Liège German R.A.C.	Bill Shepherd – Retired Peter Riley – 7th G.T. category Peter Riley – Event cancelled Pat Moss – Retired Peter Riley – Crashed Dave Seigle-Morris – 5th overall Morley brothers – 12th overall Ronnie Adams – 39th overall Sold to Mr Candler

Footnote.—PMO 201, PMO 202, and PMO 203, in its original form, were 100/6s, but are included in this table because with them the big Healey was introduced to international rally success, a foretaste of what was to come.

Reg. No.	Date	Chassis No. Engine No.	History
SMO 745	1959	HBN7-1344 XSP/18131/6	1959 Alpine – John Gott – 5th G.T. category R.A.C. – Morley brothers – 4th overall Liège – John Gott – Retired 1960 Geneva – Pat Moss – Coupe des Dames Acropolis – Pat Moss – Retired Alpine – John Williamson – Retired German – Dave Seigle-Morris – 8th overall R.A.C. – Peter Riley – 10th overall Sold to Don Grimshaw
SMO 746	1959	HBN7-1342 XSP/18131/9HC	1959 Alpine – Jack Sears – Retired Liège – Jack Sears – Retired German – Pat Moss – 2nd overall 1960 Sestrière – Pat Moss – Event cancelled Lyon-Charbonnières – Pat Moss – Crashed Alpine – John Gott – 8th overall Liège – John Gott – 10th overall 1959 R.A.C. – Jack Sears – 17th overall Sold to John Gott
SJB 471	1959	HBT7-101 26/DR/UH/113	1960 Tulip – Morley brothers – 21st overall Alpine – Morley brothers – 14th overall Liège – Peter Riley – Retired R.A.C. – Morley brothers – 3rd overall Sold to Derek Astle

Reg.	Year	Chassis No.	Event	Result
UJB 143		BN7-6686 29D/U/H7326	1960 Sebring 12 Hours Le Mans 24 Hours 1961 Midnight Sun Tour of Corsica	Peter Riley/Jack Sears – 3rd in class Peter Riley/Jack Sears – Retired Peter Riley – 12th overall Pat Moss – 1st Sports Car Sold to George Humble
URX 727	1960	HBN7-8446 29D/HU/12161	1960 Tulip Alpine Liège German 1961 Mille Miglia	Pat Moss – 8th overall Pat Moss – 2nd overall Pat Moss – 1st overall Pat Moss – 16th overall Pat Moss – Non-starter Sold to Pat Moss
XJB 870	1961	HBN7-13709 29D/RU/H25636	1961 Alpine Liège R.A.C. 1962 Monte	Dave Seigle-Morris – Crashed Dave Seigle-Morris – 6th overall Dave Seigle-Morris – 12th overall Dave Seigle-Morris – 18th overall Sold to Rudi Metzger Written off 1966
XJB 871	1961	HBN7-13708 29D/RU/H25616	1961 Acropolis Alpine	Peter Riley – 3rd overall Peter Riley – Crashed Sold to Rauno Aaltonen
XJB 872	1961	HBN7-13706 29D/RU/H25660	1961 Alpine Liège	John Gott – 15th overall John Gott – Retired Sold to Derek Astle

303

Reg. No.	Date	Chassis No. Engine No.		History
XJB 876	1961	HBN7-13707 29D/RU/H25633	1961 Tulip	Morley brothers – 14th overall
			Alpine	Morley brothers – 1st overall
			Liège	Don Grimshaw – Crashed
			R.A.C.	Morley brothers – Retired
				Sold to Don Morley
XJB 877	1961	HBN7-13710 29D/RU/H25626	1961 Tulip	Pat Moss – Coupe des Dames
			Alpine	Pat Moss – Crashed
			Liège	Pat Moss – Retired
			R.A.C.	Pat Moss – 2nd overall
			1962 Acropolis	Pat Moss – 8th overall
			Liège	Rauno Aaltonen – Retired
			R.A.C.	Peter Riley – Crashed
			1963 Alpine	Paddy Hopkirk – Crashed
			Liège	Paddy Hopkirk – 6th overall
				Written off 1964
37 ARX	1962	HBN7-18701 29E/RU/H5090	1962 Tulip	Morley brothers – 14th overall
			Solitude Race	Bohringer – 3rd in class
			1963 Tulip	Morley brothers – 2nd G.T. category
			Alpine	Morley brothers – Retired
				Written off 1963

Reg.	Year	Chassis No.	Events	Results
47 ARX	1962	HBN7-18702 29E/RU/H4971	1962 Tulip Alpine Liège 1963 Tulip Alpine R.A.C.	Peter Riley – 18th overall Peter Riley – Retired Logan Morrison – 5th overall Logan Morrison – Retired Logan Morrison – Crashed Timo Makinen – 5th overall Written off 1964
57 ARX	1962	HBN7-18703 29E/RU/H5225	1962 Alpine Liège R.A.C. 1963 Alpine Liège	Morley brothers – 1st overall Paddy Hopkirk – Retired Morley brothers – Crashed Timo Makinen – Retired Timo Makinen – Crashed Written off 1963
67 ARX	1962	HBN7-18704 29E/RU/H5220	1962 Alpine Liège R.A.C. 1963 Midnight Sun Liège R.A.C.	Dave Seigle-Morris – 8th overall Dave Seigle-Morris – 6th overall Paddy Hopkirk – 2nd overall Timo Makinen – Disqualified Logan Morrison – Retired Morley brothers – 9th overall Sold to Tony Ambrose
77 ARX	1962	HBN7-18705 29E/RU/H5454	1962 Alpine Polish R.A.C. 1963 Monte Liège	Pat Moss – 3rd overall Pat Moss – 2nd overall Pat Moss – 3rd overall Timo Makinen – 13th overall Rauno Aaltonen – Crashed Written off 1963

305

Reg. No.	Date	Chassis No. / Engine No.		History
ARX 91B	1963	HBJ8-26754 / 29K/RU/H1502	1964 Austrian Alpine / 1965 Targa Florio	Paddy Hopkirk – 1st overall / Hawkins/Makinen – 2nd in class / Sold to David Hiam
ARK 92B	1964	HBJ8-26753 / 29K/RU/H1501	1964 Tulip / Alpine / Liège	Morley brothers – 1st in G.T. category / Morley brothers – 2nd in G.T. category / Timo Makinen – Retired / Sold to Peter Browning
BMO 93B	1964	HBJ8-27537 / 29K/RU/H2173	1964 Liège / R.A.C.	Rauno Aaltonen – 1st overall / Morley brothers – 21st overall / Sold to Pauline Mayman
BRX 852B	1964	HBJ8-28477 / 29K/RU/H3160	1964 Liège / R.A.C.	Paddy Hopkirk – Retired / Timo Makinen – 2nd overall / Sold to Tony Ambrose
DRX 257C	1965	HBJ8-31336 / 29K/RU/5899	1965 Tulip / Scottish	Morley brothers – 4th overall / Timo Makinen – Retired / Written off 1965
DRX 258C	1965	HBJ8-31337 / 29K/RU/H5900	1965 Geneva / Alpine / R.A.C.	Morley brothers – 7th overall / Morley brothers – 2nd overall / Morley brothers – Crashed / Sold to Pauline Mayman

EJB 806C	1965	HBJ8/31655 29K/RU/H6162	1965 R.A.C.	Timo Makinen – 2nd overall Sold to Ted Worswick
PWB 57 (Now EG 38)	1964	(ex ARX 92B)	1967 R.A.C.	Rauno Aaltonen – Event cancelled Sold to A. H. Carter

APPENDIX X

USEFUL ADDRESSES

Austin-Healey Club (Gen. Secretary, Brian Healey),
c/o Donald Healey Motor Co.,
Warwick.

Automotive Products Ltd,
Tachbrook Road,
Leamington Spa,
Warwicks.

British Leyland Special Tuning Dept.,
M.G. Car Division,
Abingdon on Thames,
Berks.

(*Americans should contact*)
Competitions Technical Adviser,
British Leyland Motors (Inc.),
600 Willow Tree Avenue,
Leonia,
New Jersey, 07657.

Champion Spark Plugs & Co. Ltd,
Feltham,
Middlesex.

SU Carburetters Co. Ltd,
Wood Lane,
Erdington,
Birmingham 24.

The Dunlop Co. Limited,
Fort Dunlop,
Erdington,
Birmingham, 24.

Donald Healey Motor Co. Ltd,
Emscote Road,
Warwick.

Ferodo Limited,
Chapel-en-le-Frith,
Stockport,
Cheshire.

Girling Limited,
Kings Road,
Tyseley,
Birmingham, 11.

Joseph Lucas Limited,
Great King Street,
Birmingham, 19.

Lockheed Hydraulic Brake Co. Limited,
Leamington Spa,
Warwicks.

INDEX

Chiron, Louis 3, 38, 80
Church, Robin 208
Circuit of Ireland 1960 128, 178
— — — 1962 150
— — — 1963 177
Clark, Grant 159
Coker, Gerry 70
Col d'Allos 16, 136, 137
— du Cayole 93, 112
— de la Faucille 53
— d'Izoard 16, 53
— de Soubeyrand 117
— de Vars 38, 53
Colgate, John 200
Collins, Peter 18
Competitions Department, Abingdon
  106, 111, 168, 201
Cook 103
Cooper, Jackie 77, 102
Corbishley, Cyril 56
Coupe d'Argent 160
— d'Or 155
Coventry-Climax 203
Croft-Pearson, Sam 115
Croche, Domini 112
Cunningham, Briggs 38, 198

D

'D'-type chassis 37
Dalton, John 107, 200
Dermott, Brian 208
Dixon, David 155
Dolomites 55, 122
Downing, Ken 18
Driver of the Year 138
Dunboyne Circuit 177
Duncan, Ian 71
Duncan Industries 66
Dundrod Circuit 45, 56
Dunlop disc brakes 79, 83

E

'E'-type chassis 37
Easter, Paul 166
Ecurie Safety Fast 134, 139
Ehrman, Gus 178, 179
Elford, Vic 138, 139
Elliot Saloon 6, 10
Elliots 9
Enever, Roger 200
European Ladies' Rally Champions
  138, 151

Everett, Bill 51
Eyston, Capt. George 77

F

'F'-type chassis 68
Finlay, Ross 156
Fitch, John 64
Five-speed gearbox for Sprite 175
Flockhart, Ron 103
Flower, Raymond 107
Freed, Walter 42, 46

G

Gale, Guy 41
Garnier, Peter 111, 118
Garton, Mike 173, 201
Gaston, Paddy 201
Gatsonides, Maurice 76
Gavia, Passo di 55
Geneva Rally 1960 130
— — 1969 166
German Rally 1959 127
— — 1960 138
Giraud-Cabontous 63, 64
Girling disc brakes 120
Gold, Tom 139, 177, 178
Goodwood 17
— 1953 76
— Nine Hours 1952 57
Gott, John 112, 115, 122, 126, 134,
  138, 139, 142, 150, 155, 224
Grace, G. H. 42
Grant, Gregor 74
Grimshaw, Don 142, 148
Guild of Motoring Writers 138
Gurot, Monsieur 52, 56

H

Hadley, Bert 64, 75
Haines, Nick 13, 15, 16, 17, 18
Hall, Ann 115
—, Eric 208
—, Peter 18
Haller, R. 13
Hamblin, Doug 146, 148
Hambro Inc. 110
Hamilton, Duncan 40, 44, 59, 61
Hands, Stewart 155
Hangsen, Walter 198
Hanstein, Huschke von 56
Harris, John 155, 201, 203
Hassan, Wally 203